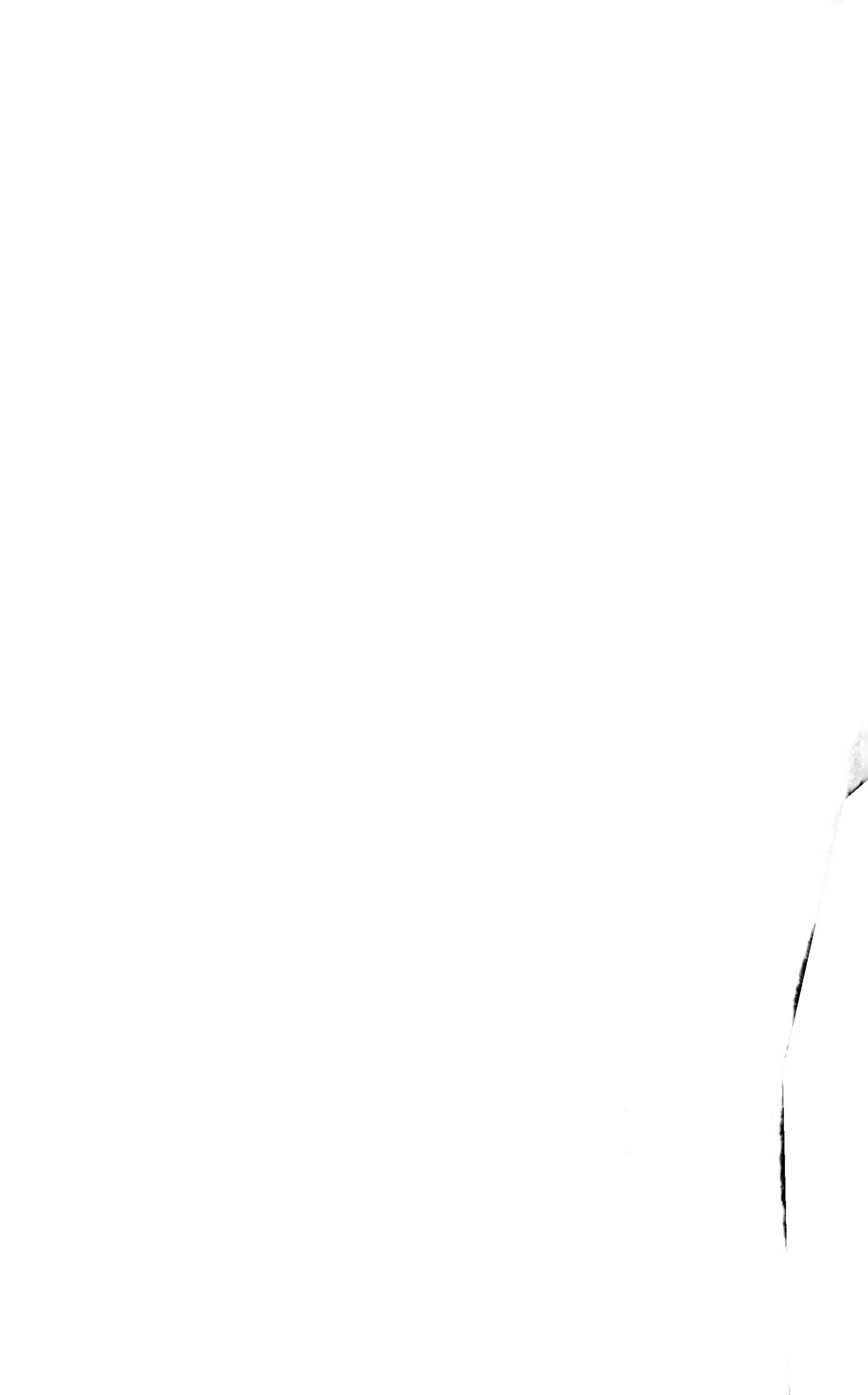

Identity, Memory, and Diaspora

SUNY series in Latin American and Iberian Thought and Culture

Edited by Jorge J. E. Gracia and Rosemary Geisdorfer Feal

Identity, Memory, and Diaspora

Voices of Cuban-American Artists, Writers, and Philosophers

Edited by

Jorge J. E. Gracia

Lynette M. F. Bosch

and

Isabel Alvarez Borland

STATE UNIVERSITY OF NEW YORK PRESS

Cover art: *El Morro*, Alberto Rey.

Published by
State University of New York Press, Albany

© 2008 State University of New York

All rights reserved

Printed in the United States of America

No part of this book may be used or reproduced in any manner whatsoever without written permission. No part of this book may be stored in a retrieval system or transmitted in any form or by any means including electronic, electrostatic, magnetic tape, mechanical, photocopying, recording, or otherwise without the prior permission in writing of the publisher.

For information, contact State University of New York Press, Albany, NY
www.sunypress.edu

Production by Judith Block
Marketing by Anne M. Valentine

Library of Congress Cataloging-in-Publication Data

Identity, memory, and diaspora : voices of Cuban-American artists, writers, and philosophers / edited by Jorge J. E. Gracia, Lynette M. F. Bosch, Isabel Alvarez Borland.
       p. cm. — (SUNY series in Latin American and Iberian thought and culture)
Includes bibliographical references (p.   ) and index.
ISBN 978-0-7914-7317-7 (hardcover : alk. paper)
1. Cuban American art. 2. American literature—Cuban American authors. 3. Cuban American philsophy. I. Gracia, Jorge J. E. II. Bosch, Lynette M. F. III. Alvarez Borland, Isabel.

NX512.3.C83I34 2007
700.89'6872910732—dc22   2007013095

10 9 8 7 6 5 4 3 2 1

Contents

Preface

For Cubans, the diaspora that began in 1959, with the triumph of Fidel Castro's Revolution, and continues to the present, has been a protracted and painful process. They have left Cuba in waves and in any conceivable means of transportation, from airplanes to makeshift rafts. Many have lost their lives in the process and others have failed to reach their goal. But even those who have succeeded in getting to the Florida shore have felt displaced, scattered, and alienated; most have suffered loneliness and some even regret. Cubans have used different strategies to overcome their personal struggles. Some have created a myth of Olympian proportions about Cuba, the paradise they were forced to leave behind against their will, and to which they dream of returning. Some have found solace in political action against the forces that displaced them. Others have intentionally tried to forget their origins and to blend in and assimilate to the places where they landed. And still others wallow in nostalgia and memories. All have had to ask themselves who they are and how they fit in their new environment. These are fundamental questions of identity that apply not just to individual persons, but also to groups. Those Cubans who live in the United States have had to face them every day and sometimes dramatically, for the country where they have chosen to reside is very different from the one they left in terms of language, culture, and values.

So who are we, so-called Cuban Americans? Are we still Cuban in some sense? Have we become fully American? And what does it mean to be Cuban American? In this volume we pose these and similar questions to a group of prominent Cuban-American artists, writers, and philosophers. The past half a century has seen an unprecedented flowering of Cuban-American talent in the United States. The number of artists is counted in the hundreds, perhaps the thousands, the writers have achieved wide readership even outside the Cuban-American community, and some of the philosophers have joined the philosophical mainstream in the United States. How have they dealt with the diaspora and their memories? What have they done to find a proper place in their adopted country? And most pertinent for us here, how has their work been affected by the experience?

This volume is related to a larger project, a National Endowment for the Humanities (NEH) Seminar that took place in Buffalo, June 11–30, 2006, on the topic: "Negotiating Identities in Art, Literature, and Philosophy: Cuban Americans and American Culture." It was directed by Lynette M. F. Bosch, Isabel Alvarez Borland, and I. In addition, Lynette Bosch and I organized an art exhibition at the University at Buffalo Art Galleries entitled, "Layers: Collecting Cuban-American Art," June 11–September 9, 2006. In the exhibition, samples of three different art collections, two private and one institutional, sought to illustrate how Cuban-American art collectors also encountered issues of identity, memory, and diaspora as collectors and how they dealt with them in different contexts. The interviews included here are selected from a group conducted with various artists, writers, and philosophers, which had the purpose of adding a personal dimension to the NEH Seminar.

The interviews are gathered in three groups, the first with nine artists, the second with six writers, and the third with four philosophers. Each group is preceded by an introductory essay and each interview is introduced with a brief biographical note about the author interviewed. At the end of each group, samples of the work of those interviewed are added. The choice of authors was guided by a desire to give a broad idea of the contribution of established figures who have struggled in some way with issues of Cuban-American identity in particular and social identity in general. The questions posed to them in the interviews were similar, although they often reflect particular situations and the nature of the work. Apart form the general questions mentioned earlier, some of the most frequently asked were: Who do you think you are and how is your work related to your identify? How did you come to be who you are? Do you regard yourself as Cuban American, as Latino or Latina, as Hispanic? Are you American, or qualified American? How has your identity been formed, how does it manifest itself, and how has the experience of the diaspora affected your work? What difficulties have you encountered, and how do you see these in relation to American culture?

In spite of similar questions and often common experiences, the interviews are surprisingly different. Not only does each interview present us with a different take on art, literature, or philosophy, but most of them explore different challenges encountered by the authors. Sometimes these have to do with personal matters, but at other times they involve social and professional dimensions. The answers reveal striking differences between the way the experience of Cuban Americans has informed their work. Mostly, the questions were treated as an occasion to get these authors to tell their stories, and what they consider important for understanding their work.

The volume begins with art because its use of nonlinguistic media makes its statement more indirect while at the same time more impacting. In literature, language is the medium, so we get closer to an explicit formulation of the issues with which this volume is concerned. Yet, literature does not explain or teach, but often uses the description of experience to entice the reader into the particularities of a situation. Finally, philosophy most openly formulates problems, whether conceptual or practical, and seeks to solve them. The volume, then, involves a progression from the less explicit to the more explicit, and from the more experiential to the more conceptual.

The preparation of a collection such as this involves substantial work of various sorts. Most interviews were first filmed and then transcribed. I am grateful to my wife, Norma Gracia, for filming most of the interviews with the artists and to Paul Symington for transcribing the filmed interviews. The cost of this process was funded through the Samuel P. Capen Chair in Philosophy, at the University at Buffalo. I am also grateful to various artists, art collectors, authors, and publishers for the permission to include works or parts of works here, and to the interviewed authors, who took the time for the interviews and consented to engage in a necessary, but nonetheless cumbersome editorial procedure. I am also grateful to Lisa Chesnel for her interest in this work and encouragement, to Judith Block for her care and attention in the production process, and to Susan Smith for preparing the index. Most of all, I am indebted to Lynette M. F. Bosch and Isabel Alvarez Borland, who have been extraordinary partners throughout the whole process. I have learned much from both of them, and I have enjoyed their partnership in the NEH Seminar and the compilation of this volume. It has been a great privilege to work with them and share their enthusiasm.

Jorge J. E. Gracia

The Cuban Diaspora: A Brief Chronology

Cubans have come to the United States for different reasons and under different circumstances. Prior to the most recent waves of exiles resulting from the establishment of the revolutionary government in 1959, groups of Cubans had lived and sometimes settled permanently in the United States. Those who immigrated permanently were primarily in search of economic opportunities, and those who came for limited periods of time were usually fleeing political oppression. A famous case involving political oppression is José Martí (1853–1895), considered to be the father of the Cuban nation. These groups were relatively small. Mass exodus from Cuba into the United States occurred only in the aftermath of Fidel Castro's Revolution. This recent diaspora may be divided into several periods and groups.

The first to leave the island were associates of Fulgencio Batista, government people who lost their jobs and were afraid of reprisals for their actions under the dictatorship. They fled almost immediately, and many of them were able to take with them substantial resources. Closely after and continuing until 1962, an exodus of professionals from the middle to the upper class began in earnest. The expropriation of property by the revolutionary government and the increasing assaults on the private sector prompted members of these groups to leave the island. The exodus accelerated after the Bay of Pigs invasion in 1961 and the declaration of Cuba as a Marxist-Leninist state, when it became clear that the political situation in Cuba was not going to change in the near future. An important component of this group are the Peter Pan children. These youngsters were sent to the United States through the auspices of the Catholic Church in order to take them out of what their parents regarded as an antireligious environment. By this time the revolutionary government had abolished private religious education and had expelled all priests, nuns, and members of religious orders who were not Cuban citizens. When the children arrived in the United States, some were placed with families, but most of them were sent to camps, sometimes with insufficient supervision. After the Bay of Pigs fiasco adults arriving from Cuba were given refugee status and provided with special assistance by the United States government in the form of a small monthly allowance and army food rations. A system of educational loans was also put in place to help those accepted in colleges and universities throughout the country. Many of the Cubans who arrived between 1959 and 1962 stayed in Miami, but some settled in other parts of the United States. Most of these exiles have joined the ranks of the professional classes.

After 1962, it became more difficult to leave the island, until 1965, when the Cuban government allowed some exits in what came to be called "Freedom Flights." These lasted until 1973. Those who left at this time were primarily family members of exiles already settled in the United States, and belonged mostly to the middle class. Many of them were owners of small businesses and workers in various trades.

The next large exodus occurred in 1980, when Castro opened the port of Mariel, presumably to anyone who wished to leave Cuba. Among those who left were some persons the Castro government considered undesirable, such as homosexuals, drug addicts, mentally disturbed persons, criminals, and political dissidents. This group is known as the Marielitos, a name derived from the place from which they left. Most of these Cubans have stayed in Miami.

The nineties saw a different kind of exodus. After the collapse of the Soviet Union and its support for the Castro government, economic conditions in the island became desperate. People began risking their lives at sea, in makeshift rafts (the notorious *balsas*), to reach United States shores. At the same time, criticism of the Castro regime within Cuba became more pronounced and certain groups of intellectuals and artists were allowed to leave the island in order to prevent unrest. These were younger Cubans, born under the Castro regime, who knew nothing other than revolutionary Cuba.

The waves in which Cubans have come to the United States has reproduced a microcosm of prerevolutionary Cuban society in this country. Whereas other immigrant groups have a certain degree of homogeneity insofar as most of them have come under similar conditions and at roughly the same time, Cubans have come here for different reasons, under different circumstances, and at different times. Also important is that a large proportion of Cubans have stayed in Miami, creating a city with a strong Cuban flavor.

Part I

The Artists

1 THE ARTISTS

Lynette M. F. Bosch

Defining Cuban-American art or what is "Cuban" or "Cuban-American" about art produced in the United States by artists of Cuban birth or of Cuban ancestry is a complex task, because the artistic production of artists who belong to these categories defies easy classification of style, subject, media, and message. Whereas the easy definition of these artistic categories can be resolved by forwarding identity as a determinant element, the implicit questions "What is 'Cuban' about Cuban Art?" and "What is 'Cuban American' about Cuban-American art?" cannot be so easily answered because issues of identity are simultaneously subjective and objective. A comprehensive or definitive definition of "Cuban" and "Cuban-American" identity(ies) has not been achieved. The attempt to determine a fixed definition of what constitutes Cuban art, Cuban-American art, or both is additionally complicated by the complexity of defining artistic identity, especially that of exiled artists belonging to different generations. This introduction to the interviews of Baruj Salinas, Humberto Calzada, Emilio Falero, María Brito, Mario Bencomo, Arturo Rodríguez, Demi, Juan Carlos Llera, and Alberto Rey is meant to guide the reader toward an understanding of how issues of identity are made manifest by visual artists, who are also Cuban exiles and Cuban Americans.

Artists are artists first and their concerns are primarily technical and visual. Visual artists, be they painters, sculptors, printmakers or architects, respond to a need to express their experience through objects. Once made, these works exist on their own terms, endowed with histories and meanings that cannot be fixed or limited by their originating circumstances. Interpretation, which is part of any "text," or object as "text," when considered within the purview of the artistic process, develops its own rules of logic while achieving context and connected meanings. Works of art produced by exiled artists of multiple identities are not easy parallels of literary, musical, or theatrical productions, because the process of making a work of art is not the same as these other creative endeavors.

It is, therefore, important to understand that the interviews conducted with the Cuban-American artists featured here are primarily artist interviews and secondarily interviews with a group interested in the expression of identity and the experience of exile.

The artists interviewed discuss their creative process within their personal, formal, stylistic and conceptual exploration involved in making objects. Each of them attempts to solve problems created by the material demands of their chosen media and in working with and around the possibilities inherent in those materials and in their manipulation. It is important to understand that visual artists are not philosophers, neither are they wordsmiths, and, while the myth of the inarticulate artist is just that, the artistic personality sees the world *on its own terms*. The artist is not interested in objectivity or in sociological, philosophical, or scholarly definitions of the subjects and experiences they represent. The perspective of artists is uncompromisingly personal and reflected in their work. The artists interviewed here have very strong individual opinions about their artistic creativity, their personal expression of this creativity, and the manner in which they view their situation as artists in relation to their being Cuban American and exiles. As artists, they do not seek "objectivity," but rather the expression of their personal vision of human experience.

Each of the artists included here represents slightly different experiences of being Cuban, Cuban American, and an exile. All were born in Cuba and have spent most of their lives in the United States, yet they are in many ways very diverse, and they came at different ages: Baruj Salinas as an adult and mature artist, Alberto Rey as an infant without memories of Cuba, Demi as a child, Humberto Calzada as a young adult, and the rest as teenagers of various ages. (The interviews are arranged in an order that reflects the different stages at which these artists came to the United States.) Except for Salinas, who came as an adult and Rey, who lacks childhood memories of Cuba, every one of the featured artists represents a range of ages conforming to what Ruben Rumbaut identified as the one-and-a-half generation: being Cuban American born in Cuba and brought to the United States as children and adolescents. The concept of the one-and-a-halfers as a social identity was popularized by Gustavo Pérez Firmat in *Life on the Hyphen* and has become a given for identifying those Cuban Americans who came to this country at a certain age. As these artists have created a body of work that reflects their personal experience, they have, at different times and in different ways, addressed their multiple identities.

Because one-and-a-halfers were partially formed in Cuba, but forced to acculturate to American culture before their Cuban identities were fully formed, their lives are truncated, cut in "half." But the halves are not neatly divided, as exile did not break their lives in even parts. Instead, the hyphen becomes a figure of fracture that creates a movable territory of negotiation that is ongoing and fluid. One-and-a-halfers are also exiles, whose sense of identity, both Cuban and Cuban-American is defined by a landscape of slippage. The hyphen is a geography of change, where one-and-a-halfers navigate back and forth between their Cuban and American cultural references on a daily and hourly basis, as events and incidents call forth reactions from their Cuban and their American parts. For those who remember their Cuban lives, the removal from Cuba represents a central memory and a break with the continuity they knew as children. The older they were when they left Cuba, the more "Cuban" they had become. For the younger members of the one-and-a-half generation, their American part represents the greater part of their lives, as the years in the United States have lengthened into lives lived outside Cuba.

Those one-and-a-halfers, who were teenagers and older children, were old enough to understand that exile meant leaving home, forever maybe. As they matured, their cognitive understanding of exile became an aspect of their experience that separated them from their American peers and defined them as being different. Those who were very young children or infants when they left Cuba, grew up in a culture of family exile, which they shared through circumstance. As they matured, association formed their identity as exiles. Thus, the exiled children and adolescents of different ages became exiles of multiple identities bound to their culture of origin through birth and ancestry, yet becoming adults in a culture that became progressively familiar as they progressively absorbed it. The response of this group of Cuban Americans to the divided self varies always, moving from exhilaration to conflict, as the tension created by the life on the hyphen fluctuates with changing circumstances. As exiles, Cuban-American artists are possessed of multiple identities as insiders and outsiders on either side of the hyphen.

For artists, yet another identity is added to these, because artists are by nature outsiders who participate in a culture and observe society in order to transform their observations into art. For the exiled artist, being an outsider takes on charged significance. For some, the moment of exile and the experience of exile may remain a fixed topos in their work. For others, it may be a passing consideration that emerges here and there in their work. Generational placement can also alter the artists' relationships with their exile identity and can affect the content and subjects they choose to develop. Each of these approaches is reflected in the work of the different artists interviewed in this book and no consensus is reached as to which approach is more or less legitimate. Yet, each artist interviewed has had to come to terms with his or her multiple identities, as Cuban, exile, and Cuban American.

The connection between identity and art in a Cuban context can be traced to the first generation of Cuban modernist artists, the painters of the Vanguardia, who were active in Cuba during the 1920s and 1930s. These artists, who include Carlos Enríquez, Wifredo Lam, Amelia Peláez, and Fidelio Ponce, sought to bring modernist movements and styles to Cuba in order to transform Cuban art from its nineteenth-century academic traditions into a more contemporary artistic expression. Simultaneously with the artistic agenda of the Vanguardia artists, Cuban cultural critics, such as Fernando Ortiz, became concerned with the definition of a Cuban identity, an identity that seemed to require articulation after the War of Independence from Spain. As Cuba began the process of postwar reconstruction, it became necessary to pull together a diverse population that included Spaniards, Africans, Chinese, and other European and Asian populations so as to create a national identity that united these groups. Ortiz's use of *ajiaco*, the Cuban equivalent of the American melting-pot, became popular on the island as a solution to the problem of the varied ethnic and racial identities that existed in Cuba. Ortiz's conceptual project became linked to the artistic efforts of the Vanguardia artists to transform Cuban art, and, by extension, Cuban society. The visual explorations and experimentation of these artists included a conscious desire to represent *lo cubano*, the essential nature of what constitutes Cuban identity.

This initial generation of Cuban artists was followed by a second, third, and fourth generations of modernist painters and sculptors, who identified themselves as the heirs to the traditions of the Vanguardia. Yet, the third and fourth generations largely disengaged from the project of linking Modernism to *lo cubano* as they began to explore a more universal visual vocabulary. These third and fourth generations, which included artists such as Baruj Salinas, Rafael Soriano, Eladio González, Gina Pellón, Zilia Sánchez, Enrique Gay García, and Hugo Consuegra, worked in styles reflecting the stylistic movements of Expressionism, Abstraction, and Abstract Expressionism, during the 1950s and 1960s. Having been born in Cuba and having become mature artists on their native island, these artists belong to a group of exiles from post-1959 Cuba, who came out of their country fully formed as Cubans and artists, with their artistic vocabularies clearly defined. When they arrived in the United States, they continued their careers in the new landscape of exile. In a manner of speaking, they can be seen as artists who continued to create "Cuban" art in the United States because their work did not immediately reflect overt changes in their identity as Cubans or as artists. For some of them, as the years passed, the need to express the realities of exile and the exploration of a hyphenated identity surfaced in their work, but for others, these events had a minimal impact on their creative production.

Artists who left Cuba as mature artists, during the 1960s and 1970s, formed the nucleus of what is now an accepted category: they became classified as Cuban Americans by virtue of their Cuban birth and their American naturalization. The artists belonging to this group who settled in Miami, began to create a market for Cuban art among exiled Cuban collectors. This nucleus eventually expanded into Miami's continuing market for Cuban and Cuban-American art. The original group exhibited in private homes, small galleries that came and went quickly, and at the Bacardí gallery. The most defined members of this wave of first arrivals belonged to the group Grupo de Artistas Latino Americanos (GALA): Baruj Salinas, Enrique Riverón, Rafael Soriano, José Mijares, Osvaldo Gutiérrez, and Roxana McAllister. GALA exhibited as a group and as individuals, and these artists became models for the younger generation of artists, who grew up in Miami, having come as children or adolescents. The GALA generation is now known as *La Vieja Guardia* (The Old Guard) and, while these artists dealt with the subject of exile and identity at different times in their work, their concerns are not the expression of a divided identity: they continue to be Cubans who have spent decades of their lives in the United States as exiles. Their acculturation has been a matter of language and choice, but their view of their Cuban selves is firmly fixed in a manner that it cannot be for the members of the one-and-a-half generation.

Identity is a significant issue for most Cuban-American artists who came to this country as children or adolescents. Thus, whereas for Baruj Salinas, for example, the expression of identity is part of a much larger *corpus* of artistic interests and concerns, for the other artists included here, the search for a Cuban-American identity, within the context of exile, can be a more pressing concern. As the members of the one-and-a-half generation have matured in the United States, their concern with their exile experience, ongoing acculturation, and hyphenated identities has been expressed in their work in diverse ways. In their interviews, these individual perspectives on exile and identity are expressed, often with divergent opinions and manifestations. As these artists address their identity, they repeatedly return to technical and artistic matters because they are artists first and foremost and their *métier* is always uppermost in their minds. As artists, their perspective is personal and individual and changing, because the identity of visual artists is highly changeable and fluid. Thus, the interviews with the artists reveal multiple levels of negotiating identities, as artists, social observers, transmitters of experience, translators of hyphenated identity, and reflectors of the experiences of specific generations of Cuban-born artists who have spent the greater part of their lives in the United States. Their contribution to this book must be taken on their own terms as artists and as exiled Cuban Americans.

IDENTITIES

____ BARUJ SALINAS

Baruj Salinas was born in Havana, on July 6, 1935, immigrated in 1959 to San Antonio, TX, and holds a BA in Architecture from Kent State University. He eventually settled in Miami in 1961, where he stayed until 1974, when he left for Spain. He returned to Miami in 1993, where he still resides. Salinas began exhibiting in Miami immediately on his arrival in 1961 and cofounded the Grupo GALA, which included: Enrique Riverón, Rafael Soriano, José Mijares, Osvaldo Gutiérrez, and Roxana McAllister (b. Argentina, emigrated from Cuba to Miami with the first wave of exiles). His awards include: Best Transparent Watercolor, Texas Watercolor Society, San Antonio, Texas (1964); First prize, watercolor, 10th Hortt Memorial Exhibition, Fort Lauderdale, Florida (1968); Special Mention, VII Grand Prix International de Peinture, Cannes, France (1971); and First Prize, VI Latin American Print Biennial, Puerto Rican Culture Institute, San Juan, PR (1983).

Salinas's painterly style is abstract with topical references to his Jewish identity and interests in spirituality (Eastern and Western) and metaphysics. Topical references to his Cuban identity recur in his paintings of leaves, or pencas, *of Cuba's characteristic royal palm trees. In addition to his paintings, Salinas has illustrated books and created prints.*

Selected Collections: Villafames Museum, Spain; Carrillo Gil Museum, Mexico; Fine Arts Museum, Budapest, Hungary; Beit Uri Museum, Israel.

INTERVIEW

Conducted by Lynette M. F. Bosch

[Bosch] "Let me begin by asking Baruj about his origins in Cuba, his career as an artist, the general artistic scene in Cuba, and the reasons why he made the choices he made in terms of the style that became his. Baruj, can you tell us about how you began studying art?"

[Salinas] "I am going to start way before, when my family came from Turkey to Cuba. They emigrated from Turkey around 1918. They first went to Marseilles—stayed a short time there, a few months—and then landed in Cuba around 1920. My mother loved art. She painted, she did blouses with oil paints. I watched her paint and I loved the smell of the paint, the colors, so little by little, beginning when I was around six, I started helping her to paint—she usually painted flowers. So I did that and then, because I loved drawing, I started doing the comic strips from the Saturday and Sunday newspapers: *El País*."

[Bosch] "So you copied and then you elaborated?"

[Salinas] "Yes, I had a bunch of notebooks filled with Tarzan, Mandrake el Mago, Dick Tracy, and Superman, which unfortunately remained in Cuba—I don't even know where. And when I was maybe eleven, I started painting Cuban landscapes with my mother's oils—at that time there were no acrylics, although we did have watercolors. . . . And I started exhibiting at school. . . . Then, little by little, I started doing typical scenes of Cuban society. Most of them I put on paper or on canvas, but I mostly did black people. I had a friend that asked me 'Hey, what's the matter with you? Aren't there any white people in Cuba?' So I started doing them as well. . . . "

[Bosch] "What kinds of subjects did you do?"

[Salinas] "There was a black man that used to come around the neighborhood with a box—a tin box—full of ice and fish. He sold fish. And there was the ice cream man, kids in buses. Then I switched to market scenes; I did many typical markets. I used to go around in a *tranvía* (street car) or in a bus, and I would go to these markets, sketch them, and then paint them at home. I didn't have a studio at that time; I painted in my bedroom."

[Bosch] "How big were these works?"

[Salinas] "The biggest work that I did maybe was 30" × 40". I remember a market scene that I did that was about 30" × 40", and all in oils. I don't know where the painting is now, unfortunately. I would love to be able to compare notes with what I did with what I'm doing now. There's always a fine line that connects all these works. If you get down to it you find a trajectory. And you being a scholar would know how to connect the points. So I started going into the Círculo de Bellas Artes that was in Calle Industria, behind the Capitolio Nacional. I was maybe fourteen, fifteen; I was the youngest artist there, among all these older painters . . ."

[Bosch] ". . . and you were self-taught?"

[Salinas] ". . . absolutely."

[Bosch] ". . . and they were probably trained somewhere and there you were, obviously, with the in-crowd."

[Salinas] "Yes. And then my mother told me that she wanted me to study. So she took me to Sara Martínez Maresma's studio and she saw what I was doing and said: 'No, let him develop by himself, don't constrain him with academia or anything like that, let him develop by himself. And so I never formally studied. I kept on painting. Then I received a scholarship to study painting at Kent State University. Once I got there, and after maybe three months, I decided that perhaps, coming from a family with no means and poor, art was not for me. So I switched to architecture, but I kept on painting on the side, I never stopped."

[Bosch] "What were you painting at that time? Because when you came to the United States as a student obviously all of a sudden there was a whole new world for you."

[Salinas] "I was doing landscapes, American scenes and also, to help my income, I did portraits. I did portraits of my friends and their parents or whatever. But I never liked doing portraits. They were very realistic, because people love to see themselves, and in a much better light than they really are."

[Bosch] "So they were flattering, idealized portraits."

[Salinas] "I remember that Juan González, who lived one block away, used to do the same thing, and I remember him telling me once that there was this old lady that wanted to have a portrait done looking like Raquel Welch, so he did it."

[Bosch] "There you are, pay me, I'll do it. That's fabulous."

[Salinas] "That tells you about human nature."

[Bosch] "But you were doing your own painting besides these portraits for hire."

[Salinas] "Yes. Now, having studied architecture, my natural inclination was to go through the influence of what I had studied—facades, buildings. But little by little I transformed the facades from something realistic to something more abstract. They were invented, although at the beginning they were from American buildings, and mixed in style—Classical, Renaissance, or contemporary.

[Bosch] "I can see why architecture would take you to abstraction because of the 3-D conceptual part of it."

[Salinas] "Exactly. But, at the same time, while living in San Antonio and working as an architect, I started showing at the Witte Museum. I won a few prizes and began to steer away from architecture. I felt constrained by the straight line, the rigidity of architecture. So I started developing a different line of work, and my evolution has always been slow. Sometimes it came spontaneously and sometimes I nudged it a little bit; I forced the evolution. This happens to all artists because we get tired, bored. I started doing works related to space conquest. I followed Apollo XIII, the moon walk, and all that. I got interested in astronomy and read a few books by Fred Hoyle, the great British astronomer and then I started painting totally abstract space . . . constellations, nebula, anything that dealt with outer space."

[Bosch] "Suggestive of form but not graphically descriptive in terms of the actual visual presentation of the thematic content."

[Salinas] "Exactly, the color and maybe a little bit of the structure, but the structure was loose, it was not architectural. That was my main subject matter throughout the '70s until I went to live in Barcelona. In Barcelona, the quality of light, the architecture, the influence of other artists such as Antoni Tàpies and even Joan Miró—although Miró's work has not much to do with my own . . ."

[Bosch] ". . . but indirectly just absorbing the idea that you could branch out in all of these different ways. That there was no set pattern . . ."

[Salinas] ". . . not, not at all. Then, my paintings started changing. The palette got grayer, the colors got lesser. Because of my connection and collaboration with poets and writers such as María Zambrano, José Angel Valente, Pere Gimferrer, and Michel Butor, I developed a concept of the language of the clouds. This consisted basically of a gray background with white as the main color of my palette—the white symbolizing clouds. I also used pictograms, ideograms, and strange alphabets like the Greek alphabet, the Hebrew alphabet, and the Iberian alphabet."

[Bosch] "Words and pictures began to come together but in an abstract way. Not at all narrative."

[Salinas] "With white as the main color. This was brought about by a conversation with my good friend, María Zambrano. I would visit her, and I would listen to her talk—because she monologued, I never had a chance to dialogue with her. Then one day she tells me—and she wrote about it—'I see you as white.' So the white became my main color, and in most of the work I did in Barcelona white is the vital element."

[Bosch] "How do you respond to it? When you use it, when you manipulate it, what is it that comes out?"

[Salinas] "I don't know . . . the idea of purity, the idea of cleanliness, . . ."

[Bosch] ". . . and as a color, when you add the others, is the white the background, the accent, the highlight, for you?"

[Salinas] "That is a good question because lately I have been using it as background. But while I was living in Barcelona, I was using it as the subject. The Chinese and the Japanese use black for their pictograms and ideograms and I used white instead of black, in a negative way."

[Bosch] "It really was your accent and your form and the subject."

[Salinas] "I developed a white calligraphy in broad forms. I did that for maybe ten, twelve years and then I came back to Miami in 1992, and color started creeping up in my work again. It had to do with the light. The quality of the light here is different than what we have in Spain. The light in Barcelona is sort of rosy and because of the gray architecture, the contrast is strange. That, I'm sure, influences Spanish artists and it did influence me very much. So I started doing paintings that related more to earth even though I still kept clouds as sort of a mainstay in my work. Lately I've been doing something I call 'Sun flares.' And the flares can be white, instead of red or orange or yellow. So white is again becoming the mainstay of my painting. One thing that I would like to insert about this trip that I have done with my work is the work that I've done with Masafumi Yamamoto—the Master printer with whom I worked some fifteen years in Barcelona. I did all my etchings and lithographs with him in his atelier. I would spend half of my day there and—it's funny because doing an etching like *Fuji-San* would take me three weeks and in that time I could have done five paintings. It is a very slow process, very involved . . ."

[Bosch] "It is a significant investment of time and energy, collaborative."

[Salinas] "A lot, yes."

[Bosch] "You don't always have the last word because you have to take the medium into consideration and the other person with whom you are working, and so it becomes much more involved."

[Salinas] "Not only that, there was a time when I would be influenced by what I was doing in my etching work, so the painting took from the etching and that developed in a different direction. So much so that a friend of mine, a poet, told me that I was becoming 'yamamotisized.' . . . There's no question that my work with him influenced me but at the same time I influenced him."

[Bosch] "It's the back-and-forth."

[Salinas] "It was a dialogue, a real dialogue. I was fortunate enough to be able to do a book, called *Trois enfants dans la fournaise*, with Michel Butor. He told me that I should do the etchings first and then he did the texts—which are very poetic—afterward. That book came out in 1988 and was shown in the Museum of Bayeux in France with a number of other artists that had been collaborating with him. We still correspond— he is an older man now, but a real swell guy. And my collaboration with José Angel Valente and María Zambrano I treasure. The work that I did with Valente, *Tres lecciones tinieblas*, had to do with the Kabala and fourteen Hebrew letters and his poetic interpretation of each letter. Like the letter 'aleph'—which is the beginning—he calls it the 'first blood.' And the letter 'beth'—which is the 'b' in our alphabet—means 'house,' *morada*, dwelling, a place to be. The book is very beautiful and won the National Prize of poetry in Spain in 1980. And with María Zambrano I've done two books, *Antes de la ocultación: los mares* with four lithographs. In these lithographs I incorporated texture, so it was a double process: first the lithograph and then the texture."

[Bosch] "You're very unusual in all of these collaborations because the idea that one has of artists is that they work alone and then they bring out what they've made. But clearly, you're fairly unique in that you keep jumping into these group projects where you're working cross-culturally in some ways but also in an interdisciplinary manner in other ways because you're collaborating with writers and with poets."

[Salinas] "It enriched me a lot and I miss it. After I moved to Miami, I haven't collaborated much because there are no etching ateliers in Miami. There's one that a young fellow by the name of Joaquin González has opened up, but it's very . . ."

[Bosch] ". . . modest in scale? And you need something larger . . ."

[Salinas] ". . . yeah, because it has a small tórculo, a small press . . . And also, I don't have the interaction with poets and writers. Barcelona is another story. It's a very cultural city, a city that is vital."

[Bosch] "It has a history with layers from the very beginning through the medieval age, the Renaissance, the Baroque, the Art Nouveau, it's all there."

[Salinas] "Yeah, we have two bookstores in Miami: La Universal and La Moderna Poesía. Over there, you walk three steps and you find a bookstore."

[Bosch] "Oh, the antiquarian bookshops also, I mean, the things that you could find if you're interested in the concept of book and what's in them. It's a major center. Now, while you're following this sort of trajectory in your own work at the same time you're looking around at other artistic productions, how are you situating yourself with the development of twentieth-century art? Were you conscious of it? Were you thinking that you formed part of something? Or were you thinking of yourself as 'I'm something different, on the side, kind of getting along. Every so often I touch base with something'?"

[Salinas] "That second point. I strive to find a language that people can recognize in me by the work and not by my signature. And yes, I received a lot of influences from the different artists with whom I had contact in Barcelona . . ."

[Bosch] "Who were you especially looking at or having contact with?"

[Salinas] "There is a guy by the name of Albert Rafols Casamada— very abstract—in the manner of Diebenkorn here in the U.S. He definitely influenced me, although his work is much more colorful than mine was at the time when I was living in Barcelona. But it attracted me because deep down I knew that I am a colorist and therefore this is really what I want to do. Also Tàpies because of the strength of his work and the power that you encounter with all the texture, all the effects that he has. . . ."

[Bosch] ". . . so those were your touch points for what was happening."

[Salinas] "Yes, but, at the same time, I was trying to do my own thing."

[Bosch] "Obviously, the big thing in terms of the discussion that we're having has to do with identity, so your identity as an artist is going to be one of the things you're going to be going for, but I'm struck by the facts that you're traveling around to all of these places: you're living in the United States, you're living in Barcelona . . ."

[Salinas] ". . . and Mexico."

[Bosch] ". . . and you're Cuban. So, how Cuban were you in all of these places?"

[Salinas] "I don't know. You see, that is what I've been told by other artists. They tell me, 'In Cuba most people paint figuratively.' But that's not totally true because I can recollect that the members of El Grupo de los Once were all abstract . . . Hugo Consuegra for example. Some were geometrical, like Raúl Martínez. Still, somehow the Cuban psyche connects better with the figurative work."

[Bosch] "You are thinking of Carlos Enríquez."

[Salinas] "Victor Manuel, Portocarrero. . . . But we tend to generalize: that also has to do with the human condition."

[Bosch] "So, the question is, How Cuban was your art, since you weren't painting the palm trees with the *bohío*, the *campesino* . . . ?"

[Salinas] "Let's get back to when I moved back to Miami and started doing a series I called, 'Penca de palma triste.' In a way it dealt with the situation that our country was living at the moment and is still living. It was a political commentary because the palm tree is . . ."

[Bosch] ". . . the symbol of the quintessential Cuban plant."

[Salinas] "So it has been said for a long time. I didn't do the whole palm tree but the branch—*la penca*."

[Bosch] "A piece of it which is very interesting considering the disjunction of exile: you're just a piece of Cuba, so you just need one piece of the palm tree."

[Salinas] "Even more, it gave me the chance to project my abstract sense of painting into the work because even though you could see the *penca*—you could also see maybe a waterfall. It could be the tail of a very exotic bird. . . . The interpretation falls in the hands of the observer."

[Bosch] "In Barcelona, how did you feel? Some Cubans go to Spain and say, 'Oh, I'm home again. This is so familiar, it's such a familiar culture.' But other Cubans go to Spain and they think, 'Whoa, these people really are foreigners!' "

[Salinas] "They really are different!"

[Bosch] "Were you more Cuban in Spain than in the United States, for instance?"

[Salinas] "Definitely. The first two years were very hard for me because the people over there react differently to different situations. I remember that once I was in a bus and I was sitting down and this old lady came inside the bus and I offered her my seat. And she just looked at me and didn't say anything, didn't move. And I thought, *This is a strange reaction to a nice courtesy.* Another time some old lady dropped something on a corner and I was standing next to her and I picked it up and gave it to her and she didn't even look at me either. And I was really flabbergasted."

[Bosch] "I find that when I speak with some Cuban Americans, they say 'When we're in the United States, we're more American, but when we go Spain, we're more Cuban all of a sudden, because of the shock of what should be the same but isn't.' "

[Salinas] "You'd think the language would unite us more and it doesn't."

[Bosch] "And yet there are people who feel very much at home in Spain so it is such an individual jump, but for you it wasn't. Now you're Jewish too . . . so now you're Jewish in Spain, the country that threw Jews out. How was that for you?"

[Salinas] "In Barcelona that's an interesting situation because the Catalans feel that they are different from the rest of the Spaniards, and they call themselves the Jews of Spain. And it's because they are more into culture, more into working; they are the real producers of industry and other stuffs in Spain. In that respect some of my Catalan friends would tell me: 'I'm not going to Madrid until they require a passport from me.' There's this . . ."

[Bosch] ". . . separatist mentality—I think it is still very much there. Recently they're starting to refuse to speak Spanish; they want to just speak Catalan."

[Salinas] "That's affecting their perception of universalism because they always talked about '*el catalan universal*' . . . Many intellectuals that speak Spanish and were living in Barcelona are leaving. And if you go to study at the University you have to really learn your Catalan because otherwise you won't be able to survive."

[Bosch] "So, if you think about your life, you have kept moving. And if you think about the history of the Jews, they keep moving. Is this part of your experience of 'I'm a Jew, I move'?"

[Salinas] "Yes. I move and I adapt. But the Catalans reject this type of adaptation and it's hurting them. After all they are only, what? six million? It's a small number in the context of the whole country."

[Bosch] "But if you think about it, how many Cubans came to Miami and refused to adapt to the United States?"

[Salinas] "I know old men who haven't been able to learn one word of English and they don't want to. Which I think is sad."

[Bosch] "So it's that closing off again of the world."

[Salinas] "And many Americans that were living in Miami moved. They didn't want to dealing with the new situation. Many have gone into Broward County, to Fort Lauderdale."

[Bosch] "Because again, it's that intransigence that doesn't allow for that opening up and deal with the global situation. Now, let's head to the Diaspora and the situation while that was happening. Obviously, the idea of exile is something that everybody came here with. So this was a Cuban exiled community. It wasn't a bunch of Cuban Americans because there's been a big shift in terms of how Cubans identify. I can remember coming—I was eight years old when I came in '61—as a refugee. And then there was the period where you were an exile. And then there was the idea that 'We're not going back, we better adapt' and so the adaptation process began. And then suddenly we were Cuban Americans. So how did you go through this and what were things like for the artistic community when you first arrived?"

[Salinas] "When we started exhibiting as a group, Grupo GALA with Enrique Riverón, José Mijares, Osvaldo Gutiérrez, Rafael Soriano, Rosana McAllister (who was Argentinian, but we adopted her). She told me once that she was Cuban, because she lived in Cuba and had to leave when Castro came. So she considered herself part Cuban. But that's why the Grupo GALA means Grupo de Artistas Latino-Americanos—because of her. Otherwise, it would have been Grupo de Artistas Cubanos. But being that Rosana was Argentinian, we broadened it. And we started looking for places to exhibit and the first place was Bacardí. At the time they had a gallery on the first floor of their building. I remember that Gloria Luria had a nice gallery in North Miami and she gave us an exhibition because we were gaining a reputation as a group and individually, because we kept exhibiting individually and as a group every once in a while. But, as a group there were conflicts—clashes of personalities. Mijares always introduced an obstacle, to do things, to move on . . . We used to meet at Riverón's home maybe once every two weeks, sometimes once a month."

[Bosch] ". . . to plan the exhibition."

[Salinas] "Yes, and just to chat and exchange ideas and see what we were doing."

[Bosch] "How did you survive financially? Because at that point it is not as if Cubans had a ton of money to spend on art and you guys didn't have much money, so how did you manage to get money for materials and sell work?"

[Salinas] "I worked as an architect—painting was a sideline—but it wasn't what I loved to do. Until I got the Cintas Fellowship for the second time in 1970 (the first time was in 1969) and I decided to quit architecture and devote all my time to painting. And it's worked out. To me, painting is not work. It is something that transcends labor. I love to be in my studio painting because I forget about everything else. I'm so concentrated on it that it is like a meditation. I concentrate on what I'm doing and I enjoy it while I'm doing it. I enjoy seeing a wide space being developed into something that has life. It's always been the most important thing in my life. And architecture was never so."

[Bosch] "Architecture was the means to the end of being able to paint and because you had the skill and there was no money you practiced that until you could take off."

[Salinas] "But remember that I had started by studying painting . . ."

[Bosch] "Right, but you were in a manner of speaking already established in the United States because you had been exhibiting here. You weren't exactly new to the American system, you understood already how things worked in the art world in the United States . . ."

[Salinas] "I had lived in San Antonio for two years, yes, and in Mexico."

[Bosch] ". . . and you were educated here in a manner of speaking, so you had a kind of advantage that some of the other artists who arrived and did not speak English, for instance, did not have. But still, it couldn't have been easy."

[Salinas] "No, it was never easy. I remember in 1963, '64, I was selling paintings for twenty-five dollars."

[Bosch] "And of course people had a hard time paying you those twenty-five dollars. "

[Salinas] "And they were buying it on time. Five dollars a week, or five dollars a month, that's right."

[Bosch] "Were these people the same who bought art in Cuba and had left collections behind or people who began to do this here?"

[Salinas] "Both. There were a lot of people who had collected in Cuba and they wanted to re-create their collections; they had left good stuff in Cuba. I have a friend who left Portocarreros, Amelia Peláez, stuff like that. My cousin, Chalon Rodríguez Salinas, left a whole collection in Camagüey where he lived."

[Bosch] "So they started going after artists that they had already owned, trying to build up collections again and then . . ."

[Salinas] ". . . substitute, yes."

[Bosch] "Can you think of anyone in particular who provided important pieces to the art world in Miami?"

[Salinas] "José Manuel Martínez Cañas for sure. Mario Amiguet, Frank Mestre . . . There weren't too many."

[Bosch] "No, I understand that there weren't crowds. So mostly you were selling a painting here and there to people who you never saw again. And who then have disappeared with their Salinases, not knowing what they have."

[Salinas] "And now some of these paintings are appearing on the internet. A friend of mine who lives in Orlando calls me every once in a while and says, 'Hey, there's a painting of yours—is that yours for sure?' And then he tells me where to go to look at it and I look at it and every time that I have looked it's been mine, yeah. So I'm talking about paintings from 1963, '64, '65. It's like encountering old friends."

[Bosch] "At that point then what you really had was this scene where these people were on the one hand desperate for culture and for reestablishing cultural patterns and on the other hand absolutely no money with which to do it."

[Salinas] "It was a tough situation."

[Bosch] "When did it get easier? When can you think of that you said 'Okay, whew, the worse is over!'"

[Salinas] "For me, it was in the '70s. And then I moved to Barcelona in 1974. I was lucky because I remember in Madrid I met Juana Mordó who was the dean of the art dealers in Spain at the time and she loved my work; she kept some of it; she sold some of it; and she put me in touch with people in Barcelona—that's where I finally landed—and then somehow things worked out because . . . I didn't know anybody there but Juana Mordó introduced me to many people, that's how I started developing a network."

[Bosch] "One of the things that comes in throughout your career is a kind of mystical, metaphysical aspect to your work. Talk a little bit about that."

[Salinas] "I think it has to do with my Jewishness and what I learned in my home—the spirituality of my mother and my grandmother. At one time I remember a doctor friend of mine telling me that I was—he kept looking at my work, he collected my work and he was not a psychiatrist but in this way brought out some of the psychology of a humanist—antisocial."

[Bosch] "Oh my God, you of all people!"

[Salinas] "Yeah, because there were no people in my paintings. He says, 'Rarely do you put a person in a painting,' and it's true. So perhaps I always had this latent feeling of abstraction toward painting and I don't know exactly where it came from—I gather it has to do with my Jewishness."

[Bosch] "The Jewish mysticism, even the Kabala, pierces through the letters, opening up other realms; you go through the material form into the spiritual world. So you think that plays . . ."

[Salinas] "I believe so, although I couldn't really pinpoint it. There's no 'a,' 'b,' 'c,' 'd' that I can really point to in my progression in painting and the way I visualize art."

[Bosch] "Abstraction for you, then, is an internal process as opposed to the art world abstract expressionism controlled by Clement Greenberg saying that everything has to be . . ."

[Salinas] "Harold Rosenberg, yes."

[Bosch] "That crowd coincidentally were doing that in the twentieth century, but you are doing something completely different that is then linked to your identity as a Jew, connecting to the mystical side of Judaism, and you're not really part of that even. So, someone comes to your work and say, 'Oh, yes, abstract expressionism.' "

[Salinas] "There is a connection, yes, but my way was different. The path was different."

[Bosch] ". . . even though it comes out at the same place. When you work on subjects, can you think in terms of thematic material that responds to the Jewish in terms of the way that 'La penca' responds to being Cuban."

[Salinas] "I did many paintings based on the Hebrew alphabet, but I stayed away from doing the typical Jewish scenes . . ."

[Bosch] "Is it difficult to negotiate and navigate the idea of being Cuban, Jewish, American, and of having lived in Spain for a while, or is it just natural—a part of a flow of a continuum of things you are and respond to and relate to?"

[Salinas] "Natural, yes. I think that it comes natural and very spontaneously and I don't perceive myself as one thing or another. Even though, when somebody asks me 'What are you?' I say, 'I'm a Cuban painter' even though I'm Cuban American. I always place myself in the position of a Cuban painter. And while living in Spain I remember that I had discussions with artists and poets and the intelligentsia, and most of them were leftists or communists . . ."

[Bosch] "Sure, because that was the intellectual fashion at the time."

[Salinas] "Right away they'd place me in the band of the *gusanos*, and I had great arguments with these people. Most of them had never been in Cuba; they only had read about what was happening but they still sided with Castro against Americans and against the Cuban exiles. So it was not easy."

[Bosch] "No, I can imagine that it wouldn't have been easy. One of the questions that I'm going to ask you—that people always ask me and most of the time I just stare at them—is: 'How would you identify as Cuban in your work other than the obvious, such as 'La Penca'? Is there anything intrinsically Cuban in what you do?"

[Salinas] "I don't think so because I developed in the U.S. I developed with the abstract expressionist movement, with Willem DeKooning, Jackson Pollock, Mark Rothko . . ."

[Bosch] "And they form also part of the larger European movement, which I think is important to keep in mind."

[Salinas] "Yeah, the U.S. art scene was enriched when the Second World War started and Max Earnst and André Breton, and even Lam came back from Paris . . ."

[Bosch] "People like Duchamp—all these waves of Europeans coming to the United States."

[Salinas] "Dada, exactly."

[Bosch] "You're connecting to that also."

[Salinas] "I definitely think so, yes. Not perhaps directly but indirectly."

[Bosch] "Indirectly, you formed part of this global movement. And of course other Latin American artists with whom you are also familiar are also part of that continuum. And this brings us to a close. Thank you."

August 16, 2005
Interviewed in the artist's home, filmed by Norma Gracia, transcribed by Paul Symington, and edited by Jorge J. E. Gracia.

A SENSE OF PLACE

— Humberto Calzada

Humberto Calzada was born in Havana, on May 25, 1944. He emigrated to the United States in 1960 and settled in Miami. He received BA and MBA degrees from the University of Miami (1966 and 1968). He began exhibiting in Miami in 1975 at the Bacardí Gallery. Calzada received a Cintas Foundation Fellowship from the International Institute of Education, NYC (1981); a Purchase Award, Museum of Modern Art of Latin America, Organization of American States, Washington, DC (1978); followed by a Painting Fellowship from the Fine Arts Council of Florida (1980).

He is unusual among Cuban and Cuban-American artists in that he depicts only architecture and landscapes, with few objects, in his paintings. Calzada seeks to re-create an imaginary Cuba based on his memories and research of Cuba's architecture, spaces, and landscape. His goal is to render an idealized vision of Cuba that records a simultaneously engaged, yet objective analysis of the island's history as seen through its buildings.

Selected Collections: Denver Art Museum, Colorado; Panama Contemporary Museum of Art, Panama; Ponce Museum of Art, Puerto Rico; Museum of Modern Art of Latin America, Washington, DC.

INTERVIEW

Conducted by Jorge J. E. Gracia and Lynette M. F. Bosch

[Gracia] "I understand that you are a trained engineer, and even practiced for a few years, before you began your career as a painter."

[Calzada] "After I graduated, I worked for IBM for three years, but I wasn't happy, so I quit. I came back to Miami and taught engineering at Miami Community College for about three more years, and at the same time I was building houses. I got a contractor's license and built houses. But I wasn't happy with that either. I then took painting as a hobby, just trying to find something else. . . . It wasn't until 1975 that a friend of mine came to my house and said, 'I'm friends with the director of the gallery at Bacardí, and in their office building they have a gallery, would you want to have an exhibition there? By that time I had maybe twenty paintings, so I said 'Well, I never thought of that.' But she encouraged me and arranged for the exhibition. I sold most of the works at the show, so I thought, 'Maybe I can make a living out of this!' That was the start; by the following year I had liquidated everything I was doing and jumped into painting. It was rough the first couple of years, very rough, because I had to practically give away my work."

[Gracia] "Yeah of course, and I'm sorry I was not around to pick it up! Did your wife work to keep you going?"

[Calzada] "She had not worked before, but started working when I started painting. She worked for a year at a law firm—it was the toughest year."

[Gracia] "When I look at your work and that of other Cuban Americans, I ask myself, 'Is this his personality? What is it?' Because it is a kind of celebration."

[Calzada] "If you look closely, there is also a bit of sadness sometimes and loneliness and all that. But I think that you can express that through beauty. And you can express it through ugliness also."

[Gracia] "Exactly. The first thing that comes through is the beautiful. Then you can go into the work and see something else, but the beauty is just fantastic. Now, are your compositions made-up, or are they something you copied?"

[Calzada] "It's all made-up and I didn't know that much about materials when I started. so I used watercolor—very cheap watercolor, those little trays they sell. That's why some of the color has faded and it's untempered. I did maybe five or six paintings in this style and kept one."

[Gracia] "When I saw you paintings for the first time I thought that you had been an architect at some point. Then I found out that you had been an engineer. But architecture is behind it all."

[Calzada] "Yeah, I love architecture. I come to any houses being built and I dream—I think that I would have been a good architect."

[Gracia] "You have many series, have you kept paintings from all of them?"

[Calzada] "No, unfortunately not. There are periods from which I don't have any. Supporting a family with painting, you have to sell. I had some I wanted to keep but . . . "

[Gracia] " . . . they had to go! It is interesting that you have done some anecdotal work. You began with it, then moved away, and now you're returning to it. It looks as if you are trying to put everything together perhaps, integrating your whole work, and making remembrance part of it."

[Calzada] "Yes. Then I went from the anecdotal work to one in which I did stairs and I started doing walls that had no ceiling, and then

I went to ruins, and then from the ruins I went to the floods. Floods have a lot of symbolism. It's the ultimate disaster that can happen."

[Gracia] "So they have to do with what happened in Cuba. What are the great influences in your work?"

[Calzada] "De Chirico, Magrite, and then, among the Cubans, Amelia Peláez because of her use of vitrales, although my use of them is completely different. I love the luminosity of hues in her paintings. When you look at her paintings you see the inside of houses and the vitrales and the fruits, and all of it put together; it's a crazy composition but it has a very Cuban feeling."

[Gracia] "Light is very important for you."

[Calzada] "Light, yeah. Around 1975 I did many black surroundings where you can see the light through into an interior. These paintings have to do with my memories of interiors in the old Cuban houses, they were very dark in order to . . . "

[Gracia] " . . . make them cool. So you closed everything and then there were little windows at the top of the big doors, but everything else was shut."

[Calzada] "When I painted this studio—we built this house in '79 but the studio was done in 1993 because the original studio was just the size of a room and it was hard painting in it—I made my Cuban door, and laid a black and white floor. Then I ordered a lamp, which is a replica of the lamps used in many homes in Cuba."

[Gracia] "Well, you do have a lot of memorabilia around you."

[Calzada] "I've tried to make a fortification around me to stay Cuban."

[Gracia] "Tell me about it. How is it that you feel?"

[Calzada] "I have never really become reconciled with the idea of stopping being Cuban. You get your roots when you are thirteen, fourteen, fifteen years old. And at that time, when the revolution came, I remember dreaming a lot about my future. Although my family was always very pro-American and we loved to come to the United States and all that, I never wanted to become American. I wanted to keep the old way, be Cuban and then come here whenever I wanted. So I have created this world around me. I swear, sometimes when I'm painting I put on Cuban music and I open these doors in the winter, when it's not so hot, and I am in Cuba."

[Gracia] "And you have a Cuban backyard. And you eat Cuban? And you live Cuban!"

[Calzada] "Oh, yes."

[Gracia] "Everything! And your art? Clearly you make architectural compositions, but they are Cuban in many ways. It is all going back to your roots as it were. But are you a Cuban artist or just a Cuban-American artist. How have you negotiated that dichotomy? How do you feel when people catalog you or peg you and say that you are Cuban."

[Calzada] "It doesn't bother me. I hear a lot of BS about 'an artist is an artist and I don't want to be cataloged.' I am an artist, but I'm also Cuban. I don't know how the two fit together, but basically my art and inspiration come from the Cuban culture and my Cuban roots. So it really doesn't matter to me whether I am called a Cuban artist, a Cuban-American artist, or just an artist. But I do identify myself basically as a Cuban person, I am very, very Cuban. I don't know if it's something that I've worked hard at or it just comes naturally. I've never felt the desire to integrate—although I have a lot of American friends and I can function in the American world perfectly. I've never felt like losing my identity or anything like that."

[Gracia] "And as an artist, how do you feel? Do you think about these things, about how you fit in the art world? Whether you have a niche?"

[Calzada] "No. Right from the beginning a lot of people gave me advice, 'If you want to succeed, do this, or do that,' but I ignored all that because it wasn't me. I do what I want, if the art world likes it, fine, and if not. . . . I'm not going to work with a mold and I know there are many molds. I don't know if you have the same thing in philosophy or in writing, do you?"

[Gracia] "Exactly the same!"

[Calzada] "You have to make a choice. Maybe you can get more ahead or faster ahead by going by the mold, but I didn't leave a career that I didn't like to go into something and then do whatever is not me. So I set with my own sail."

[Gracia] "But it's a tough thing because to succeed in art, as in philosophy or anything else, requires approval from groups of people who control what gets through, as it were. And if you don't fit what they want, you have a tough time."

[Calzada] "To begin with, being a Cuban exile already puts you in a situation in the art world. In 1985 I went to Paris to try to get a gallery. So when I went with a list of over ten galleries and I called them on the phone to make appointments, I did not get an appointment for a single one because I am Cuban living outside Cuba. 'Ah oui. Where do you live?' 'Miami.' Oh, 'mais non, non.' I was not able to show my work there just because I am Cuban from Miami. That's strike number one. Then if you don't conform to the type of work that is acceptable, then you are out. Still, I've done well. I'm not superfamous but I've been able to do what I want and be happy."

[Gracia] "There is one more thing that you have done and that is that you have been able to survive just painting, which how many artists can do? And then there are some painters that survive just doing paintings but what they do is not quite good, and your work is good! Now tell me something about the medium. You use acrylic primarily?"

[Calzada] "Acrylic on canvas or on rag board."

[Gracia] "And then you also do serigraphs of your works."

[Calzada] "Yeah, I had done some serigraphs before, but then around 1999 my wife and I decided to ask for a loan to the Small Business Administration and with that money we did several editions, and it's generated a good side income. When your work starts getting expensive for young people or for offices or for second homes. . . . people don't want to go over a thousand dollars in such cases."

[Gracia] "We've been talking about the very strong aspect of your work and of yourself as Cuban, but how do you feel about this whole Latin American thing and the Hispanics, and so on? Have you taken any interest in, say, Latin American art? I noticed that you have exhibited in Venezuela."

[Calzada] "Yeah, I have exhibited in Chile, Venezuela, Peru, Panama, El Salvador, and Puerto Rico."

[Gracia] "So, they know your work there. Have you become interested in any artistic creations and artists from those parts of the world?"

[Calzada] "I follow what they do and I read the magazines on Latin American art. I don't collect it because I don't have room where to put it. I collect just Cuban art, and just a few pieces because I don't have much space or money. But I am interested in Latin American art. I follow it as much as I can."

[Gracia] "Well Humberto, is there anything else you would like to say in this interview? Do you have any beef? An ax to grind?"

[Calzada] "Not really. I just wish there was more freedom in the sense that in the modern art world they have substituted one dictatorship for one tyranny."

[Gracia] "What about the Internet? Do you think the Internet might actually help break some of this monopoly of opinion?"

[Calzada] "It could. I read the other day—and this is not related to art but to politics—about a blog or blogs. These are people who express views that do not get into newspapers because they are censored."

[Gracia] "There's always censorship of one kind or another, no question about it. Now, let's go back to the way you begin to work. You tell me that your compositions are made up, but many artists say that they have to begin with something and then they make up things out of it. But you don't begin with something that you're looking at. You begin with an idea?"

[Calzada] "Sometimes I start with something, anything. Sometimes I do sketches. For example, when I have a commission, I show the collector some alternatives. But when I don't have a commission, sometimes I just go to the canvas directly, drawing on it."

[Gracia] "And how much work do you do a year? How long does it take you to get through some of these paintings?"

[Calzada] "I always work on two, sometimes three, pieces at the same time. Some years I produce a lot, some years I produce less, it all depends. That one, for example, took me almost a month to get where it is, it's still not finished, that's a commission too. I still have to do a little railing. Originally I was going to do it without a railing, but I feel that it needs a line here showing a hint of the banister."

[Gracia] "I see that almost everything that you're doing now has some kind of landscape in it which it didn't before."

[Calzada] "Yeah. A lot of it comes from places where I have been in the past six or seven years. Now I see a lot the landscape. Many things in art require digestion, they come out later, and you don't even know what it is."

[Gracia] "Your work deals primarily with architectural elements but you've never gone to machines, you've never gone to automobiles, you've never gone to any other type of artifacts. You concentrate basically on the architectural side. And the other thing that I notice is that you haven't gone to big buildings or anything like that."

[Calzada] "No, they don't interest me at all."

[Gracia] "Your interest is primarily in immediate living quarters."

[Calzada] "I'm going to show you something. I always think of Cuba, but it is an empty place because I don't know anybody there, I don't have any relatives there that I know."

[Gracia] "Empty. No one is there. You are trying to reconstruct something, but different than it was.

Humberto is showing Norma and Jorge a picture of the dining room in the Calzada's house in Havana.

[Norma Gracia] "Ah, the floors!"

[Gracia] "In many ways you're trying to re-create or bring back the past but in a different way, because you're transforming and making it much more beautiful than it was. And you know there's something about this that is common to other Cubans. Cubans often think about the past in Cuba and they talk about it and I often say, 'Well, that's not exactly how it was, that's how one would have liked it to have been.'"

[Calzada] "Right, right. As in an eulogy, when you know the guy was a big son of a bitch but in the eulogy he is said to have been great!"

The interview resumes a couple of days later, with Lynette M. F. Bosch as interviewer.

[Bosch]: "One of the things that Humberto and I have talked about over the years is his interest in historical architecture. So, Humberto, I wonder if you could say something about the way that you traveled around Cuba when you were young, the impression that the architecture you saw made on you, and how that comes out in your work."

[Calzada] "My father was born in the area of Trinidad, so we used to go back there every year to see a couple of aunts he had in Cienfuegos. Then we would go and visit Trinidad, which had some beautiful neo-Classical architecture and had some houses with the typical central court-yard which dates back to the Romans. They always had a fountain. Trinidad is one of the oldest cities of Cuba, so it had architecture you could admire. Some houses were completely furnished with pieces that were dated back to colonial times, all the way back to the 1700s and the 1800s."

[Bosch] "What was the architectural style of the colonial houses? Was it neo-Classical, Baroque, or what?"

[Calzada] "It was not neoclassical, that comes in at the end of the nineteenth century. The colonial architecture of Trinidad is Spanish ar-chitecture adapted to the climate. It's very similar throughout Latin America except for adaptations to materials, climate, or customs."

[Bosch] "What in that architecture resonated with your idea of what it was to be Cuban in Cuba at that time? What were the things that you looked at in architectural style, the specific details, that made you think 'that's mine, that's what's me.' "

[Calzada] "Everything. I don't think I specifically looked at it that way, but I integrated the whole thing inside me. For example, the house that most inspired me belonged to my uncle, and all the family reunions took place there. His wife was a pianist and the daughter of a famous composer that was from the Netherlands but lived in Cuba. And so she would play songs in the piano, and when you listened to that in that setting, you had no choice but to become really Cuban. To experience that and to see all of the foliage outside and all the tropical plants really made an impression on me."

[Bosch] "So it's the combination. In terms of thinking about your work within an art historical context, you're pretty unique in choosing to make architecture your metier so to speak, because when I think about the range of subject matter, presentation of thematic content, your work really stands out in that. How do you see yourself within the continuum of Cuban and Cuban-American art from this particular perspective where you chose architecture as . . ."

[Calzada] "I think not only in Cuban art but also in Latin American art, architecture is a theme that is not uncommon, maybe mixed with other things, I do it exclusively some others do it . . ."

[Bosch] "That's what's unique about you, you do it so exclusively."

[Calzada] "Yeah, but before me there was also Emilio Sánchez. But architecture is my main interest. I haven't been that intrigued by the human figure. I haven't been that intrigued by other things but architecture, light and shadow, and perspective have always fascinated me."

[Bosch] "How did you get interested in perspective because your technique in this is fantastic."

[Calzada] "I don't know—it's something that always fascinated me because you would create this new dimension. After I started doing it, I started reading a little bit, and I learned that it was a dirty word in art. But I didn't know that at the moment, and once I learned it, I didn't care. So what, I wanted to do it. I didn't know that it has almost been banned from the university."

[Bosch] "Right, how dare you introduce the third dimension. When one looks at your floors, one always thinks of Vermeer for instance."

[Calzada] "A few artists have really fascinated me and the Dutch painters are among them. The use of light and of the floor, the use of geometry and perspective, they have is fabulous."

[Bosch] "I see much in your work that has to do with the idea of Renaissance perspective, Renaissance-Baroque imagery. How do you interweave your interest in Renaissance and Baroque artists with Cuban identity?"

[Calzada] "I love Renaissance art. And what I have to do is to take it to Cuba—it's not that far away because I introduce a few elements and I'm there. Introduce some stained glass or wrought iron work . . ."

[Bosch] "So, you don't see a conflict between, let's say, being Cuban and then reaching to the European."

[Calzada] "No, in fact being Cuban has always meant trying to reach out to the whole universe. I guess from being an island, we are very self-contained but at the same time we're always fascinated by anything that comes from the outside. We have created Cuban music by borrowing from everybody and then Cubanizing it. We did that with many things in our culture and it's great. Another thing, in culture very few things are really original, it's all borrowed, and rehashed and then reproduced."

[Bosch] "It's a mixture, a new mixture that comes out. One of the other things that I think is very characteristic of you, and again, I think pretty unique to you, is the way that you do, for instance, the stained glass. We've talked about the idea of memory in your work and how you remember similar windows. You invent pretty much everything in your interiors, your exteriors, but when you think back into, let's say the creative sources of that particular motif—the windows—what comes to your mind when you start to make the windows? Do you remember specific windows?"

[Calzada] "Yeah, I remember specifically the ones in my uncle's house. But I remember also windows I saw all over Cuba. I remember very much looking—as a kid—at the reflection on the floor that the glass would produce and being fascinated by it. It's a connection of light and shadow. If you look at Cuban art, the presence of stained glass is almost everywhere. It is such a strong visual element that you have no choice but to ingest it and throw it back out."

[Bosch] "If you think about the history of Cuban art going all the way back, who are your favorite Cuban artists when you think about looking for inspiration, who do you admire? Who would you identify as being quintessentially Cuban?"

[Calzada] "Amelia is one of my biggest fascinations. The day I hung the Amelia I own, I told my wife, 'I smell black beans.' It's like a a synthesis of everything Cuban. It has the wrought iron rail, the colors of the stained glass, the Baroque, everything. It's so like her."

[Bosch] "Tell us something about the series that you did that combines literature and art. Where did that come from?"

[Calzada] "It came from reading José Martí's poem called 'Dos patrias' which means 'Two motherlands': Cuba and the night—opposite but they're both the same. From there on Martí goes on to describe the situation of Cuba. He's talking about the late nineteenth century, but you think he is talking about the situation now, because it's just very similar, very sad."

[Bosch] "What did you want the spectator who sees the series to experience?"

[Calzada] "I tried to convey the beauty of the nights in Cuba. But every painter falls short. You have it in your mind but you feel that you're not really able to reproduce it."

[Bosch] "I wonder if you can talk to us a little bit about what things were like in Miami when you first started exhibiting your work in terms of the larger scene of Cuban-American art. Who were the artists who were active, because there was a generation of the older artists."

[Calzada] "I started exhibiting in 1975, but between '65 and '75 was mainly Soriano, Mijares, and Salinas. I started more or less at the same time as Falero."

[Bosch] "Then your friend, Arturo Rodríguez came from Spain. And then Demi joined the group. When you all exhibited, the idea was that you were Cuban Americans. How much of that played into how the exhibitions were organized?"

[Calzada] "The Miami context is different from anywhere else. The whole group was Cuban-American so the issue didn't come out as much as it would have been elsewhere."

[Bosch] "Right, so it was more that there happened to be a bunch of Cuban Americans here, you were all artists, and you were of course Cuban-American. Another thing I'm very curious about is that you have an almost classic Renaissance way of working in that you're always very accessible to patronage and patronage demands. You think of your work within the architectural structure of the house where it's going, for instance. I've heard you talk about going and looking at the place and taking measurements. And this really is a very unique way of working that links directly back to Renaissance practice. This idea of the work in situ, that it's designed specifically for a place."

[Calzada] "Yeah, because I think this idea that artists are demigods is recent. Renaissance artists thought of themselves more as artisans. There was not so much snobbishness as there is now. I like to paint something and people go and buy it, but if somebody wants something a special size—I don't see anything wrong with that. I really don't."

[Bosch] "Because it's again the idea of the collaboration between the place where the work is going and you."

[Calzada] "It's challenging. In fact, I think I can produce a better painting if I see where it's going to be hung. Then I can imagine how it's going to look and then I work my sketches in that direction."

[Bosch] "As opposed to a kind of haphazard, 'well here's the painting, I create my own world' and then somebody takes it and they put it somewhere where it may or may not fit in."

[Calzada] "Exactly. Sometimes, it happens in my house. Sometimes I buy a painting of another artist and it doesn't go on the wall where I intended for it to go—it ends up on a completely different wall because that's where it goes well."

[Bosch] "Yeah, it's a way of making sure the work is going to fit the context. Which, again, is something that goes directly back to Renaissance practice and yet it's very much a part of the contemporary world. Good, so we're done. Thank you."

August 15 and 17, 2005
Interviewed in the artist's home and studio, filmed by Norma Gracia, transcribed by Paul Symington, and edited by Jorge J. E. Gracia.

ART ON ART

Emilio Falero

Emilio Falero was born in Sagua La Grande, on August 18, 1947. He emigrated to the United States in 1962, as part of the Peter Pan Operation. He settled in Miami and studied at Barry College (1969) and Miami-Dade Community College (1967). He began exhibiting in 1969 at the Library Gallery of Miami-Dade Community College's North Campus. He has received the Ziuta and Joseph James Akston Foundation-Award (1976), followed by the Society of the Four Arts, Palm Beach Award, and a Cintas Fellowship Award from the Institute of International Education in New York City (1976).

Falero works in a representational style with Renaissance/Baroque quotations within a philosophical framework that seeks to juxtapose spirituality and the alienation evident in contemporary culture.

Selected Collections: Cintas Foundation, New York; Metropolitan Museum of Art Center, Miami; and Miami-Dade Public Library System, Florida.

INTERVIEW

Conducted by Lynette M. F. Bosch and Jorge J. E. Gracia

[Bosch] "Emilio, I'm going to build a structure for the interview that begins with you in Cuba, how you came to the United States, and then how you began to develop as an artist. We're particularly interested in your philosophical, religious, and spiritual base, how you identify yourself as an artist, and what it means to you to be Cuban, Cuban American, and a Cuban-American artist. So start by telling us a bit about your early childhood training as an artist."

[Falero] "I had a pretty normal childhood in Cuba; I went to kindergarten and things like that. In kindergarten they used to give you drawings and things to draw and the teacher told my mother that I had a certain inclination to art. According to my mother—I don't remember this at all—that was one the first indications that she had that I could be an artist. Then in grammar school—I went to a Jesuit school and they didn't have art classes at all—but in my notebooks I used to draw things all the time, along with the numbers. Then one day, one of the brothers who was from Galicia in Spain called my parents and showed them some of the drawings—and said, 'You see, he spends some time of the class drawing these things, but don't tell him anything, because he's going to be an artist, and it's normal that he does that. We would like for him to pay more attention in class, but you should buy him things that he can use to do art at home.' Later on, I met a neighbor—Juan Carlos Llera's father—who used to paint also. He had some friends in my home town that were from San Alejandro, and they used to talk about art and show paintings. I was very young—about eleven years old at the time—but I used to sit with him, looking at his paintings and how he painted. But later on I began to paint with him. I learned from him some techniques and outlooks on art. After the Jesuits left my home town, new priests from an order of the Sacred Hearts of Mary and Jesus came, and they were very young and knew a lot about art. They sung very well, they knew music, they knew art; art was very important to them as an order."

[Bosch] "So all this formed part of your world . . ."

[Falero] "Yes, and it shatters all the stereotypes. You can't put human beings in compartments. These priests had a lot of life in them, although they were very religious. One of them used to paint in the parish—my school at that time (secondary school) was in front of the park where the church was—the plaza, in the center of the town. And when I finished my classes I used to go there and he let me sit and look at him paint. He told me not to 'talk to me' because he didn't have much time, he had a lot of things to do. But he had a little time to paint. He sometimes showed me how to mix colors and so on. He used to paint in a very interesting style to me at that moment. It was a combination of impressionism with some of the ideas of the luminists. He was from Mallorca and he used to paint seascapes with the things typical of the Balearic Islands. I learned many techniques from him, particularly a very good use of the spatula."

[Bosch] "How much did you learn from books at the time?"

[Falero] "My father had the *Enciclopedia Espasa-Calpe*, and I used to look at the different art pieces in the encyclopedia. I also had some books from the school, and also my grandmother gave me some books. And then, the first year after the Revolution, came an exhibition from Havana. It was like a sample of the National Museum."

[Bosch] "Was this the first time that you actually saw works of art in the flesh, so to speak?"

[Falero] "I had seen some of the Baroque paintings that were in the school and in the parish—they had beautiful paintings, particularly one in the Baptistery that was from a Dutch artist. But the first time I saw modern paintings was in that exhibition, although coming from my home town, I wasn't ready to understand that type of art. Then I came to Miami, and I went to the Belén school, but I used to spend some time at the library looking at things. At the same time I was going to Belén, Soriano was teaching there and he introduced us to abstract painting and took us to different museums to see art, which he'd explain to us. I was also painting with him but he said that it was the exposure to abstract paintings and museums that helped me to understand the concepts and gave me an incentive to read more about abstract painting and about the artists. So I went to a library and met Margarita Cano, and we became friends, and she gave me books and allowed me to look at files she had."

[Bosch] "When you were doing this—which was a kind of informal art history study—what painters were you drawn to?"

[Falero] "Very weird painters. One was Dalí because I was attracted surrealism. Then I became very interested in the Mexican muralists. My interests went in different directions. Also I was interested in the Baroque, the Renaissance, the Gothic . . ."

[Bosch] "You went global and across time."

[Falero] "Yes, because I had the books. I didn't have to do much, just go to the library and get books. Then in Miami I started studying architecture. I thought in my naïveté that architecture was more art. But when I started, I realized there was no art in it, it was just something in a straitjacket, with things that came already done. Everything was set for windows, everything came already made, and you just put them together. I felt this sort of thing was not for me. I remember this professor I had that taught renderings and the first rendering I did was my idea of the building but in the sunset. When he saw it he said, 'Oh, this cannot be a rendering at all. You have to do the trees in this form and this and that.' And I said, 'Why do I have to do that? You want to see just a building? I am showing the building in all its details, but why do I have to follow that style? I can have another style to do the renderings.' Which actually it came to pass later on—things changed, and they were doing later what I was doing at that moment."

[Bosch] "You were a man ahead of your time."

[Falero] "I learned that architecture wasn't for me. I spent a lot of time in the library, looking at paintings. I also took drawing classes, life drawing classes, which were very good because you had the models and somehow you learn a lot about drawing from the model. I had a good teacher of drawing in one of the classes that was a very good friend of Duane Hanson, and he moved to New York, he was like a hippie in New York. He started doing cartoons of people, and he left completely his work while he worked on cartooning. But at that moment in college he used to look at me drawing and then he took me aside and he gave me some good counsel. He told me to buy certain books and helped me to perfect my look at paintings. The way you look is very important to draw, you have to learn how to do it. Then I changed my major to art in college. I had some classes with Consuegra and Duane Hanson and others. In painting classes I didn't learn much because at that moment they just told you to express yourself, that was it, they played some music and told you to express yourself! So I had to look for other avenues to learn about techniques and things of that sort."

[Bosch] "But at the same time you had an education that, within the context of the classic art academy education, included all the things that were part of the curriculum. On your own and in bits and pieces you got the techniques and the history, and you put it all together. Now, at this point you're still in school but you are starting to exhibit, so did you start to now think that you were a professional artist?"

[Falero] "I exhibited at student shows. Then I started working with a landscape architect because I couldn't get a job in architecture. But the landscape architect saw my drawings and said, 'This is what I want, because the way I was taught to do them in architecture school I don't like. I don't care about the building, I care about the trees.' Then I met Juan González and we became very good friends. We had meetings and spent a lot of time talking about art. That was very good for me because it gave me an incentive."

[Bosch] "I remember you told me at one point that you wanted to travel, you went to Washington."

[Falero] "Yeah, and then to New York in 1971 or '72. I did some works also for a restaurant in New York and I took the opportunity to go to museums and galleries, so I saw a lot of art and got a sense of what was happening."

[Bosch] Did this change the direction of your art?

[Falero] "When I left Miami I started doing some abstract work. I took a motorcycle and developed abstract shapes out of the motorcycle. And those shapes then became the main elements in a series of paintings that were abstract. At the same time the shapes were kind of organic and had some geometrics also. It was more like a spatial thing, like the cosmos or cosmic things; like a dreamworld. Then I started including in the paintings faces of women from the classical tradition. At first those faces were blurred—if you didn't look at the painting very closely you would miss the human touch in the painting, you'd see only an abstraction but they were there. Later on the faces became more important and the abstractions receded to the background. I began taking the faces and women and men from works of art from the Renaissance. That's how I became interested in what they later called 'art about art.' At that moment there was nothing like that; what you saw was the actual painting—in Pop art they had sometimes the Mona Lisa, but it was something sporadic. Nobody talked about this in the art world; they didn't talk about 'art about art' or anything like that. I received much criticism from some professors. They said that I was doing something that was not good because the Mona Lisa was dead when they invented the photographic camera and there was no use anymore for realism. They were very, very stern about this. But somehow I felt like doing these things more, I don't know why. And all of a sudden they have this big exhibit at the Whitney that was called 'Art About Art.' And they had biennials in the Whitney, and they had a lot of this type of art in them. And they wanted González to move to New York. But he was criticized because they said that he was kind of crazy, doing this sort of thing, going back in time."

[Bosch] "Did you let this stop you for a moment? I mean what did you think when they said these things to you? Did you just say 'I know who I am as an artist and I know what I have interests in'?"

[Falero] "I had started doing this and I continued. I wasn't selling paintings or anything. I just did it. So all of a sudden I was in the middle of a trend and everybody was calling me and it felt strange. But it happened and there were people doing this all over the place, but nobody knew about it because it wasn't written about in the magazines. I realized then that there is something in art that is like an undercurrent that flows and another thing is what you see published. There is a gap of ten or fifteen years between what you see published and what has been happening for twenty years before or even more."

[Bosch] "So what you think is current isn't really current."

[Falero] "It isn't current in the sense that it is contemporary. It's more what is being assented as contemporary. Also at that time I had a crisis in faith in New York. I was one day in the subway and these Hari Krishnas were singing, and they gave me a booklet, and it was a long trip to Queens, so I had time to read it. It looked to me very strange, but all the same something came to my mind that said, 'If you were born in India and your family were Hindu, you'd be Hindu also.' It came to me that all religion is cultural and faith is the product of culture. So I lost my faith completely, and I felt very weird because it was as if the floor had fallen out from under my feet. For me everything lost its bearings. Then I went to a priest that I knew there in New York and I told him about what had happened and he told me, 'You have to go to 102, where we have a house in which we work with poor people and with the gangs in the street. And there you will find your answer.' I went, but it didn't help, because my problem was intellectual. I had to find answers outside the actual world. So I had an experience one day. I was coming from the

Museum of Modern Art, walking down Fifth Avenue and passed in front of St. Patrick's and the bells were ringing. I entered St. Patrick's and saw these Japanese people taking pictures. And I felt like if I were in Bangkok taking pictures of the pagodas. I didn't have any religious feelings or anything like that. I walked to the apse—it was very quiet, nobody was there—only three or four people praying. There was an image of the Virgin Mary in the chapel, on stained glass. And it was a contrast with the street because it was rush hour. So I felt peace there, sat down and started wondering—nothing about religion or about what I saw in the museum— but it felt so good there because it was quiet. I spent one or two hours there, a long time there. When I got out of there, I went to the subway and the Village because I wanted to see some of the galleries in the Village. And when I got out I saw a place where they sell used books and I got this urge to look. And then I saw this shelf full of books and I went to the shelf and I saw a book and I got it out, and it was Gabriel Marcel's *Creative Fidelity*. I didn't know who Gabriel Marcel was, but the title told me that it had to do with creativity. So I started reading and all the questions I had Gabriel Marcel answered in that book in a very, very strange way."

[Bosch] "What was it specifically that you suddenly realized to which here's an answer?"

[Falero] "In a nutshell, he said that your relationship with God, or what he called the mystery of being, was personal. Even when you have this intellectual or cultural thing, that is part of you but it is not when the real you meets the real Thou, the I and the Thou. This thing has to happen, otherwise you are not having a covenant, a real relationship—and he said that in order for the relationship to be true and good it has to be one of fidelity. Fidelity is the key. Then I realized that faith is a gift that God gives you, there's nothing that you fabricate or do for it. If you do, then what you get is not faith, it's something else. This faith is a relation- ship; it has to be personal. Then I got some more books by Marcel, and started spreading out to other books. I went into Nietzsche because I got very interested in atheists. I said, 'How do they see this?' Because this is what Gabriel Marcel does, he opens you to other possibilities, because he's very considerate of all the others. So I got a lot from reading Sartre and Nietzsche, et cetera. And I was also trying to see their lives because I thought that their philosophy had to be connected to their lives. I wanted to see how they lived and how what they believed manifested itself in their living. So I started looking at things differently—even scientific knowledge many times is belief also, because it is not only the fact but it is how you interpret the fact. Gabriel Marcel was interested in creativity and all that. I discovered that he also had some books on creativity. Some of these books were also about art, so I became interested in aesthetics. I read a lot of that, about art on art, art for art's sake. Leo Tolstoy has one that is against art for art's sake. So then I realized that there were different ways of looking at art, so I tried to make up my mind by reading all these things. Then I reached a conclusion I still hold—although I've changed it a little bit—mainly that the history of art is not so much dialectic in the sense that one school is in the other and then you get a synthesis and so on. In reality there is an undercurrent that is like a chain that unites everything. And the styles and the art manifestations are in the end of man because each human being as a human being is looking at this world, and somehow he intuits how things are and he portrays that. In a way, art is like an X-ray, not only a photograph of man, but an X-ray. It goes deeper, it goes into the spirit of man and comes out in the works of art. Picasso had his idea of man and Velásquez had his own. And the theme is the same, it's the artist in his studio, the other one is the apprentice of Velásquez, see. So what you're looking at is how an artist or a man saw man in the sixteenth century and how modern art sees man in the twentieth century. When you see the differences then you have many questions: Why so different? Why one sees it this way and the other one the other way? Then I turned to essays of people like Ortega y Gasset, who differed a great deal in their views. But at the same time, there is something that unites all this—that is the same man who's producing them. And somehow you can communicate through art to the artists of the Altamira caves. Today you can see an Altamira painting and be moved by it. You can be moved by a Chinese work, and the century does not matter. And so there is something that breaks all the boundaries that schools fabricate, because there is something that unites all of them. It's that we are human and we all express our spirit. It's as if today we read a letter of a mother to her son in the Renaissance let's say, you can feel the feelings of the letter and somehow they become very real to you, they speak to you. The letter transcends the lifespan of the mother and there's a reality in it that is between the words because it is not actually in the words but it is something that is between the lines of the words that somehow hits you as real, living, it's not dead. Paintings have that also, they are living things, and they communicate to you something that is alive, that is not dead. When you see a painting that is dead you think 'This is bad art,' usually. And then you have it in the twentieth century, in the Renaissance—they are shallow, they have nothing there and you get bored with them very soon. The same is true of the theater. You can see the same play many times, Shakespeare or whatever, and it tells you something new every time. But when you see one that is not good, once is enough and if you see it again there is nothing there for you."

[Bosch] "So at this point that you're working on the art on art series you're firming up your faith again."

[Falero] "Yeah, little by little, because I needed to comprehend also and to study more what all these things have to do with man. What's the difference between Michelangelo's *David* and Bernini's *David*? But if someone does a David and he's not an artist, then it won't have the life that Michelangelo's has. So there is something that is the same and something that is not the same. Some people put a lot of emphasis on the theme or the psychology or the sociology in a novel—they see the sociological aspect—and it is good in a painting also that it reflect all that—but that's not what makes it beautiful or what makes it a work of art; there's something else there, and that 'else' is something that I was trying to get at in this moment in my life. Then I realized that every work of art is like a window that is opened for a vision toward the mystery of being. We live a mystery, we are a mystery to ourselves. We go into ourselves; our deepest self is a mystery to us, we cannot grasp it completely. And we cannot analyze ourselves to death because everything we analyze becomes something else in the process, on that Sartre had a lot of ideas and he is very interesting. So somehow when the work of art is really alive and transmits something to you it's the same as when a flower or a tree or a landscape or the moon makes you transcend it and communicate with what is mysterious. That mystery, that transcendence of things—that's what makes it appealing and that's what makes you awe. Because art should leave you speechless so that you communicate at a level that is not thematic. This is what you receive in poetry, that's what you receive in every work of art. The actual elements of design or the music are like a carrier, like a vehicle that lets the artist communicate that experience of the mystery of being, which he had as an inspiration and you receive. That's why people didn't understand van Gogh at first because they didn't have the vehicle yet, so they had to learn how to use that vehicle. But later on they found it beautiful. Today people love van Gogh. During his life he couldn't sell one painting because nobody liked them. So somehow people learned how to appreciate them . . . But in the end, it was because what van Gogh saw was so beautiful and so mysterious that he was able to put it in the paintings."

[Bosch] "So you began working on the series and then all this is happening in New York but you come back to Miami."

[Falero] "Yes—I was going through these ideas also at this moment—so I started putting this art on art series."

[Bosch] "And you started exhibiting it."

[Falero] "I went through all these experiences with other artists."

[Bosch] "Because you came back and you were suddenly part of this whole Cuban-American generation movement that was starting."

[Falero] "Yeah, another thing is that, although I didn't realize it, I had also the influence of Cuban art—of my experiences. And I became aware of it when I started translating some of these images into a language of the fauvists, I used Matisse and Picasso. But somehow those paintings related more to the tradition of Cuban art."

[Bosch] "So you started to double connect to being Cuban because you're here in a Cuban-American community and now you're connecting to the history of Cuban art at the same time that you're actually becoming a part of the history of Cuban art in exile in Miami. How did being an exile at that point have an impact on you?"

[Falero] "One thing that I experienced as a Peter Pan was a sense of security even before I left Cuba. I felt that it was like God wanted me to do this transition. I received that the day of our Lady of Charity. I was in the Church in Cuba, it was September the eighth in 1962. They had this celebration of Mass—and I stayed by myself after that and I went before the image of the Lady of Charity, I prayed there, nothing special, you know, just looking at it, but somehow I got this insight there, very deeply, that no matter what, everything was going to be okay. I got this message and I didn't know why I was receiving it. And a wire came right away after that. So I had to leave without my parents and the only thing that I knew of Miami was the name of a man that was waiting for me at the airport."

[Bosch] "But you were certain that it was going to be okay."

[Falero] "Somehow I received this fortitude. It was something very weird. And when I went to the camp I saw that other people did not have that, some people were very disturbed."

[Bosch] "You were in the boys camp. What was the age range?"

[Falero] "Sixteen to nineteen. I was there for a year and then I went with forty boys to the Jesuits and we went to Belén. We were living on a road which is now St. Jude. So I realized that somehow I was doing what God had wanted me to do."

[Bosch] "What was the difference that you could see between you and the others who did not have that assurance?"

[Falero] "I saw extreme cases. There was this guy that used to go into the pool—we had a swimming pool there—and he used to go like this and like that and you ask him, 'What are you doing?' and he would say, 'I'm rowing back to Cuba.' He did this almost every day for hours. Some kids invented things. Some came from Cuba without their parents and their parents never called them from Cuba. And we had a public telephone, and all the calls came to that telephone. So whenever someone called, people used to yell, 'Falero! You have a call from Cuba.' But some guys invented their own calls so they had these calls and they were conversing—and people waiting to call on—and they were conversing and conversing. And we found out later that it was all invented, no voice was on the other line. They couldn't live with the idea that no one was calling them so they invented their own calls. Things like this give you an idea . . ."

[Bosch] "But you somehow navigated through all of this."

[Falero] "Yeah. I went through all of it until my parents came from Cuba. When my parents came from Cuba I had to work on my own because I felt responsible for them.

[Bosch] "So how Cuban do you feel? How Cuban American do you feel? Do these categories mean anything to you?"

[Falero] "Yes, they do in this sense. When I was in Cuba around the age of fifteen I knew pretty well what was happening. I knew that I was persecuted. In secondary school, in my class, I was one of two or three who didn't sign to be revolutionaries, so we had a lot of pressure. Also, some professors at our school were jailed because they expressed their opinions about political ideas and such things, so they were jailed because of it. Also I used to go with another youth from the parish to the country side, to the mountains near Sagua La Grande to teach the catechism and provide instruction in religious culture . . . But the government was carrying out the antireligious campaign and that conflicted with what we were doing. So we were told to stop what we were doing. So I felt that I couldn't be myself. Another thing was that my parents saw that they couldn't accept my growing in that atmosphere. So they asked me if I wanted to go to the United States. So we decided that I should go with them to the sugarcane company where my father worked—it was in another town in another area of Cuba—and leave school. There I was asked why I was not in school, and they proposed to me to study art somewhere in the Soviet Union. So we were telling them that I was not going to school because everyone else was studying art elsewhere. Eventually the telegram giving me permission to leave came, and I was free to leave Cuba. But I came with a very good idea of what I was doing. My parents consulted me, without my consent they wouldn't have done it. I saw that somehow we needed to rebuild Cuba because the government was distorting history and introducing changes that weren't beneficial. They were really destroying things, redoing things, rewriting things . . . In a way that it wasn't recognizable. We needed to form ourselves more here, to know the real history, who was Martí, and so on. I felt that people coming out of Cuba would eventually lose that knowledge. Then, when I decided to paint, I tried to paint what I felt and not be guided by anything political. Because Cuban politics was really messed up. So politics were not my issue. I was interested in culture and religion and the way of being. I saw that if you're Cuban and you are religious you don't have to do religious art or Cuban art, you just do art. And somehow in that art you have the Cuban and religious aspects. Because if you do it too much then somehow it ceases to be a real thing, it doesn't come from within, something really felt or believed."

[Gracia] "I was wondering something about the art itself, for example, the painting that you have there. How did you think about this particular painting . . . how did you decide on the topic?"

[Falero] "It came almost as an afterthought. The paintings I was doing before this one were based on still lifes. I just took pictures of tropical fruits under a certain lighting. And then I had these impressions that I have within my soul of when I left Cuba, what I saw there, what I saw as a child there, and some of the experience of coming here. It is not thematic, I cannot talk about it very well, but I felt the sea when I came to live here—in Cuba we lived by the river, which was in the middle of the city, and the contact with the sea was very short. And when I came here I lived by the sea also, every morning I looked at the sea from my window and there was a new seawall on which we used to walk. And then I moved to another place where there was also a bay, so every morning I saw that and at night I heard the sound of the sea. So somehow I appropriated this and also the idea of fruits that get old and dry. So somehow I put these together and I started to paint. And I wanted it to be like in an evening or late afternoon, to have something Romantic about it. But at the same time surreal in a way. But what I wanted to capture more was the mystery of the thing that we are talking about. In one painting I did a child dressed in a white robe. And he had doves flying above him, the sky was a very dark blue, the sea was present, and there was a seawall. Somehow I felt that the child captured the experience I was talking about when I left Cuba. The robe became the clothes of the Virgin Mary that covered the child—something like that— and the doves were my parents and since they had died, they were like the souls of my parents. That's something that I came up with later on. When I composed the painting, I didn't know exactly what I was doing. But somehow along the way I saw that the painting had some connections with those experiences. Something similar happened when I started the painting that is here. I saw this photograph of a painting of Goya, and I don't know why I associated the fruits with the woman portrayed in the picture. So I put her in there, there's also a sunset in the background. But somehow it was two things all the time and they did not relate well. So I kept working on it and then I realized that I should divide the painting into two. But it still did not work, so I decided to open a window on a wall. Then I put the sea in because somehow the sea was very important, but it needed to be darker. And so I put the moon and then I thought of the bird. So I played with that idea. Then I put the Morro fort from Havana. The walls then become more of those of the fortress. And somehow, there is the Hispanic tradition with the tropical thing but I don't know. There is a lot of that in there. And I added some tropical trees, but they are not palms because I thought also of the historic Miami. But it is mysterious, I don't know."

[Gracia] "It is for others to interpret it. This is a good point at which to end the interview. Thank you, Emilio and Lynette."

August 16, 2005
Interviewed in the artist's home, filmed by Norma Gracia, transcribed by Paul Symington, and edited by Jorge J. E. Gracia.

THE JUGGLER

— MARÍA BRITO

María Brito was born in Havana, on October 10, 1947. She emigrated to the United States in 1961, as part of the Peter Pan Operation. She settled in Miami, receiving a BA from the University of Miami (1969), a BBA from Florida International University (1976), and an MFA from the University of Miami (1979). Brito began exhibiting in Miami in 1978. Her first exhibition was at the Twentieth Annual M. Allen Hortt Memorial Competition and Exhibition, Museum of Art, Ft. Lauderdale. Brito has been the recipient of several prestigious awards including, a Florida Arts Council Fellowship (1979), a Cintas Foundation Fellowship from the International Institute of Education in New York City (1981), an Artist-in-Residence Fellowship from the Djerassi Foundation (1983), a National Endowment for the Arts Fellowship (1984), another Cintas (1985), a Florida National Endowment for the Arts Fellowship (1988), a Pollock-Krasner Foundation Grant (1990), a South Florida Consortium Fellowship (1992), a Virginia A. Groot Foundation Grant (1994), and an Individual Artist Fellowship from the Florida Department of State (1996).

Brito's work is focused on representing internal and external states of mind and on the roles individuals are forced to play as they seek to perform the various roles assigned to them by family, culture, and society. Her work is associated with a special emphasis on the roles women play in Cuban and in American culture. She is a multimedia artist, who combines sculpture, installations, ceramics, drawing, and painting.

Selected Collections: Olympic Sculpture Park, Seoul, Korea; Archer M. Huntingtom Museum, Austin, Texas; Art in Public Places, Metro-Dade Center, Miami; and National Museum of American Art, Washington, DC.

INTERVIEW

Conducted by Lynette M. F. Bosch and Jorge J. E. Gracia

[Bosch] "I'd like to focus this interview on María Brito's art and especially on the idea of identity—negotiating identities—traveling between cultures through the visual arts and also addressing how María comingles her artistic vision with her personal experience and also with

42

how the trajectory of being exiled, of having a dual identity—of really having multiple identities—functions within her life insofar as it plays a role in her work. María happens to be an old friend of mine and she and I have discussed these topics over the years and so I know that she has a lot to say. But I think it would be a good idea to start by asking her to tell us a little bit about how she began as an artist in Miami, because she is part of a larger group of Cuban-American artists based in Miami who reflect a very particular experience of exile rooted in the Cuban culture and experienced here. So, María, tell us, how did you begin?"

[Brito] "I never ever imagined that I would be a practicing artist. It just happened by chance. I enrolled in a class at the art center—Miami Art Center. It happened after completing a few courses and receiving a Bachelor's in Art Education—in essence, it was my coming together and learning about ceramics and touching the material that led to my career. It is as simple as that."

[Bosch] "So next you started exploring a three-dimensional medium and discovered a whole world."

[Brito] "Absolutely. I had experienced different subjects in school, I had never experienced clay. And I think it was because it was a dirty medium—one gets so dirty—and I was brought up differently, I wanted to be a nice, a very dainty student. I had two sons and after the second was born I was ready to go back to school. But clay interrupted everything and that led me into what I've been doing now."

[Bosch] "Do you think that the introduction to clay made you become an artist as opposed to somebody who was thinking of a practical career—let's say, art education or teaching art? What do you think made the transformation from being pragmatic to 'I'm an artist'?"

[Brito] "To me it was a revelation to be able to make a three-dimensional object that you could touch and feel. So here you're, dealing with a feeling that you cannot touch, you cannot describe as an object, but clay made possible to express those inner feelings. To me that was quite a revelation. I had never dealt with any other type of material where I was able to accomplish that. I wasn't looking for that, but it so happened that clay offered it to me and it was quite surprising."

[Bosch] "What themes did you begin with once you began to understand that you could actually express what was inside in this three-dimensional form. How would you say you began to do your trajectory of thematic material?"

[Brito] "Pretty much the same way I've dealt with it throughout my career. I dealt with issues that I had at the time: personal issues, family issues. And dealing with the material and putting objects made out of clay in juxtaposition to one another created, for me, a certain tension that reflected what was going on in my mind. Since then no matter what type of material I've used, it has always been the inner self that has come forth in these works."

[Bosch] "We've talked about how you went from ceramics to the construction of wall pieces, to installations, and incorporating paintings. We've also talked about how you see the multiplicity of roles that you have in your life that come from being a woman, from being Cuban, from being Cuban American, from being a mother, a daughter, a wife, a sister. Can you talk about how you identify yourself? Where does you sense of 'who I am,' 'what I am,' come from? How would you say it projects into your work?"

[Brito] "I think that what projects into my work is, again, those feelings, tensions, that are perhaps caused by all those multiple roles. I see myself as a mother. For instance, at one particular time in my career my sons were of an age where I was able to relate to some of the things that they were doing and at that time came some pieces related to childhood. They did not approach childhood with nostalgia. It had to do with feelings and what went through my mind as a kid. I was able to go back to those times prompted by activities that my sons carried out and to which I was able to relate."

[Bosch] "Those memories took you back to Cuba, but now in the United States how do you feel about how Cuban are you? How American are you? How do you go between those two?"

[Brito] "The only way that I can describe it is by saying that in my mind perhaps I'm more American, in my heart and in my emotional make-up I'm more Cuban. So I'm practical. I've been working in this format, the social format of this country, so I'm formed as an American in many ways. But my inner self is very Cuban."

[Bosch] "If you think about the idea of balancing this issue of identity, you're balancing all the items that everybody balances, because you have all of these multiple roles to fulfill in your personal life. Then you're also pushed into a situation where people are perhaps looking at you through the filter of 'Well, how Cuban are you?' and then the filter of 'How American are you?' So you really have a kind of hyphenated identity—which side of the hyphen do you fall on, the Cuban or the American side?"

[Brito] "It's hard to tell. I think it's half and half. And I say it because I don't know that I'd be able to function in any Latin American society, including Cuba, given the way daily activities are carried out there. I don't know. Then again my work doesn't have to do with the place where I'm living, or so I think. Meaning that I could be doing the same thing here as well as anywhere else because the work deals more with my personal experiences."

[Bosch] "Masks come up in your work a lot and the idea of duality and things transforming and changing and things having two sides. Could you talk about that in terms of specific works in which you began exploring it?"

[Brito] "It's very simple really. It has to do primarily with the inner self and the self that projects to the outside. We all have dealt with this at one time or another. It began simply, with a simple concept . . ."

[Bosch] "Can you think of some works that you began specifically exploring this?"

[Brito] "Yes, there is one sculpture, one small self-contained environment, called *Room of the Two Marías* where just by chance—and this happens in my work a lot, not necessarily accidents but things that do happen in the process of building any one piece or constructing any one piece, I guess I'm attentive to everything that goes on—I was working on two masks which were going to be treated differently. How? I did not know. One was a pristine mask, very pensive, very calm looking; and the other one I had to rush, in a way, in the sense that I wanted it to dry quickly so I could go on with the piece—I put it outside and before I knew it, it was raining. The mask became distorted and there was what I was looking for. I could have made another mask which was similar, but this distorted mask became the other self, the other part of the self. So that's one piece that comes to mind where I deal with the issues we were talking about."

[Bosch] "And then more specifically taking them to, let's say, the Cuban-American negotiation of identity, can you think of a work where you then pursued this idea of the hidden, the public, the private, the past, the present?"

[Brito] "*El patio de mi casa* comes to mind. It's a three-dimensional piece, a self-contained environment—as I like to call them for lack of a better term—where one side of the piece evokes the outdoors. And there's a bed, a crib—it is sort of a mixture of both—and that whole side has to do with the past. On the other side of the piece there is a kitchen where changes take place; it is a metaphor, which I realized only later on, when other people talked about the piece. Much of my work happens that way. I don't intellectualize the work at all, I would say, or minimally, as the work develops. I like to think that the work takes place on more of a gut-level and that it is more spontaneous, there's a lot more interaction between the work and myself than my intellect—it is not about coming up with an idea and carrying it out. Of course, there's that germ of an idea on which I work, or with which I work, and as the piece develops things happen and I take advantage of whatever happens. It's a sort of communication established between the work and myself. I see the need of a certain piece and take it from there."

[Bosch] "One of the things that I've always found interesting in your work is its additive nature where so many found objects are incorporated. To some degree, this idea of the assembly of random pieces that come to your attention that you think 'this needs that,' 'this needs this,' 'there it is,' to some degree I think it is a process somewhat analogous to the idea of constructing an identity. Because when you're constructing a dual identity you're pulling things from your environment and you're reconfiguring them into completely new patterns. Is this something that you think would be an accurate description of your work?"

[Brito] "I have never thought of it that way but it is certainly possible. One of the things about my work in general is that consciously I work up to a point beyond which I think everything is explained or that the work becomes obvious. I don't know why I brought this up in relation to your question but anyway, there's layers, and layers and layers and it's like a narrative, but if you leave the end open for interpretation I think the work becomes more appealing, more universal in nature . . ."

[Bosch] ". . . because everyone constructs an identity out of this and that and the other and you don't know exactly what piece you need and you make it up as you go along."

[Brito] "Exactly. A piece that's called 'Whitewash' comes to mind. It's, again, an installation, a self-contained environment which is basically a cage, a human-scale cage. Inside is an environment that can be construed as a home environment, even though all of the details are not there. I showed that piece somewhere, I forget where, and I was lecturing, giving a slide presentation, and after I finished I took questions from the audience. There was this older woman who was a Holocaust survivor, and she was able to relate to that type of confinement and imprisonment—not necessarily imprisonment but confinement; and it's not necessarily physical but also emotional and psychological. So this again goes back to what I was saying, leaving enough information there."

[Bosch] "You and I a long time ago talked about something that I think is shared by many Cubans who came to this country and has to do with this additive, spontaneous, sometimes maybe haphazard, quality of gathering objects. Remember we talked about how Cubans would pick up junk?"

[Brito] "Including my family!"

[Bosch] "My family too! Can you talk more about that in terms of being part of your creative process and, again, thinking about how we construct these identities out of other people's garbage? Tell me about where you would go with your family."

[Brito] "Along Coral Gables Way, an upper-class neighborhood. The word spread like wildfire among Cubans that the residents there would, every so often, throw out discards. They included sofas that were beautiful, and chairs, and lamps, and what-have-you, and so there was a whole procession of Cubans just arrived from Cuba down that road. My mother was a terrific seamstress and she reupholstered for the first time ever—it just took a little imagination and a lot of know-how on her part—many of those pieces. You and I were talking about that and I remembered that I thought, well maybe. . .”

[Bosch] “. . . the idea of sampling and reconfiguring. Because that process of transformation is such an integral part of the experience of Cubans—you didn't have enough money at the beginning—so you took the discards of other people but at the same time they were American discards that you were now reconfiguring to this Cuban-American identity. I remember you talking once about how you would go around in your truck looking for things—of course, this was later on when you were already an artist—and then bringing them home and putting them in the garage. It became yours so to speak. One of the things that has interested me about this reconfiguration of identity and the recontextualization of signs of identity is the way that you incorporate Renaissance and Baroque art in your work because to some degree this addresses the idea of the larger Hispanic identity that Cubans share with Latin Americans and of the course the idea of culture and connection. When did you start looking at Renaissance and Baroque imagery and what did it mean to you? Why were you drawn to that?”

[Brito] “To begin with—and this is something that you and I have talked about before—because of all of my different roles and I was going to school at the same time, I had very little time to educate myself; not only with everything that was going on in the art world or that had gone on before, but also visually I had very little visual information that I could draw back on. So that's been one of my hang-ups for a long time. I think also—and I'll get to your question in a minute—that ignorance and lack of knowledge of what had been done and what was being done at the time helped me tremendously in developing my own iconography and exploring my own ideas without any idea whatsoever what ‘art’ should look like, which was very important. In reference to those periods that you mentioned, little by little I became more interested in looking at what had been done in the past and what is being done in the present in the world of art. But I connected very much with the work of Fra Angelico, Duccio, and Giotto and Mantegna especially. It has to do with what I perceive of their work as being frozen in time. My sculptures have that feeling. I'm talking about the environment—the small environments— that I've created. They all have this feeling that something happened and the work is almost a snapshot—a photograph—that you take of a particular moment in somebody's life—and I saw in these works of Duccio or Mantegna, that feeling of the frozen . . ."

[Bosch] "You talked about photography in your work. You incorporate a lot of photography into the work and then you talked about this idea of a photograph as being suspended in between reality and a painting and then again of capturing that moment in time that becomes timeless. There is almost a threshold of consciousness here. When you think about incorporating specific photographs, how do you go about making the choice, because once you've put your image into your work, your work is identified with you, it's a piece of you that you're exporting as it were for the public consumption so it's your perfect 'private going public.' What makes you choose certain types of photographs over others? Consider *The Traveler,* for example, where you integrated a painting of that little photograph of you as a little girl."

[Brito] "Right, and actually, the incorporation of that image into the piece created the title. The piece did not have a title up until that time. In terms of incorporating anything, including paintings of photographs, into a work, it's intuitive. Thinking back to when I was working on the *The Traveler,* I chose that little image because there was innocence in it; it was me as child, but to be honest with you, I don't know, it's a very intuitive kind of thing."

[Bosch] "In terms of a journey, one thinks about the process of exile and, again, the formation of identity. Exile has a certain external aspect to it. You see the person go from one place to another, so there's travel in terms of space and time, and the title of the work is *The Traveler.* Do you ever stop to think about the identity of an exile as being something that is a journey that had a beginning in one place and then undergoes a metamorphosis as it goes through? And how does the idea of being a traveler in that sense relate to you as an artist? Because the artist also travels and that's also external—being an artist in some ways is a form of exile because you're never like other people. So, there's always that sense of separation."

[Brito] "But then again, I don't play the role of an artist. I don't live the life of an artist . . ."

[Bosch] ". . . How would you characterize it, then? What do you think an artist is?"

[Brito] "Well, going back to when I was younger, the idea of an artist to me was something very foreign to the way I carried on with my life. I was a mother, I enjoyed the family, while to me an artist was eccentric. Everything that I was not, including those stupid roles that are assigned to artists."

[Bosch] "So, how do you relate the idea of exile and of a journey, and the idea that an exile is transported from one place to another—which are intrinsically different—to the idea of the artist. For the artist is also intrinsically different, you're a traveler and an observer because this is, again, something that an artist does. How would you link up with these ideas in terms of your role as an artist and your being an artist, your identity as an artist, given that you don't think you are an artist because you're not insane and you don't do strange things and you're normal. And you are an artist! And you're a very well-known artist! How do you deal with that?"

[Brito] "To me, María Brito is somebody else and María Cristina is me also but in another role. To begin with, I was born María Cristina Brito, my name changed over the years because of marriages, so I've been a number of people. And I've come back to María Brito, minus the Cristina, and that's sort of a stage name . . ."

[Bosch] "So when María Brito goes into the studio, who doesn't go with you? María Cristina stays behind?"

[Brito] "I disconnect all phones and I make sure that I don't hear them, and I try to disconnect myself from the rest of the world. It's difficult many times, but that's what I try to do. I go into this place that's my own and nobody else's. I'm willing to share everything else but not that . . ."

[Bosch] "And then there's María Brito who has to do openings and has the shows and plays 'public artist.' Who's that?"

[Brito] "That's the one who smiles all the time."

[Bosch] "What was the most exciting thing that happened to you as an artist when you said 'Wow, I've arrived! I really did jump there.' "

[Brito] "It happened when I was in Seoul, Korea. I was commissioned to do a piece for the Olympics; actually, the educational-cultural part of the Olympics that took place in Korea in 1988. I went there with my husband at the time, all expenses paid by the Korean government and it was just a big, big party. And there was one point during our stay there where the artists were asked to go by themselves to this opening of a huge sculpture park. It was decorated with balloons—the Korean people really went out of their way to show the world how much they had accomplished since the war. So I was in this wonderful place surrounded by sculptors from all over the world in the most beautiful setting, and I happened to ask someone who had become a friend—a sculptor—'What day is today?' And it happened to be the same day that my dad had passed away, so here I was in this incredible environment and I knew he was there with me. And in terms of my professional career that was the highest point. That personal touch made it ever so . . ."

[Bosch] "What was the piece that you did for them?"

[Brito] "It was a piece based on a work I had done a couple of years before. Again, it's a self-contained environment. I learned of this opportunity, around five months prior to the time it had to be shipped over to Korea. So there really wasn't that much time. Not only that, I was supposed to be working with materials that I had never dealt with before, outdoor type of materials. The logical thing to do was to go back to a piece that was already thought out and realized and translate it into a piece that used outdoor type materials. I was fortunate to engage the help of Gay García, master Gay García—a wonderful human being and a terrific sculptor. He helped me put the piece together. We used steel and aluminum. And the piece was shipped over to Korea. We took buses to different sites throughout the park and when my piece came up I thought I'd faint."

[Bosch] "I can imagine. You mentioned Gay, and one of the things I wanted to talk to you about was your part in a continuum of Cuban art coming to the United States, and forming part of the history of Cuban art which extends to Cuban-American artists, the idea of generations. So when you worked with Gay García, you worked with one of the major classics who came out of Cuba to this country already as a fully formed artist. Do you think about your place in this continuum? How do you see yourself in relation to the generation of Gay García?"

[Brito] "I don't think about things like that, I don't. I think that anything that would make me feel 'Whoa, María Brito the sculptor' would affect my work in the studio. I am a humble person, and when I go in there I have all the fears of a beginner; all the concerns, and there's no BS-ing. You're facing your own mortality so to speak and you're facing your work and you're going to be as honest as you can be."

[Bosch] ". . . so you don't think that 'My role is this'—but do you feel yourself connecting to a history? Leaving aside these sorts of 'ra, ra, hoopla,' how do you feel about being a 'Cuban-American artist'? How do you deal with that?"

[Brito] "I see that there's a need out there for labels and I'm fine with that. I make my work and I get satisfaction out of showing it. So if it's shown under the context of Cuban-American art, that's fine, and if it's shown in the context of sculptors or work by sculptors, that's fine also. It's my work and whatever is out there, is what it is."

[Brito] "Maybe that's the reason, yeah. Maybe that's the reason."

[Bosch] "You talked about how an artist is this crazy person, but if you really leave aside what the world thinks about artists, what do you think being an artist is? What makes a difference between you, as an artist, and me? I'm not an artist, you're an artist."

[Brito] "I don't know what makes you tick. I wouldn't know how to compare the two because I don't know you that intimately at all. So I guess an artist is someone who is a sponge in many ways. It's like your whole psyche, your whole emotional make-up—and I'm speaking for myself, I am the only point of reference—is being channeled that way. I work from my own emotions, my own perspective, although some of the pieces also reflect what has happened to others and how I perceive their emotions. Now I'm looking more at the international and national scenes in terms of human beings, not politics—the human aspect of situations taking place all over the world, including this nation. It's always the human aspect . . . the individual story."

[Brito] ". . . yes, the individual pain, that sort of thing. A few pieces have come about because of this new interest, or maybe a change in focus."

[Bosch] "Right, expanding into a larger world from the more Hispanic world. That kind of thing. Jorge, do you know of anything that has been left out?"

[Gracia] "Oh, I think that you have covered everything very well. But one aspect that interests me is the woman side of it. There are two things that I think I want to ask you. One is, you are a woman artist, there's no question about that, and does that affect your work? Do you feel that it affects your work? Do you feel that it brings into the work something that would not be there otherwise?"

[Brito] "The way I see it is that a woman is also a human being. I'm not being feminist in any way, and all human beings share so much that my work is not particular to one or another sex or ethnicity or even nationality. We're all basically the same, and that's what I ultimately concern myself with."

[Gracia] "With the basic humanity that we all share, so you're not really exploring any particularities?"

[Brito] "I may have done that in a piece or two, but I don't think of my work as being feminist or as being concerned with a woman living in this country or in this century. It's beyond that I think."

[Gracia] "The other question I had has to do with the art world itself. It's a difficult world, I assume it is. I know the philosophical world is very difficult. There are cubicles, there are people that basically determine who goes forward, who doesn't go forward, at which time and so on. There are galleries, curators, collectors, and art historians, and the artists are trapped in many ways in this very difficult environment, and they have to eat."

[Brito] "To begin with, ever since I decided I was going to continue doing what I was doing, I realized that I had two children to feed and I had a mortgage to pay and what-have-you. Thankfully, I had a lot of support from my parents and both my ex-husbands in that respect. So I feel like they have contributed to my career as well. But I always had a job outside what I was doing in my work as a sculptor or painter, so that I felt that I had the income necessary for me to function and, at the same time and most importantly, not to compromise the work. To me it was, 'You do not touch this! This is not to be touched!' And as far as what you said about the art world being difficult, I think that it's a matter of what your goal is; it's as simple as that. My goal has always been to do the work, that's what I derive the most enjoyment from. I've been very fortunate to have had good galleries representing my work. I'm not a salesperson—I'm the worst salesperson in the world—so I need Bernice Steinbaum to help me. She would love this!"

[Gracia] "And she certainly does a very good job!"

[Brito] "I think that my role—and I can't speak for others—is to produce the work, and the rest I can't deal with. It would fragment my life too much. It would take away time from the studio and that's why artists need someone they can trust and represent their work."

[Gracia] "I have one other question that occurred to me. I see two things in art. I see an aesthetic dimension—is it aesthetically pleasing?—and I see a cerebral part, the thought behind it. You have talked a lot about the intuitive factors in your work; basically you 'work from the gut,' that was your expression wasn't it? There are some Cuban artists whose work is very aesthetic and there is less evidence of thinking in it, although there are others that are more cerebral and less aesthetic. So, how do you see your art, and how do you see your aim? What are you trying to do, balancing these two areas? The thought behind it and the aesthetic element?"

[Brito] "The intellect has to come in at some point, during the process otherwise I don't know what would happen. The intuitive aspect of it is this—it's hard to describe it because it's a process, and how do you describe a process? The germ of the idea comes not when I'm taking a shower or sleeping or daydreaming, it comes through hard work. I go in the studio, whether I have something going or not, I go there—I'm very disciplined when it comes to that—and sit around or pace the floors or go through my sketchbook to look back at some ideas. So, a germ of an idea comes forth. Something that I can't even draw because it's not formed. It could be a theme, perhaps, an impression, this, that. If it's going to be a sculpture the process is different than if the piece is going to be a painting, and that I decide early on. The processes are totally different."

[Gracia] "Let's say, let's take this painting here behind us. I think this is very aesthetically pleasing, isn't it? You can't help looking at it, and so we go, 'Oh, that's nice' and so on and so forth. Yet there are all sorts of things going on in it—there are these lines, these ropes coming down, there is this wrapped-up baby—and you are supposed to be the baby—and then the sky with all these clouds. So let's say that you're in the process of creating this painting, are you at any moment thinking 'I want to make this a beautiful object,' or are you thinking 'I'm trying to develop this particular idea'? Or you are not actually paying any attention to any one of those things and you're just working at it and things intuitively come through?"

[Brito] "The beautiful object part doesn't come through. It's trying to solidify, to give form to a feeling more so than anything else. And how do you substitute, or what type of imagery do you use in order to make this feeling visual? That's the challenge. So if you're dealing with entrapment, not only physical but especially emotional, how do you deal with it in a form? This baby, obviously cannot move around very much, even though wrapping it had some use at the time for certain reasons—it still does and it's meant to be good for the baby. I'm looking at the irony of how it is good for the baby. I'm dealing with the idea, thinking about the idea, playing around with thoughts. As far as the piece, this particular piece was meant for a sculptural piece, an environment, but it didn't quite fit the piece visually. So as I was painting it, I left this area of it dark. So I just daydream sometimes. You look at something and start thinking—it is like players in the theater, or positioning players in a stage—and I start."

[Gracia] "Well, I think that's it."

[Bosch] ". . . We've wrung you dry! Thank you."

August 11, 2005
Interviewed in the artist's home and studio, filmed by Norma Gracia, transcribed by Paul Symington, and edited by Jorge J. E. Gracia.

IF QUEBEC WERE IN THE TROPICS

____ MARIO BENCOMO

Mario Bencomo was born in Pinar del Río, on July 26, 1953. He emigrated to the United States in 1968, then went to Spain and New York City, before settling in Miami in 1968. In 1975, he received a BBA from Miami-Dade Community College. Bencomo began exhibiting in Miami in 1979, at the Library Gallery at Miami Dade Community College's North Campus. He has received a Cintas Fellowship Foundation Award from the International Institute of Education in New York City (1984–85), a Purchase Award from Second All-Florida Biennial (1987), and an Award from the Boca Museum's 38th Annual all Florida Exhibition (1989). In 1992–93, he was awarded an Individual Artists Fellowship Award in Painting from the Division of Cultural Affairs, State of Florida.

Bencomo's style is abstract with suggestions of organic forms and thematic subjects based on his interest in spirituality, environmental and political situations, and sensuality. He frequently explores the movements of natural forces, such as wind, water, and climate. He is concerned with the spiritual dimensions of human activity and with the erosion and transformation brought about by contemporary cultural realities.

Selected Public Collections: Archer M. Huntington, Museum of University of Texas, Austin, Texas; Detroit Institute of Art, Detroit, Michigan; Metropolitan Museum of Art, New York; Museum of Modern Art of Latin America, Washington, DC; Panama Contemporary Museum of Art, Panama; Polk Museum of Art, Lakeland, Florida; and Ponce Art Museum, Puerto Rico.

INTERVIEW

Conducted by Lynette M. F. Bosch

[Bosch] "Mario, tell us about how you first began to understand that you were an artist, that you were a painter."

[Bencomo] "The painting came later. I always wanted to be a writer. But ever since I was a kid, I used to color from botanical books. I used to copy the illustrations and then I would have these incredible fantasies with the Latin names of the flowers and the plants."

[Bosch] "And then being an artist simply became something else that you were doing in a very natural context, just being there, being Cuban, and then realizing that 'well, I have this other part.' "

[Bencomo] "I was in Cuba but it's so normal being a Cuban in Cuba. It's so normal being a Swede in Sweden. I'm from Pinar del Río and people didn't go around saying, 'I'm proud to be Cuban.' "

[Bosch] "So you're out of Cuba now, what does being a Cuban mean to you? In Cuba it means nothing other than that 'here you are.' "

[Bencomo] "Out of Cuba means you are out of your element. Otherness increases. You become more aware and more focused of how displaced you are."

[Bosch] "But you went to Spain first."

[Bencomo] "I'm very lucky I did. Very lucky that the transition was from one dictatorship to another. It was very good for me to see both sides at such an early age."

[Bosch] "So at this point you come to the United States, and you're an adolescent, you're aware of all these circumstances. You want to be a writer, you want to be a poet. How do you come to realize that actually it's things that you need to be making, works of art? How did you make the transition from thinking of yourself as 'I want to be a writer, I want to be a poet, to I'm going to be a figural visual artist?' "

[Bencomo] "It was the next best thing I could do. Because I had an ability to understand color and to understand line and a keen eye. Many of us, in any creative field, just want to do something. It's a chain. I remember the first time I ever saw a painting in the Prado—that's something that I took from Arturo Rodríguez a long time ago; that was his experience too—the first time we saw art was at the Prado, I said 'so this is Velázquez!' And then I came to New York and a friend of mine was living in Brooklyn and she said, 'Mario, I'm going to take you to the City.' And she took me to a place I'm sure was MoMA, and I saw Rothko's work. That's the only thing I remember and I said, 'Wow, look at all that space!' I had just come to New York from Europe, my first time. And I said, 'This is where I am! I am in this big, insecure and scary space,' and maybe later looking back at that moment I realized that maybe for Rothko America was uncertain as well. The spaces were so immense and unfathomable, the vastness of it!"

[Bosch] "Then you began to paint. Tell me about your first show."

[Bencomo] "My first show was at Dade County Community College, at the library, that's why I'm a library pusher. That's why it's so important to have libraries. They give you an opportunity not only to read and see but to show works when you're beginning. I think it was called 'The Insularity of the Rectangle,' and I was worried about habitat and dwellings, and it had a lot of Rothko influence. Actually, I think that's gone away. And it was a good show. I got my name in the paper and I'm like, 'Oh my God, they took me seriously.' "

[Bosch] "Then you began the Torquemada series?"

[Bencomo] "Yeah, that's the Castro of the Catholics. And in a bad sense of course—yes, politics has always been there but from an intimate point. It's just an awareness that all this can change tomorrow. It's like, 'this is the last frontier' and a lot of those pieces were called 'The Last Frontier.' I had gone back to Spain after high school here, because I wanted to go back to Europe—I thought that I would be more comfortable there. And I kept on going back but I think that as any new American, you develop this sense of home here, of space."

[Bosch] "You get used to the spaces and you get used to the culture."

[Bencomo] "And you have this background of people that are just like you and I came here from other places and you say, 'Hey, this is organic. This grows.' These experiences expand and we feed. I'm feeling like a little scavenger shark. I'm feeding from everything."

[Bosch] "Now, after you have the first show, you go back to Europe. Tell me about the series of themes and subjects that you've done."

[Bencomo] "The Torquemada series was very young, very early. Because of the political conflict in Cuba, I was horrified to learn about the Spanish Inquisition, and how ignorant even Catholics are about it, and what a great loss Spain had. And what a gain Amsterdam had—The Netherlands at the time, and northern Africa, with the Jewish diaspora. So I was fascinated by how history repeats itself, and dogma, religion."

[Bosch] "And you also have a Jewish identity."

[Bencomo] "On my mother's side—very secular—and it's only on her side. I think the only time religion was relevant was when my mother said, 'Think of Goodness. Goodness would always come, will always be with you and the angels are with you.' But I grew up very secular and I'm very grateful for that. It just gives you a little bit of an edge."

[Bosch] "And yet you have a tremendous interest in spirituality, which turns up in your work as well."

[Bencomo] "Yes. I was talking with a critic last night, in the show— and he said, 'This new work is drawn from poetry,' and I said, 'Yes, painters do read poetry sometimes.' And he said, 'What about gender?' And I said, 'Genders have always been there since the beginning of time, but poetry is never the same when one reads it.' "

[Bosch] "Your work then comes out of all of these varied interests."

[Bencomo] "Yes, I think that, yes, it does. In that respect I do not have this patriotic responsibility that other painters have. And I always wonder, 'What does that mean?' To be a patriot. I think artists have no political role and if there were one, it would be a humanist role, not a regional one. Even though that could be naive because I will always be a Cuban American. Why, am I going to be a Cuban Norwegian, or . . . ?"

[Bosch] "No, because circumstances put you here and that's really the inescapable fact of exile that you ended up in the United States."

[Bencomo] "And how blessed our experience has been; at least mine. Because had I not seen what Stalinism was as a child, which I was very much aware of—fear—and had I not realized that fascism was tied with religion such as Spain was, and had I not seen the horror of runaway capitalism—and injustice, racial injustice—such as I had never in my life considered, that a human being because of color could not marry somebody else of a different race or couldn't even get a drink of water in certain places."

[Bosch] "Now, you have gone back to Cuba? What was behind that decision?"

[Bencomo] "I was going to Panama for a show—I had a show at the Museum of Contemporary Art in Panama—and on the way back there was bad weather. And the pilot excused himself because we were going to fly over Cuba. And it was right there, under me and I said, 'What's the fear here? It's a little island. What is stopping me? Nobody has the power to control me or anybody else—the boogie man is there but that's not the only boogie man in the world, and that boogie man does not define me as a person, as an artist, or as somebody that was born in Cuba. I am that.' It does not matter how untypically Cuban I might be because I don't do 'ethnic work' or I don't do sociology in my work or there's no religion. There's no ethnography in my work. I'm going back there! So, I started thinking about that and I went back in 1996 for the first time, and I've returned many times."

[Bosch] "When you went back, did you engage with the art world in Cuba?"

[Bencomo] "Not the first trip, and in fact I really haven't. I was approached by certain institutions there and I have to say there are many incredible people working in Cuba! But I only know the capacity and the interest in what artists are doing outside Cuba who were born here."

[Bosch] "But they knew who you were when you went back."

[Bencomo] "They knew. Cuba is not a vacuum for everybody. And what I realized was that we had friends in common in Rome or in Paris. And there are people who say, 'The only thing that matters is that you were born here and you are of here. This belongs to you.' "

[Bosch] "Did you feel that when you went back? Because you have fairly developed memories of Cuba until you were fourteen."

[Bencomo] "Yeah, you know how it is sometimes. I was sort of like a voyeur, you know, like a spectator."

[Bosch] "Because you go back and you observe."

[Bencomo] "Yes. I'm supposed to be Cuban, and these people that I see, they're just like us. They are Cubans as we know. They're not little [puts fingers up to head pretending that he has horns] . . ."

[Bosch] "Right, they're just people."

[Bencomo] "And they're people who are interested in what we are interested in. Some are nice, some are not. But who handles grants here, for example? I mean, who are the museum curators who control everywhere?"

[Bosch] "And it's all political, again."

[Bencomo] "Yeah, it's all political. And I think, 'What did it do to me?' Because I'm not as criollo as maybe my demeanor is more reserved. Maybe I'm more introspective, something . . ."

[Bosch] ". . . the American part has done."

[Bencomo] "Cubans are very spontaneous. I try to be a little bit more cautious for obvious reasons. Having to play the odd man out. But that would have happened to me also had the situation not changed in Cuba. I would have been the same guy and probably neither you nor I would have been living there because there's a history in Cuba."

[Bosch] "So you went back to Cuba and you have one of your paintings in the National Museum there. How did that come about?"

[Bencomo] "I have a cousin who has access to art events and art institutions. This is a cousin with whom we used to do blocks together when we were kids. He stayed, I left. And we have a lot in common. He's a brilliant, brilliant man. And he showed me a center where American, Latin American, and European art were going to hang, because the Museo Nacional would be only for Cuban art. So I asked him, 'What happens when I die, where would I be hunged?' And he said, 'What do you consider yourself? Just think for a minute and tell me an answer a minute from now.' But I said, 'I want to be in the museum with the Cubans.' And he said, 'Well, you know what you have to do.' And I said, 'But they don't want me.' And he said, 'How do you know? Who is 'they'?' Just as here."

[Bosch] "Who is 'the theys' that everyone worries about?"

[Bencomo] "I never say, 'he,' you know Fidel or Bush or any other."

[Bosch] "Or any other name. It's always, 'they don't.' "

[Bencomo] "Transitory figure of authority. 'They!' Yes, I am part of this country. I am a product of this country and I love Cuba. I love it. And I said, 'I want my work here.' So years later it went. It's the first time that the work of a Cuban-American artist or how 'they' said, 'an artist who had not developed in Cuba' was put in the National Museum."

[Bosch] "Which painting did he send?"

[Bencomo] "It's called *Anima Mundi*. I selected it specifically. It was a bureaocratic process. And when that went through, I was happier than when the Metropolitan Museum in New York acquired my work. Because I can die now. Isn't this tacky? But I did my part. And it was for the benefit and enjoyment of the Cuban people. That was how the work got in there and it stays there. I'm so relieved, because I would always be against power. I'm basically anarchist. We are all anarchists. Do we have any political faith?"

[Bosch] "Now tell me about your series 'If Quebec Were in the Tropics.'"

[Bencomo] "I suffer from wanderlust."

[Bosch] "Yes, that need to travel."

[Bencomo] "That need to travel where I want, and why."

[Bosch] "Let's go look."

[Bencomo] "Let's go see, let's open the theater and be a spectator. And how wonderful it is! I tell American friends and French friends and Italians: Can you imagine what it is to have a passport? This is the immigrant, this is the political guy speaking here. Can you imagine the luxury of having a passport and going places?"

[Bosch] "So Mario, tell me about the exhibition 'On the Tropics.'"

[Bencomo] "I had that exhibition in Puerto Rico and I love myths. And I was thinking about Narcissus and looking at the poem, so I said, 'Huh, the tropics.' I'm from there and I love going there and so much of my imagery comes from that organic world there. And I was thinking about the essential and the erotic in everything in the tropics and how that translates. So all of a sudden I saw Narcissus, instead of looking on the water and being in love with his image, actually penetrating the tropics. Just taking it over, making it his own, blended with him. And so the tropics have always been very important as a theme, it's my myth. It's like a little fountain that I have, that I pulled that from. And it went very well."

[Bosch] "And how did you get to Quebec being in the tropics?"

[Bencomo] "Canada, I have always gone to Quebec—to Canada and to British Colombia, Vancouver—where I discovered a painter called Emily Carr. I wrote you from Vancouver and told you there's this movement that I love."

[Bosch] "You did, we now have to add Canadian to your identity."

[Bencomo] "BC identity."

[Bosch] "BC?"

[Bencomo] "What is a Canadian? You're Quebequois or you are from BC. But my focus has mostly been on Quebec because it's an otherness, an otherness, an otherness. It's so nice to be not an Anglophone, a Francophone, but an Alophone, or something else. And it's a very generous society, the arts, and there's a lot of stuff going on in Quebec—and in Canada in general—but Quebec, I go there a lot. One time I realized,

'What about if this city that I love so much, Montreal, if this city was in the tropics?' Would I like it as much? Because I don't live really in the tropics and I said, 'Well, I'm so comfortable here; I can read hours and hours on end and I can draw and it's peaceful.' I'm in North America but not of North America. And I started the series, mostly as I do with my work in hotel rooms. A little rental for the season."

[Bosch] "Traveling, traveling."

[Bencomo] "Wanderlust, we got the bug. The aviatory flu has nothing on us. And finding inspiration and to me it's just like another window. I remember that I told you, 'Oh, Lynette, you should see the . . .' and then you said 'The seven or the nine or whatever, the Canadian painters,' and there's this whole mystical Canadian art and how much Whitman was important to the Canadian, sensual painters. And there's this whole inner life that is very French. The French neurosis, of which many of us suffer from, acquired of course as if we needed any more. But I started seeing Quebec bloom in January; you could relate to that."

[Bosch] "Yes, all too well."

[Bencomo] "It's such a shock going from Montreal to Havana, because they are totally different places. So I started imaging that and the palette was cooler. And I said, 'My God, this has the coolness of ice. This does not have the fire of the tropics. I never thought of that. So I wonder what happens in Iceland."

[Bosch] "What would be, if I were to ask you where your next series will come from?"

[Bencomo] "Well, I'm leaving for Haiti tomorrow. That's it."

[Bosch] "And we will wait and see. Thank you very much."

April 8, 2006
Interviewed in the home of Inés Ydanda Bosch, transcribed by Paul Symington, and edited by Lynette M. F. Bosch and Jorge J. E. Gracia.

THE HUMAN CONDITION

——————————————————————— Arturo Rodríguez

Arturo Rodríguez was born in Las Villas, on February 6, 1956. He emigrated in 1973, going first to Spain and then settling in Miami in 1976, and began exhibiting in Miami in 1978, at Florida International University, after having exhibited in Spain in the mid-1970s. He has received a Florida Arts Council Fellowship (1980), a Cintas Foundation Fellowship, International Institute of Education in New York City (1982) and another Cintas (1988), as well as a Visual Arts Fellowship, South Florida cultural Consortium (1988), and another Florida Arts Council Fellowship (1990). Later, he received a Florida Arts Council Fellowship (1991) and two Florida Individual Artist Fellowship Awards (1990–91 and 1998–99).

Rodríguez has produced a body of work that is focused on the representation of the internal state of alienation and transformation of the exile. Psychologically incisive in the depiction of the emotional trauma experienced by the exiled, Rodríguez's paintings are characterized by a semi-abstract style, where disjointed, floating, and contorted figures float through imaginary interior and exterior spaces.

Selected Collections: Miami Main Public Library, Florida; Metropolitan Museum of Art, New York; the Jerusalem Museum, Israel; Polk Museum of Art, Florida; The Norton Museum, West Palm Beach, Florida.

INTERVIEW

Conducted by Jorge J. E. Gracia

[Gracia]: "Arturo, let's begin with your art, and then at some point we're going to jump back into your life and how you became an artist. You have a very distinctive style which develops in various ways. So, how do you conceive your art, how do you see it?"

[Rodríguez] "The first thing is the human being, the presence of humanity, the human figure."

[Gracia] "You have no paintings of landscapes alone or paintings of artifacts, or . . ."

[Rodríguez] "No, nothing."

[Gracia] "So, your subject is always the human being."

[Rodríguez] "My art is concerned directly with the physical, philosophical, and psychological states of the human. How can you put that into painting, when painting is the opposite of philosophy, or—it's something that is a language in itself—and you have to use language very cautiously? You don't want to tell a story, you don't want to state a philosophy, you don't want to teach or say anything to people with your work. It comes out of the painting. The paint dictates your thoughts. Paintings become objects, but you have to put so much work in them, it's such a long process. Just mixing colors, waiting for them to dry, regulating tonality, how can you do this better, erasing this drawing, going back, and all that process is what ends up in the painting, but there is also an image and the image that comes from that process is a human figure and you can always see it in my work, the body in various stages and in situations. That's about it, also it's a very unconscious process."

[Gracia] "And the human figure takes center stage in the painting. That is, it does always—I'm just looking at one of your paintings from here, a very large one, and I see that the human figure there is centered. Well, in fact, there are several human figures in the painting. I count five. But there is a huge one in the middle in a very difficult physical position as it were, maybe an impossible one. And then two figures on each side. But there's practically no landscape, no context, no buildings, nothing but those persons."

[Rodríguez] "Right, that's the idea, how you can convey all these things and make it essentially human, the distortions. Because one figure has the head coming down his back, which is impossible. But mentally, this makes a statement about this discomfort, about violence, about pain, and sadness, but also about life.

[Gracia] "In many ways you are unlike many other Cuban-American painters. They are concerned with buildings or situations or things that do not necessarily involve humans. Lots of vegetation, for example, or memories of Cuba. But you are centered on this, on some idea of a human being. So, how do you begin to paint? What is it that comes first? Is your idea a conceptual notion that you then explore?"

[Rodríguez] "You have a concept and the concept is that you want to paint, and it is a human figure in certain ways, certain contexts. Then you have to work to paint it, which is the most important part for me. In conceptual art you have a concept and you don't do that much work—you have the finished piece—because you say that this is the concept. It's like Duchamp's *Urinal*. He'll say that's art. He didn't make the urinal. He just said that's it. In my case, I think about it but what I think needs the work, and you get absolutely lost in the work and lose contact with the concept at the beginning. That's what painting is; it has such a strong interest that you get lost in it. You start with the work and then the work dictates itself. You don't know why you do it. You are in a fog. And it's a great feeling but it's also very disturbing, and you don't feel comfortable at all. I don't enjoy painting. I do it because it's a necessity, but not because I like to paint."

[Gracia] "It's one of those things that you have to do, but you would rather not do if you could, but you can't get away from it."

[Rodríguez] "Yes, like Samuel Beckett, 'I can't go on, but I will go on.' You have that fight, and it's a fight. It's something that you take to the canvas with the colors, but the painting never comes out the way you want it. In the end you like it, but only for ten minutes, and then you want to do another one. In my case, sometimes I go over paintings for years, I retouch them. And when I haven't seen one of my pieces for a while that I thought it was great, I see it as something terrible and I don't want even to look at it. I want to retouch it, but they don't let me, of course. And I feel that's a shame . . ."

[Gracia] "Ah, fortunately people buy them and they don't give you a free hand. Otherwise, there would never be an end to your painting. You see, I'm siding with the enemy here."

[Rodríguez] "There was an anecdote about Bonnard. There was this guard at the museum who saw this old man and he had this little box with paints and he started retouching a Bonnard. And the guard immediately seized the old man and took him away. And you know who he was? Bonnard! That tells you the level of obsession you can get into with painting. Paintings become infinite. In a way you could always be working on the painting and never finish it."

[Gracia] "Do you think that is a result of the fact that you yourself are changing and therefore when you look at a painting ten years after you have done it, you see something different than you saw before? Then you want to bring the painting to where you are now and move forward from there. But then it's not the same painting, is it?"

[Rodríguez] "Yes, exactly, no, no it's not! That's why I don't do it."

[Gracia] "Ah, we won't allow you to do this, and certainly not with the painting of yours I own! You have to do a new painting, so I can buy another."

[Rodríguez] "You keep painting because you get tired of the ones you have done, you need a new idea. I always work on new things. But there are certain parts in a painting that you can never change. They come not because you want them, they are just there. And you don't want to touch them—that's inconceivable—because they wouldn't return. Another aspect of my work in watercolors is that I don't make any drawings at all. Everything is absolutely improvised so, unlike the paintings, I can't erase, I can't do anything because what I do is determined by whatever comes out of the water with the brush, that's it. But then I do ten water-colors and choose two and the rest is trash. I like improvising. That's what I like so much in music also, the artists' expression and improvisation—but they have a structure, over which they improvise. Also in my work I get lost because I try to improvise. The work itself tells you where to go. You start seeing it, because painting is all about seeing what is right in front of your eyes. And what you see in the morning is different at night, because. . ."

[Gracia] ". . . the light changes."

[Rodríguez] "The light, the time that you have to work on it. This face that is now red, may be black at the end of the day. Painting has a lot to do with time, with space, with so many things. Painting is very complex."

[Gracia] "So, when do you think that you are sufficiently done to sell the painting or to put it in an exhibition, or declare it finished? Of course, if you had your way, it would never be finished. But let's suppose you do not have your way, because after all you do finish paintings all the time and say something like 'Okay, this is pretty good.' "

[Rodríguez] "Somebody said 'you never finish a painting, you abandon it.' "

[Gracia] "Ah, alright, a very clever thought."

[Rodríguez] "That's why you have a clear conscience afterwards. But sometimes it's good to abandon them because maybe there is such thing as overpainting, and getting the painting too heavy and then it doesn't work. You have to have this balance between so many conflicting things and that's what makes the tension of the painting, at least in my work. I have so many different things from the same images, that sometimes I want to make it little, sometimes I want to make it more strong. Just to get to that is a struggle."

[Gracia] "And how much of the painting is you? Clearly the painting is doing a function for you, for your feelings, for your ideas—you are working something out, although you may not be clear about it."

[Rodríguez] "Because you work a lot with your subconscious. Once you start getting into the work, the actual work of painting, you get lost. That's where the subconscious takes in a lot of stuff that maybe happened to you twenty years ago or just five minutes ago. These things start coming out like the brushstrokes. You know, by the way, that my painting has a certain direction, all my pieces go from the right to left. That's the way I paint almost everything. I cannot go left to right, because then they start twisting. Still, my paintings have many directions, the compositions are very complex and the brushstrokes come from everywhere. So I have to turn the paintings around to get the different directions. I rotate the pieces as I go. To me, this is very important because a lot of my work is painted upside down, not the way you see it. That makes it more abstract, but it makes it also easier for me to see that abstraction; I see the actual painting, the language of the painting itself, but I don't have the image of anything, although it's there."

[Gracia] "Does that mean that the paintings themselves could be hung upside down?"

[Rodríguez] "If you want to, they work either way."

[Gracia] "Now let's go back to your subject matter: the human being. That's the center of everything for you. But is it the human being in general that you are concerned with, or are you also in a way, painting yourself? Many painters seem always to be painting themselves in one way or another. How much of you is in your paintings?"

[Rodríguez] "Everything. It's always me, the way I see the world, but it's not narcissistic. I don't paint myself all the time."

[Gracia] "But you have done self-portraits?"

[Rodríguez] "Oh yeah, because it comes with the desire to see how you see yourself through all this fog that is painting. And you see who are you. And you can be one thing in one painting, and one thing very different in another. If you take Rembrandt's self-portraits—and he did a lot of them— it's almost like a different person in each one of them, but all of them are Rembrandt. In some of them he is a subtle painter, in some he is an actor, in some he is a very young, cocky painter. So many things. That's what the self-portrait does for you. But also it's something that you have on your hand that is very easy to get to because you are there. Sometimes I paint my own hands, or my feet. I have certain things that I want to resolve in a face. I go to the mirror, it's there, so I put it in. A lot of my work is about my inner feelings. But also there is a distance, a big distance. You don't want to get emotionally involved with your own work. You have to keep a distance be- cause it can become oversentimental or emotionally overworked. You always want to keep a distance from the world, from reality."

[Gracia] "You have now a very substantial body of work and you have been at it for a long time—how do you see yourself in the art world? What do you think is your main contribution to painting?"

[Rodríguez] "At this point in time, anything can be art. We are in the twenty-first century, you can take anything, make art out of anything and then put it in a museum. If you believe that there is an avant-garde or progress in art, that everything is getting better and more sophisti- cated, it's not! No, a lot of contemporary artwork is manipulated by collectors, galleries, museums. Art is going to be art, especially painting. It's based in the Paleolithic. So that's an essential impulse in the human being. That's the way I see it: I need to paint, it's a necessity. I don't paint to make money or be famous or anything. I have to be there every day, almost every day—work. And if I don't do that, I don't feel complete. At this stage of the game, there's not a real center. I don't care that much about that at all. I just want to do what I want to do every day, and I've been able to survive, without making concessions to what is . . ."

[Gracia] "Fashionable?"

[Rodríguez] "Yeah, that's the word. I didn't want to use it but you said it."

[Gracia] "You are your own man. This brings up an important question because you said that you have been able to survive without having to change what you want to do, to cater to a particular audience— maybe a museum audience, or expert audience, or collectors, or whatever. Many artists are able to support themselves by having other jobs in addition to the art, but you have been able to survive as an artist."

[Rodríguez] "There is an element of luck in all this that nobody knows. Since I was twenty-two years old, I've been living off my painting. I've never done anything else."

[Gracia] "How many Cuban-American painters have succeeded in doing that? I bet not many."

[Rodríguez] "Yeah, but I think if you work hard and are serious about what you do, and consistent in what you want to say, you'll find people eventually. It's like a trip in which you want to go to see just how it ends. You keep painting and painting. I want to see my limitations? What are, you know, my assets?"

[Gracia] "You showed me some of your recent paintings, in which there is a great deal of humor. Before you were a very serious painter, almost tragic in many ways, concerned with hard issues. And concerned with them not in a light manner but in a heavy, thoughtful manner. And now you are dealing with serious topics but in a lighthearted way, and using humor. That's a huge change. There's also a color change, you've become more colorful. So, what's this about? Are you really changing?"

[Rodríguez] "I am always changing. I don't know where it's going to end. This funny business started about three years ago. My wife had colon cancer and then breast cancer, and then came a cancer of the thyroid—so many black things! And I started to laugh at the serious things. They threw so many things at me and I'm laughing. But it's not a crazy laugh. Just when you see so many black things, you start to look at the lighter side. So this series has a lot to do with that. I'm not escaping from the bad things, on the contrary I'm dealing with them. I'm not a very positive person, but the context is also very human and also full of follies, and it's called the human comedy. It's like Balzac, it's an ongoing process that you'll never finish because it's absurd. I wanted to concentrate even more on human beings without any landscape, nothing surrounding them. Almost all of the paintings are very stark: you don't see any background, just based on the caricature—but it's not a caricature. Many of them are based on real people that I painted realistically and then I distorted them. It's all about these different feelings. Because you have drama but also this sense of the absurd. And also in the way I am, I'm not a very serious person. In my everyday life, I'm always joking and I'm very sarcastic sometimes. That's what's coming out now. But maybe I'll go back, but I don't plan things—they have their own life, and they finish if and when they want."

[Gracia] "So you have a good sense of humor. Does that have to do with you being Cuban?"

[Rodríguez] "There is a lot of that Cuban character in those paintings. One of the factors of Cuban painting is caricature. Everybody did it. Carlos Enríquez, even Ponce—it is surprising to see Abela also did a famous caricature in the newspaper. A lot of the Cuban character is like that. It's universal and also serious. In my case, it had a lot to do with the way I am. I don't do anything Cuban but it's there."

[Gracia] "So there is a Cuban connection. There is a traditional Cuban caricature and in a way you are doing something similar although they are not caricatures."

[Rodríguez] "Right."

[Gracia] "Yeah, what about the previous work? Some of your previous work has to do with topics that are the result of the Cuban situation, like the Balsas—we even see the island in some paintings."

[Rodríguez] "Yeah. I left Cuba when I was fourteen years old. That's an age in which you aren't completely Cuban, you're not completely anything. I went to Spain for three years and then came back here, to Miami. So many changes of culture and different friends leave you rootless or displaced. I understand very well the sense of displacement, and that's tragic, but also, if you think about it, it's an advantage, because you're not Cuban, you're not American, you're not Spanish. You start seeing life from a distance and that helped me a lot in my work. To see that this is too Cuban, or too American or too European. You're not completely Cuban, you're not completely American. I don't speak good English, I don't speak good Spanish."

[Gracia] "But you paint well, that's the important thing, isn't it? That's your medium."

[Rodríguez] "I'm glad I do it right, because I can't even dance, unlike (almost) all Cubans."

[Gracia] "Tell us, how did you develop your technique and the style you have?"

[Rodríguez] "I'm a self-taught painter. I have never been to any art school."

[Gracia] "So how did you start?"

[Rodríguez] "Just by myself. I had an aunt in Cuba that was a teacher and she had painted for a while. At that time in Cuba there were no oils or anything of the sort. But she had kept a small box of oils. I painted very thinly and used very little canvas—she only had also one roll of canvas, which I clipped very small. I wasn't part of the government. My family already was leaving Cuba, so I couldn't get the grants and support others got. I was considered antirevolutionary, even when I was twelve or thirteen years old. I wasn't part of the worker's paradise. So I started painting on this little canvas and saving as much as I could because there was no more. Then I turned to wood. And then I left Cuba, when I was almost fifteen years old. Even today I save and I am very systematic about cleaning my brushes. When I finish with a tube of paint, it's really finished. Then I went to Spain and I started doing a lot of reading by myself. That's how I learned. Then I came here, went back to Spain, and kept working and going to museums. The best way to learn how to paint is to go to museums and see the masters."

[Gracia] "But what about the tricks of the trade because there are all sorts of tricks to painting. Maybe I shouldn't call them tricks, let's say techniques. How to do this and how to do that?"

[Rodríguez] "I read a lot of books, but also it's trial and error. You want to know which medium works; I did ten paintings and ten different things and then I threw them away. But I was learning. Now I use just a very simple technique, just a little bit of medium and color, that's it. I used to be very elaborate preparing the canvas. Sometimes I still do it, because I get a kick out of it. I prepare the rolled canvas with glue and sand and I stretch it—I love to do that, but sometimes I don't have the time and sometimes it's very difficult, especially with a big canvas. But the technique has been getting simpler. The painting takes you where it's needed, and with so many years of working, it's like a second nature. So, they just come out, they almost lead me by the hand."

[Gracia] "Was there a moment when you became a painter? Were you in high school then?"

[Rodríguez] "I always wanted to be a painter. They used to throw me out of classes because all my notebooks were full of drawings. And I always was a terrible student, always drawing. And I like to read a lot. I have many friends who are poets and writers, and I like to do my own research and explore my thoughts. It's like in painting. I want to do it by myself. I want to crash and start all over and go back again and that's what prepares you to survive. There are so many critics, so many people that don't like your work. It's very hard, it's the hardest. But, you don't care."

[Gracia] "How did you feel when they first said, 'Oh, this is no good.'"

[Rodríguez] "You never like it, but you understand that there are people that have different points of view from yours. I myself like certain painters and certain others I don't like. I respect them, but I don't like them. The same happens with music. You like some type of music, and some type of music you don't."

[Gracia] "Now that you mentioned music, that's very important for you. You always paint with music in the background, don't you?"

[Rodríguez] "Always, yes. It's part of my way of painting. The brushstrokes are made with music. I use different music sometimes for the same painting. I could use a flamenco for one part of the painting, and then Debussy. Music makes you emote, you get a certain energy from it, a certain thoughtfulness. Everything is there in the music, that's why I have eight thousand CDs."

[Gracia] "I see that the whole house is filled with CDs. You have to paint a lot and sell many paintings to support your—well, what you would call it? Vice? Musical vice?"

[Rodríguez] "Miami Vice."

[Gracia] "One last thing about the technique. You have chosen a certain technique and a certain medium. The question is: Are these essential for you? You talked about watercolors also before."

[Rodríguez] "Yeah, I draw from life exactly without any attempt to distort—exactly what I see. A boxer needs to run, and a painter needs to draw; especially from life. You can draw your own style—and maybe distort it; and I do that also—but to keep my vision clean and ordered, I draw from life. It can be anything: a hand, a finger. You look at the subject and draw it exactly without any attempt to distort it or to make a statement—it's a very cold way of doing it. That keeps your vision. I like watercolors, ink, sometimes I paint in acrylic—much less. But my favorite way of painting is with oils. Because I'm used to it, the colors, the labels. You know what to expect. All this is part of painting because you're a worker at the end. That's why I did a self-portrait painting, but I call it *The Worker* not *The Painter*. You work with color, with materials that somehow get transformed in a piece because you get the olive green and when you see the tube you put it on the paper and you alter it so much that when it becomes the olive green at the end of painting, it's transformed, it's alchemy. That's why I like to read about alchemy. A good painter realizes painting is alchemy. The best proof that alchemy works is that in painting the medium is transformed into something else."

[Gracia] "Yes, something entirely different. Now, Arturo, what have been your major influences as a painter."

[Rodríguez] "I think everything. I've been influenced by painters, poetry, cinema, books, novels, philosophy, everything. It's as if you made a *batido* in your head. You prepare your unconscious level, and then you throw it out. For example in the poetry, I did a whole series of paintings based on Rimbaud's *Illuminations*, and the fact is that I always read a little bit of poetry every day. You know, it could be one poem, it could be a whole book but . . ."

[Gracia] "You don't write poetry?"

[Rodríguez] "No, thank God. What appeals to me in poetry is that it doesn't have an order. It's the closest to painting in all the arts—poetry is so plastic."

[Gracia] "I like to call literature, great literature, art with words. So, it's the same thing that you're saying. As a painter you have oils, canvas, and you use them. And the poet is doing the same thing, but with words."

[Rodríguez] "With words, yes. I have a *Macbeth* DVD by the Royal Shakespeare Company and it's very dark. All you see is the face of the actors. Everything is black. But what is wonderful about it is how the drama, without visual effects, comes to life because of the words and the acting—that to me is the perfect painting. In a way, it's like the *Meninas*, it's perfect. It's nothing more or less. This is the kind of thing I'm interested in and poetry gives it to you; a great book or music gives you that. But music is more worklike to me. Poetry is more mysterious and it takes longer to assimilate. Many of my works are based on poems. Many images are based on images from poems. It's unconscious because there is not an order. There is only the order of the words—and in painting the order is that of the colors, the composition, and the drawing."

[Gracia] "But what about other artists. Have they influenced you?"

[Rodríguez] "We would be talking for hours telling you my influences, because everybody influenced me. You know, sometimes I don't like a painter at the beginning and then I end up liking him at the end. And vice versa. I was talking to somebody yesterday about that. You like a painter and ten years later you don't. To me it's an open eye, an open attitude. I love Mondrian, for example."

[Gracia] "I would think that you would."

[Rodríguez] "And yet, he is as far from me as possible. I like Duchamp. What I don't like is to have one mentality, that this is the only thing that works, or that this is not new enough or not trendy enough."

[Gracia] "A lot of control."

[Rodríguez] "A lot of control and created interest. But anyway that's another interview."

[Gracia] "But you know, considering your almost exclusive interest in the human being, if you were going to integrate Duchamp in your work, you would have to have a man using the urinal in the painting. Don't you think?"

[Rodríguez] "Maybe I will. But the point of the Duchamp urinal is that you're not going to use it. But why not? It could be."

[Gracia] "So there you are. And this brings us to an end. Thank you very much."

January 4, 2006
Interviewed in the artist's home and studio, filmed by Norma Gracia, transcribed by Paul Symington, and edited by Jorge J. E. Gracia.

FOR THE CHILDREN

Demi was born in Camagüey, on October 6, 1955. She emigrated to Puerto Rico in 1962, and then came to the United States in 1971. She settled in Miami in 1978 and received an AA degree from Miami-Dade Community College. She began exhibiting in 1987, at the Cuban Museum of Arts and Culture of Miami. She has received a Florida State Visual Artist Grant (1992–1993).

Demi's paintings primarily depict children represented as caught in circumstances beyond their control. She is an advocate for the rights of children and creates works that reveal a variety of forms of neglect, abuse, and emotional trauma brought into the lives of children by adults. Her style is semi-abstract, complex, almost pointillist in its visual impact and characterized by brilliant color and complex form.

Selected Collections: Fort Lauderdale Museum of Art, Fort Lauderdale.

INTERVIEW

Conducted by Jorge J. E. Gracia

[Gracia] "Demi, why don't we start the interview with your name because this is a very intriguing name. I was looking at the Internet and I put down 'Demi' and then there were all sorts of things that came up that were interesting, such as 'Demi Moore.' "

[Demi] "I wish I could look like a Demi Moore!"

[Gracia] "So, how did you choose this name? This is not your real name, is it?"

[Demi] "No, it's not. And I'm not going to tell you my real name either."

[Gracia] "Well, you told me already earlier, but I won't repeat it."

[Demi] " 'Demi'– like 'demitasse' means half, small. To me it has two meanings I always liked. First, it is something cut in the middle—I was taken out of my country and it's as if they cut me right in half. And I always paint children; no matter how much I try to paint adults. Also Demi is my alter ego. Demi can reach places and do things that I think my other name would never allow."

[Gracia] "Your other name—which will remain unmentioned—is more, let's say, serious, substantial, and you like the playfulness of Demi."

[Demi] "Yes."

[Gracia] "So, when did you decide this? Did you start painting first or 'Demi' was a name that you chose for yourself before you painted?"

[Demi] "I changed my name to Demi long before I knew I could paint. I discovered that I could paint only when I was twenty-eight years old. I was a late bloomer—I never knew I could paint before. I knew I was very sensitive to music and I always had a desire to express myself, but I didn't know how. I even took theater classes at night at Miami Dade Community College, and they helped me a great deal. But I never went to museums. I didn't know what an art gallery was, or what art was. I lived in my own little world at twenty-eight years old, a terrible world!"

[Gracia] "So, first of all, I want to know something about how the painting came about and then I also want to know something about your past history, what you thought was very important—lamp posts in your development. So how did you begin to paint?"

[Demi] "I was a bookkeeper, and very unhappy. We'll talk about my life later if you want to because my life plays a very important role in my paintings. I always think that my whole life has been in preparation for my paintings, because it's thanks to all the things that I have gone through that I can paint the way I do. I have always been in training—very tough training—for my painting. But going back to when I was twenty-eight years old is exciting. Like I said, I didn't know that I could paint. Then I met a person, and that was Arturo Rodríguez—a Cuban artist—and the impact of knowing him on me was so revolutionary, so powerful, that it changed my life completely. It was like my life stopped, turned around, and began anew. He taught me how to channel all the negative energy that I had in my life into positives and my life changed completely to such an extent that for the first time I was proud of what I was doing, and I began to love myself. And I began to love people. It was a miracle."

[Gracia] "And how did this happen exactly?"

[Demi] "First I saw his paintings at a gallery and I received a great impact because he had a painting in the exhibit that to me was me. It portrayed a person divided into many parts. And I said, 'that's me!' because that's the way I always felt: cut up in pieces. And I fell in love with the artist, even without knowing him. And I met him that night, and he liked me too!"

[Gracia] "And the rest is history, as the cliché says!"

[Demi] "And it was beautiful, and we fell in love with each other. Then I began to know him also as a person. And in many ways, he was the first person that cared about me, the first person that was interested in listening to what I had to say. He showed me a lot of compassion because my life was terrible; I hated everybody and I hated myself. I was a very twisted person. And he showed such compassion for me. I saw so much innocence in him, even though he painted very strong stuff. But, to me, he was like a clean soul. Then he took me to live in Spain for a whole year, and he only said, 'Demi, I want you to clean your mind of whatever happened in your life. I want you to look, experience, and listen. Don't give any opinions, clean your mind and learn.' That's what I did for a whole year. It was the first time I could listen to someone teaching me what to do. He taught me about music, about the arts; he took me to museums, he took me to the theater. He showed me so many beautiful things that I did not know existed. I knew some existed, but I had not wanted to experience them before because I was in such a negative mood in my life that I didn't want to accept anything. But from him I could. Accepting these things and watching him painting for a whole year in Madrid captivated me. It was such a mystery to see how from a white canvas, he would create life, like a god! Originally in Madrid, my days were spent going to stores. And I didn't care what he was doing in the studio. But then, after I began to experience what he was doing and was captivated by it, I stopped going to the stores and began to spend time watching him paint. After we came back to Miami after that year, I began painting. I asked him for a small piece of canvas and a brush and I began painting."

[Gracia] "What a wonderful story! It is extraordinary because clearly you were inspired by him and his work, and yet your paintings are completely different from his. It's like day and night. I don't see anything in common. Am I missing something? I am looking at one of your paintings right now behind the camera and I'm looking at one Arturo made on the other side of the room, and they look so different!"

[Demi] "Right."

[Gracia] "So how did this work?"

[Demi] "It is as if I have been in training for my whole life. From the beginning, I began painting with my own style. Painters sometimes have difficult times in finding out their own style, in finding out what they really want to paint. Not me. The moment I began painting, I knew what I wanted, how I wanted it, and that it had to be children. I knew what I was doing. It was a miracle; it's very mysterious. It's the same way with painting itself: it's a mystery. I don't know how I do it."

[Gracia] "Thinking about this, it seems that you were fascinated, for example, by color because your paintings use a lot of color. They are very colorful. And at the same time there is an extraordinary amount of—I don't know how to call it—detail. They look like tapestries. They have a sense of cloth, material—you used the word 'embroidery'; this fine putting together of cloth and little strands of thread. This is very different from what Arturo does. Had you seen any painter that inspired you? Did you start with someone in mind? How did this come about?"

[Demi] "It was like an explosion. Remember, I was twenty-eight years old. I had such an interior life that had never been opened before. I was a very lonely person from the time I was a little girl. And I would create my own life, like the colors. I know the colors is where it comes from. I used to find pieces of glasses of different colors in the garbage and I would collect them, and wash them, and dry them and look at them drying in the sunshine. And when the sun would hit them, it was so beautiful. In a way, I was trying to find some happiness, some enjoyment in what was a sad life. It was a defense mechanism. I used to love doing that. So I know the colors come from there. Then, twenty years later, when I began painting, it was as if somebody had opened up something that had been closed for twenty-eight years."

[Gracia] "And just poured out in enormous quantities, not quantities of paintings, but quantities of the intricacy and detail and overflowing . . ."

[Demi] "It did pour out. Some people call my paintings decorative, because of what they see as ornaments in them. Some people call them a madness, and they do have a lot of madness in them. I use hundreds of dots, little lines, hundreds of flowers, hundreds of lines. And I create a kind of claustrophobic atmosphere also. They are creations of what I have felt. I'm always in confrontation with something—life and death. Remember, I had a home and then I didn't. I had a father and he was killed. I had a country and then I didn't have it anymore. It's always a confrontation. Life, death, light and darkness. And I create these hundreds of dots and lines and flowers—it's an insane atmosphere because that's what I have always felt. The hundreds of dots is also a very important element in my paintings because it helps me to unify the whole—the whole thing that I'm doing. It unifies the color, the space, the figures. The painting has movement, it has energy."

[Gracia] "Now some of the impressionists used similar kinds of technique, like Seurat for example, little dots. But your use of them is very different in many ways. But did you see some of those paintings in your trip to Spain, and perhaps they had some impact on you?"

[Demi] "I get influenced by everything. I can look at a newspaper and be influenced by an ad—a hat. I made a very big painting called *The Changing of Hats*, after I saw an add for hats. I open a book and if something touches me, eventually it will come out in a painting. Every year for the past thirty years we have traveled to museums, to see the masters. That's how I learn too, by looking at the masters and the brushstrokes, the use of the colors, the balance of the paintings. So I have been influenced by everything."

[Gracia] "When you married Arturo, he already had a career as a painter and was devoted completely to painting. So, did he teach you techniques and things of this sort, or did you try to develop your own?"

[Demi] "Remember, I didn't know anything so Arturo taught me about the kind of canvas and colors to use. The best thing he did, however, was that he never interfered with my own style. He accepted the style immediately. I began painting children without any hair and I know he didn't like that. He said, 'Demi, why don't you put a little hair here, and a little bit there?' And, 'Why do you have to do it like that?' But I could not do it. Like I said, since the moment I began painting, I had strong convictions and nobody could change them. I knew I could not put hair in my children's heads. And it had to do with taking away the cuteness children have. I didn't want people to look at my children and say: 'Oh, look how cute they are!' You see, I do not paint about all kinds of children. I paint about children that have had conflicts, have lost their innocence in some way. And I wanted to inflict on them respect, as in a monk. But now I'm painting children with hair."

[Gracia] "I'm looking at some of them."

[Demi] "But that was after twenty years. And I mix them in a painting and you can find children with hair and without hair."

[Gracia] "But the classical ones that you used to do had no hair, and they also were surrounded by an overflowing of finery. And yet their faces are somewhat serious and enigmatic; sometimes sad, certainly capturing your attention. They are not lighthearted children. So there is this contrast between this extraordinary finery—which suggests wealth perhaps, well-being, and happiness, pleasantness—and the faces."

[Demi] "I have always been very poetic. I like flowers. But if you look carefully at some of the garments—these beautiful garments—they are very claustrophobic."

[Gracia] "Yes they are, they trap the child!"

[Demi] "But you have to look very carefully. If you keep studying my paintings you will always find something happening, some kind of confrontation the child has. Also the child can be in a very wealthy position but be trapped in a very unhappy life. But it's interesting that people began buying my paintings right away. I was amazed. I said. 'My God, I can make a living at all this!' "

[Gracia] "So what happened? You started painting and you accumulated a few paintings and then you had a show?"

[Demi] "No, collectors would come to buy Arturo's paintings at the house."

[Gracia] "And they saw yours."

[Demi] "I would hide them. I would put away the little things—I used to paint them very small. But then one day Arturo began showing them because he was proud of them; he was my teacher. He was teaching me and I was growing, and the collectors began buying. Then they gave me an exhibit and I sold everything, and I couldn't believe it! I really enjoyed doing it. I was beginning—through my paintings—to understand my life, which to me was always a mystery, a dark spot. I couldn't find myself and I have found myself through my art. That's why I love what I'm doing. I have such a big respect for art because of what it can do for a human being."

[Gracia] "Both to the one who produces it and to the one who doesn't produce it."

[Demi] "Exactly. I have letters from people telling me how much they have been touched by my paintings. And that's such a gift from life. I never expected it; at twenty-eight I thought my life was over! Over! And then this miracle happened through art. That's why every day of my life is enchanted by the art that surrounds my life: by my husband's art, by the art that I produce. I still cannot believe that I can do it. But it's also a struggle, because the moment I begin painting, a little voice says to me, 'You cannot do it!' You cannot do it! You cannot do it!' "

[Gracia] "And also it's very clear that you are not what one would call a prolific painter. You have few paintings."

[Demi] "Right."

[Gracia] "But you work at them endlessly. We were just talking about one that you mentioned in your studio. You've been working at it for a year and it's still not done."

[Demi] "And this collector has been waiting for a whole year for it. For me to paint is very painful, because I paint through the unconscious, with my unconscious, and by elimination. I begin with an idea and I begin painting—very prolifically here and there—and then all of a sudden I start eliminating, and putting, and changing, and putting more and more. With a blade, I erase everything, I scrape everything, and I begin again because I have to create in stages, in layers, and destroy the layers. It's like I'm copying my own life. A layer came over my life, toppled my interior, and then I have another one and another one and that's the way I paint. It's very painful, with all those little dots and little things. Everything is done by me with little brushes. At the end you can see all that struggle, all that energy coming out, and that touches. . . . People either hate or love my work. Those are two strong emotions and I love them."

[Gracia] "Indifference is what you cannot take, but it would be difficult to be indifferent to your paintings, I think. Do you find anybody that is actually indifferent? I think I can see people saying, 'Oh, I hate that!' and other people like ourselves who say, 'Oh, my goodness, this is wonderful!' But to be indifferent, it's almost impossible. That person must be someone who doesn't have an inner-life or no appreciation of the complexity of art and the beauty of it. So, in many ways your painting has been a catharsis or has provided a catharsis for your life and has brought it to a level in which you have become productive and rich. You probably should tell us a little about the past because it's a very tragic past. And I know this is painful—we don't want to create pain for you—but insofar as it was the background of what brought you to art, I think we need to have you say something about it, although perhaps briefly."

[Demi] "When I was five years old, my father, who was in the military was executed by the Cuban Revolution. Immediately, my mother sent me away to another country to be with relatives that I didn't know. So, in a second, you could say, I lost my father, my family, my home, and my country. That's strong stuff!"

[Gracia] "You became completely lost, as it were. And at what age did you leave Cuba?"

[Demi] "I was seven years old. And it was very hard. But in order to survive I created a world for myself. I would look for colors which made my life happy. I was separated from my mother and my two sisters, for almost nine years. Then we came together again, but I had to start to know them all over again, to love them, which was very difficult. I moved in with them, in New York. And that also was very painful because I did my last year of high school in New York and I didn't know the language. And the people at the high school laughed at me. I would sit down to eat lunch and they would disappear. It was something terrible. So I began having these confrontations. And look at this, I'm fifty years old and I'm still crying when I remember all these things! I had confrontations with my family, with the school, I didn't know the language. But I learned a little bookkeeping and I got a job and then I moved down here to Miami. That's when I felt like a very twisted person. I hated everybody. I wanted to die, and I met Arturo."

[Gracia] "And that was your salvation."

[Demi] "Yes."

[Gracia] "But you know, Demi, many of the greatest artists and intellectuals and writers have had very painful lives and experiences. And they have been able to overcome them in some way—maybe sometimes not even overcome them. In fact, I don't think many of them have overcome them, but those experiences have made possible for them to produce a kind of art and literature that has the kind of depth that helps establish it forever. It makes it universal because it strikes a chord with every other human being who has suffered."

[Demi] "I always say that I had a lot of bad things happen in my life. I have had three bouts with cancer, one after the other. That was tough. So I have had physical and emotional—how do you say?—storms in my life. But if you compare all I have suffered with the blessings I have had with my art, I welcome it. Because the suffering makes me a better human being. It makes me a better artist. It makes me appreciate the gift that God has given me: by giving me such a husband, such a friend like Arturo, and by giving me the art that I can create. So, it's beautiful. I'm happy."

[Gracia] "That's wonderful. Now let me ask you, how do you feel as a Cuban or Cuban American? How does this play in your art, is your art inspired by Cuban themes? Some of the games your children play are very Cuban. And in other paintings you have depicted First Communion and other things that are very much related to Cuba. But how do you feel as a Cuban or Cuban-American artist? This is too complicated, so let's begin with two questions: Do you feel that you are a Cuban artist or a Cuban-American artist? Or is there any difference between the two in your mind?"

[Demi] "I have tried to do universal painting that cannot be associated with any country because every place in the world has children suffering, children going through suffering—their parents die, they get killed. This is a universal pain that children experience, with the loss of innocence. And the games, they all play games. But I cannot deny that I have a wound as a Cuban—as a person who comes from Cuba, because I was born in Cuba. And I can never forget that my home was destroyed, that my father was killed in such a terrible way; this makes me Cuban, because those sufferings come from Cuba. It was caused by my own Cuban brothers and sisters. And I am Cuban, so I paint. But I do not paint Cuban—even though I have some Cubans in my paintings—but . . . I don't know how to say it."

[Gracia] "That your experiences as a Cuban, in relation to what Cubans have had to suffer, has in a sense informed your painting."

[Demi] "Exactly, now you see how you said it better than I did."

[Gracia] "No, no, I didn't. But anyway, you mentioned in our conversation before the interview something about Frida Kahlo; that you admire her. So, I'm wondering how you feel about Latin American art."

[Demi] "I love Frida because I identify with her as a woman, with her suffering—but I also identify with Velázquez. He has been a great influence on me. And I also like the Renaissance painters. I love Fra Angelico and Filippo Lipi, and all the little things and the delicate kinds of ways they paint. And I love the English artists. One is Palmer—very few people know him—and Dadd—'Dadd'—he was insane. All his life he was in an asylum, and he would paint these strange-looking girls with these magnificent dresses too, with flowers. And nothing would make sense, but I love him."

[Gracia] "You never considered painting abstract or anything of the sort."

[Demi] "Not yet!"

[Gracia] "That's right, it could be, couldn't it? It's an interesting question, because you have a couple of series that are more simple than the very elaborate ones, but you seem to be painting elaborate ones still. So, you are not, as it were, abandoning the former style and moving to another but sort of developing various types of things at the same time."

[Demi] "Exactly. I have collectors that don't want my paintings to change."

[Gracia] "They want you to do the same thing."

[Demi] "Always the same and . . . I paint for them too, and I paint the other way, the ones with less figures, less colors. I love to do different styles at the same time. It will always be a Demi. It will always identify with me and my way of thinking and my experiences. But I do—I like to do different things at the same time."

[Gracia] "Well, Demi, we are about to finish the interview. But before we do, let me ask you if you want to say something else?"

[Demi] "My language is painting and I'm terrible at speaking."

[Gracia] "But you have done a marvelous job of speaking today."

[Demi] "Maybe I have a thousand things more to say but I don't know how."

[Gracia] "Well, let me ask you one more thing. You mentioned that you paint for some of your collectors who want you to do certain things, and not go away from your style. And yet, you want to feel free to do other things. How important is the audience for you?"

[Demi] "Let's be honest. The economic . . ."

[Gracia] "It's very important!"

[Demi] "It's very, very important. And I have to yield to it. But whenever I feel like doing something else, I will do it and they will wait until I can do whatever they want. It is natural for me to do different things and then all of a sudden I begin doing the same thing back again. It's very easy for me to change and come back again. I do not have specific stages. I am very flexible."

[Gracia] "And now with this business about the art world and the galleries and the shows—does that play an important role in your choice of themes, topics, or career?"

[Demi] "I try not to pay attention to anything like that. I am in my own world. I know it's important to pay attention to what's going on in the world, but I decided not to pay attention because it would upset me. Sometimes you see things that are not well done, but I'm not going to get into that."

[Gracia] "Right, right."

[Demi] "I live in my own world and I'm happy where I am. My life is full, just trying to survive in my own life: my health and my paintings, that's my whole life. Nothing else matters."

[Gracia] "Very good, then. Thank you very much for a wonderful statement of your painting and your goals. I'm sure that everyone who reads the transcript or sees the interview will be moved by your life as an artist. And of course, they will be moved by your work."

[Demi] "Thank you."

January 4, 2006
Interviewed in the artist's home and studio, filmed by Norma Gracia, transcribed by Paul Symington, and edited by Jorge J. E. Gracia.

A SEARCH FOR UNITY

JUAN CARLOS LLERA

Juan Carlos Llera was born in Sagua La Grande, on January 26, 1965. He emigrated to the United States in 1972 and settled in Miami. He began exhibiting in 1993. That year, he was awarded "Best in Show" at the 35th Annual Memorial Hortt Competition Exhibition, held at the Museum of Art, Fort Lauderdale.

Llera works in a multiplicity of techniques that combine oil painting and digital imaging, and realism with abstraction. His body of work can be contextualized within spiritual traditions that seek to unite the material to the spiritual and the abstract to the representational.

INTERVIEW

Conducted by Lynette M. F. Bosch

[Bosch] "Juan Carlos, you and I have known each other for some years now; we've had many discussions on these topics; and I think maybe what we might do is start with the obvious Cuban-American subject and then work from that to the more universal aspects of creative identity . . ."

[Llera] ". . . the more abstract."

[Bosch] "Exactly. Just to fill in the background, tell us a little bit about how you began to think of yourself as an artist, when you came to this country, your connection to art, just give us a sense of your biographical origins."

[Llera] "Contrary to the idea that to become an artist is an act of the will, I think that much of it has to do with circumstances. It has to do with a number of factors that come together at a point in time, and for me it was no different; it's no mystery, and no act of magic. It's where life took me circumstantially. My father was an artist . . ."

[Bosch] "That's right, your father was an artist—how old were you when first began to think of yourself as coming to be, or as being, an artist?' "

[Llera] "I didn't know anything else. I opened my eyes and my father was painting, and much of my identity came from my father, emulating him, wanting to be like him. In this respect it was literally bred into me."

82

[Bosch] "How would you think of your artistic origins and the idea that you're Cuban American? What does that mean to you? What does being a Cuban American mean to you?"

[Llera] "In essence, although Cuba obviously has a very heavy Spanish influence, Cuba is in the Americas, so the conflict between, say, the New York school of art and Cuban-American art doesn't exist, for me. Also having been raised in this country as a Cuban American, I am able to fuse both sides, the Hispanic side and the Anglo."

[Bosch] "There's not so much a high sense of balance that blends into a unit?"

[Llera] "No. Yeah, exactly, it is a beautiful balance. It's rather like two juxtaposing forces; I see it as a marriage of two cultures that work very well together."

[Bosch] "In terms of thinking about the themes that you pursue in your work, can you talk a little bit about how you started in terms of working style, what kinds of subjects interested you in the beginning, and how you see your development, because I know the work you're doing now is very different from the work that you were doing at the beginning?"

[Llera] "On the surface it is very different, but in essence it's actually the same. I began to do photo-realism, then I did strict realism, but all of it had a heavy mystical, a spiritual end. I was attracted to Caravaggio, Monet, the Spanish School, and at the same time—once again, going back to the Cuban-American issue—I was attracted to Motherwell, Barnet Newman, and—having come from Emilio Falero, with whose work I'm sure you're familiar—Mondrian and Vermeer. So, although on the surface the work appears to be physically very different, it's not."

[Bosch] "I've always been interested in the sort of spiritual/philosophical aspect that you pursue in your work and I wonder if you could talk about the search that you have undertaken and the goals that you had in this kind of metaphysical exploration into which you launched."

[Llera] "The goals are purely selfish, meaning that they amount to a search for personal freedom—freedom from concepts, freedom from anything that will bind you, anything that will hold you down. In that respect, I have searched for nothing more than freedom: So, why not realism, abstract expressionism, San Juan de la Cruz, Santa Teresa? Why not?"

[Bosch] "So when you look at these categories of representation, thinking, and being, do you do it thinking, 'I'm an artist. I work with all of these concepts. I interweave all of these things into the visual product?' Where do you situate yourself within this continuum of thought that you're identifying as freedom, as spiritual, and as metaphysical? Where are you?"

[Llera] "I'm just one big paradox like everybody else. To me, human existence is a paradox. So, in the new series of works that I'm doing, I define it as a creature having the knowledge and the foresight to know that one day it will come to an end, yet at the same time having the same genetic code or messages that any other creature has, that is to survive. How do you marry the two? To some people it's an afterlife, to some people it's the attempt to reconcile the fact that in a hundred years we're just going to be bones. It's all about meaning—I hope I answered the question."

[Bosch] "Yeah, you did. So what you're essentially hoping to do in the work is to make something concrete . . ."

[Llera] ". . . for myself. I'm looking for a marriage between abstraction and realism—in the case of Emilio Falero, between Vermeer and Mondrian—I'm trying to reconcile and find a common denominator."

[Bosch] "You're looking really for a kind of material/spiritual balance."

[Llera] "Absolutely."

[Bosch] "A sort of unity."

[Llera] "Yes."

[Bosch] "How do you relate this to your identity as an artist—because, if you think about it, being an artist is being different from people who aren't artists? You're in a position where you're almost a permanent exile."

[Llera] "Indeed."

[Bosch] "How do you think about it, or does it even play a role in your work, in your creative process?"

[Llera] "It's actually one of the driving forces, that very feeling, that very difference, an almost neurotic energy. Much of the creative process comes from sheer insecurity, sheer neurosis at times, and circumstances."

[Bosch] "Can you tell us a bit about the kinds of subjects that you represented as you moved from, let's say, photo-realism to abstraction, and mention particular works if you wish? If you think about the time you began to produce work that you considered professional, at what moment did you say to yourself, 'I'm part of this art world'? What were you doing, what were you working toward?"

[Llera] "In professional terms?"

[Bosch] "When did you start exhibiting? What were you exhibiting? What were the moments that were milestones for you?"

[Llera] "I don't believe I've ever really felt that way, although one of the pieces that I produced won a competition . . ."

[Bosch] ". . . and that was a capstone . . ."

[Llera] ". . . basically—the newspaper articles came out, and that launched me into a professional environment. Now, did that change anything else? No. It's been like a tree that has been growing all the time."

[Bosch] "So, what were your first subjects?"

[Llera] "The first group were collages. I was juxtaposing the delicate with the brutal, I was juxtaposing this with that. Then I moved to a series that became religious, where I was juxtaposing the material by putting it into a different context. For example, I created a crucifixion of me, nailed onto three closet doors."

[Bosch] "When you put yourself into a work in that way, how did you—again, to go back to the idea of identity—identify with the work that you were making? Was it about you? Was it you watching? Was it about other people?"

[Llera] "I think it's always about me. I think it's purely selfish in that respect."

[Bosch] "Was it based on things that were happening in your life? Or thoughts you were having? Things you were reading?"

[Llera] "Delusions, yeah."

[Bosch] "I know you read tons and that you're always injecting yourself into what you're reading and what you're thinking."

[Llera] "Exactly."

[Bosch] "So, it's a piece of you that floats out there in individual form that has to do with what's in your head at the moment, what you're reading, what is stimulating you, and then it manifests as this work of art that is a piece of your thought process."

[Llera] "Absolutely, it becomes an extension of you."

[Bosch] "Would you identify yourself as being an emotional artist, an intellectual artist? Where is the gravity center? Where do you create from?"

[Llera] "You mean, a rational artist versus a romantic?"

[Bosch] "Yes, do you create from your guts? From your heart? From your head? Where does it come from?"

[Llera] "I don't know. I think the day I realize where it comes from will be the day I stop working because it doesn't come from any one place in that respect. It comes from a life force inside of me."

[Bosch] "It's something that simply generates."

[Llera] "It generates and it has a life of its own and it does whatever it wants when it wants it. In this new series that I'm working on now, I began to explore the idea of some nudes, but the moment I began to work it became clear that there were not going to be any nudes, but landscapes instead."

[Bosch] "Talk a little about how you make this new work, because I know that it's a fairly complex technological process. Again, it reflects yet another aspect of your creativity and your identity as an artist— you've moved away from the standard of the artist as the guy with the paintbrush pushing around paint on a canvas and have become a different kind of artist."

[Llera] "Having a great teacher like Emilio Falero means that it's always about the work, it's always about the expression. In this respect, it doesn't matter what I utilize to create the work. I can utilize paint, I can utilize a video camera, I can utilize anything, it doesn't really matter. But how did I choose to incorporate the digital medium into it? Because, first of all, I'm proficient at using it, I've been working on it for a long, long, long, long time, so it's second nature to me, just like the paint. For me, the marriage of the two made complete sense. Once again, another marriage; bringing two things together."

[Bosch] "Again, it's the reconciliation of two seeming opposites that's where you've placed yourself as a Cuban American, as an artist, somebody who navigates tradition and innovation."

[Llera] "Completely. There are pieces that come out of, say, a German romantic. You sit there and say, 'How does this come out in a digital medium?' "

[Bosch] "How do you start? Take us through a particular specifically."

[Llera] "I begin a piece by creating an abstract on a piece of paper. And, at that point . . ."

[Bosch] ". . . now, where does the abstract come from?"

[Llera] "I paint it."

[Bosch] "So, at that point, you're doing a traditional painting."

[Llera] "Yes. I could do the abstract or, alternatively, I could be photographing or drawing or painting something else. Then, all of a sudden, I see the abstract, I see it, I bring out the abstract—I digitize it, put it into a computer, I bring the other image into the computer—inside the computer I marry the two—I can print it back out, repaint on that, if I want, redigitize it, bring it back into the computer, paint on it again. I can go back and forth a million times."

[Bosch] "You're navigating through these worlds of *techne* in the old sense of the technique of the actual hands-on and then in this new kind of removed technological world where you can manipulate anything you want, create things that don't even exist."

[Llera] "I can create things utilizing this medium that would be futile to try to paint. It would take me six months and I'd never get what I'm after. So, there's no point. How can—in an age where the Internet and computers rule our life—there not be an expression of that medium?"

[Bosch] "About the images that you're creating now, you said that you were setting out to merge the material and the spiritual, the abstract and the representational, how do you think you've achieved that?"

[Llera] "It's a challenge. For example, in the series with the telephone poles, I think I was pretty successful in finding the solution—but that solution is different from the solution in the new series on which I'm working."

[Bosch] "...and this very new series, tell us about it."

[Llera] "It has to do with impermanence, with the idea of time. That's the blanket umbrella. Right now, you've caught me in the midst of it, so for this particular section which is going to be fifteen paintings, I haven't found the right name."

[Bosch] "One of the things that has always struck me about you—and we can talk about this again within this context of identity—is how aware you are of these generations of artists—you talk about Emilio, your father, you are friends with Baruj Salinas, how do you see yourself within the continuum of Cuban art, Cuban-American art? Is it a generational thing?"

[Llera] "If I don't see a conflict between Mondrian and Vermeer, how do you think I see myself?"

[Bosch] "As being merged in the unity of..."

[Llera] "...exactly. Just one more..."

[Bosch] "...one more Cuban American, Cuban artist..."

[Llera] "...just one more guy with a paintbrush."

[Bosch] "When you talk with Emilio and Baruj, and—obviously, being Cuban American—when the experience of exile comes up, how do you see yourself as being similar and different in the way that they're looking at it?"

[Llera] "Than Emilio and Padura or Baruj?"

[Bosch] "Because you're younger than all of us, so your perception of everything is intrinsically different simply because of the general placement of who you are."

[Llera] "In the context of these other artists, how would I see myself? That's not easy to answer because I think I just see myself as an individual . . . there will come other younger artists than me that will . . ."

[Bosch] "...so, you're simply a stage in what is happening? One of the things that always has struck me about you is the great friendship you have with Emilio and Baruj, but also with others; I've always thought about you and this integration within the group in this very personal way, but at the same time you're part of a group that is drawn to Renaissance and Baroque art. I wonder if you could talk about what it is that draws you to the Renaissance and the Baroque? Because even in this new work that you are doing now I see that influence. Tell us about your exposure to it, your initial interest in it, and how it gets incorporated into your work."

[Llera] "The tendency of any artist is to try and be innovative, and I studied art at a time where most of the professors I had studied under the New York School. That was their training, and they would push abstract expressionism. That's where they felt comfortable. Of course, being somewhat of an artist you choose to go the other way and you choose to explore something else. Plus, in the idea of being an exiled Cuban American, there is a fragmentation or a cutting off of a cultural identity in a certain sense. So, what do you go back to? You go back to the Hispanic, you go back to the icons, you go back to the visual icons in that respect."

[Bosch] "How do you relate that to the interest that you have in spirituality?"

[Llera] "Like Kandinsky, I think all art is in essence spiritual. Ultimately, the well or spring from which art stems is the creator, whoever that is, or whatever that is. Art is the imitation of a creative process. In that respect, it becomes spiritual, it becomes good art, for all good art is spiritual—I'm going on a limb here, I just said it, I just said 'all good art' . . ."

[Bosch] ". . . value judgments!"

[Llera] ". . . exactly! 'All good art!' "

[Bosch] "How politically incorrect of you!"

[Llera] "All good art, in essence, transcends its surface. If art does not transcend the surface, it just sits there, it doesn't talk about human existence, it doesn't talk about what we're doing here, it doesn't talk about anything else. And this is, in essence, what's all about. No matter who it is, whether it be Warhol, Motherwell, or Juan González. It's not that you go after the spiritual, for even the most materialistic of artists who would love to give that up sometimes can't."

[Bosch] "So it comes after you."

[Llera] "It comes after you."

[Bosch] "And it grabs you, and then there you are."

[Llera] "You have no choice."

[Bosch] "You have to pursue it. I've always been impressed by how much you read and how much you think because if someone were to ask me to categorize you, I would think of you as being a very thoughtful artist in every sense of the word. Not that you illustrate your thought, but that you're always reading, you're always thinking and to me your work comes out of a very profound complex philosophical base. So, I'm wondering if you could talk about the kinds of interests that you have in terms of what you read, why you read it, and what you are reading at the moment? What's made the biggest impact on you?"

[Llera] "Philosophically? Lately I've been reading the same thing that I've been always reading, to tell you the truth: St. John of the Cross."

[Bosch] "You're very Catholic in your reading taste."

[Llera] "Sometimes. For example, I'll read the Dalai Lama."

[Bosch] "What brings you to St. John of the Cross so repeatedly?"

[Llera] "The language. The mysticism. It's just very iconic in that respect."

[Bosch] "Does your interest in the Renaissance and the Baroque respond in anyway to the fact that you're a Cuban Catholic? Do you think about this or is it just something that you gravitate to instinctively?"

[Llera] ". . . it's something I enjoy."

[Bosch] "So it fits into your general experience?"

[Llera] "Yeah, in essence. I would definitely put it that way in a certain sense. Obviously, it's a different time, it's a different age, it's a different language. Today I think you would find a different way to express it."

[Bosch] "Which is what you're doing in this new series because especially the sense of time and space. When I think of St. John of the Cross I think of something that, if I were trying to give a visual form to it, it would have a sense of the ongoing, and this is what I see in the new work that you're doing. The possibility within infinite space that connects to the larger universal. Is this part of what you're trying to find and negotiate?"

[Llera] "In essence, at least for the artist, art is somewhat selfish. This means that, for example, when I was reading Montaigne, another one of my philosophers (Marcel and Montaigne are my favorites), one of the things that struck me was that he juxtaposes two ideas of human knowledge. In the scientific method one becomes objective to your subject to a point where you understand your subject but you never experience it. When it comes to mystical models, as with St. John of the Cross's, you're not talking about understanding your subject, but merely experiencing it. These are two very different ways of knowing your subject or your object. St. John of the Cross absolutely has no understanding of God as a fact, this understanding of God is irrelevant and could probably be completely a hindrance to him experiencing God. So, once again, do you understand the color red?"

[Bosch] "Of course not, you just recognize it, you experience it."

[Llera] "You experience an abstraction, you experience a beautiful sunset, the moon. You don't understand beauty, you experience beauty. And thus, the connection between mystics—St. Theresa, St. John of the Cross—and art."

[Bosch] "One of the things that comes through in all of your work is this presentation of beauty at a time when so many artists are turning away from it. You always embrace it. Your work has always been gorgeous and at the same time it has the ability to walk through the material into the spiritual, take you into the sublime through the beauty of it. Are you an artist who consciously thinks about creating beauty or does the beauty just happen?"

[Llera] "It just happens. Beauty is all around us and the mystical experience is all around us. Artists walk down the street and find an object and put it on display. How many people passed that object on the street and never saw its beauty? Well, you take it, you put into its context in a museum and all of a sudden you are experiencing beauty. But when I speak of beauty I'm speaking of it in a very broad sense . . . not something pleasurable. There's a very big difference between something pleasurable and something beautiful. They're two very different things. Something can be incredibly displeasurable and yet be incredibly beautiful. The idea of turning away from beauty, period, horrifies me as an artist."

[Bosch] "I"m looking forward to seeing your future work."

August 11, 2005
Interviewed in the artist's home and studio, filmed by Norma Gracia, transcribed by Paul Symington, and edited by Jorge J. E. Gracia.

LANDSCAPES OF THE MIND

ALBERTO REY

Alberto Rey was born in Agramonte, on August 7, 1960. He emmigrated to Mexico in 1963, and then to the United States, in 1964. He settled in Barnesboro, PA, after 1967, with brief stays in Brownsville, TX and Miami. He received a BFA from the Art Institute in Pittsburgh (1981), a BFA from Indiana University of Pennsylvania (1982), an MFA from the State University of New York at Buffalo (1987), and an MA from Harvard University (1988). He began exhibiting outside Miami in the early 1980s.

Originally an abstract painter, Rey turned to realism as he began to explore his Cuban identity. During the 1990s, Rey focused on depicting Cuban landscapes, combined Cuban and American locales, Cuban cultural objects, such as bars of guava and bottles of rum, and portraits of Cubans and Cuban Americans. He lives in Fredonia, NY, where he is Distinguished Professor at the State College.

Selected Collections: Albright Knox Art Gallery, Buffalo, NY; Bronx Museum of Art, NY; Brooklyn Museum of Art, New York; Burchfield-Penney Art Center, Buffalo, NY; Castellani Art Museum, Niagara University, Niagara, NY; El Museo del Barrio, New York; Fort Lauderdale Museum of Art, Fort Lauderdale.

INTERVIEW

Conducted by Jorge J. E. Gracia

[Gracia] "Alberto, let's begin with two questions: How did you become an artist? And, when did you know that this is what you wanted to do?"

[Rey] "I started doing art when I was in high school—let me give you a little background. I left Cuba when I was three, moved to Mexico for two years, and then Miami, and I ended up spending most of my adolescent life in a small coal mining town in western Pennsylvania. The idea of making a living doing art seemed ridiculous. At the time I made art because I enjoyed it, but I never really thought of it as a career choice. My parents didn't think it was a good idea either, so I went into college to study biology in the hopes of one day becoming an oceanographer. I also enrolled in some art courses and, much to my parents' dismay, I switched from biology to art. I went to a couple of different schools and concentrated my efforts in making a career out of illustration. I soon realized that I wanted more control over my work and switched to fine arts. That's where I'm at now. It wasn't an easy road to get here. I often wondered if I had made the right decision because trying to make a living as an artist was very difficult, but since I had no other options or a safety net to fall back on, I continued to work through those difficult times. I am now a professor at the State University of New York at Fredonia."

[Gracia] "In going back to the period when you were an adolescent and you were discovering yourself, and then in college when your parents weren't particularly thrilled about your plans, did they put up an active opposition to your ideas?"

[Rey] "Before I went to college I was offered a scholarship at West Point Military Academy. After realizing that I did no want to spend my life in the military I dropped out. This was a difficult pill for my father to swallow. I had dropped out of West Point and then switched from biology to art. My father and I did not speak to each other for two years. My parents were always worried that I wouldn't find any employment. My father has two doctorates, my uncle is a doctor, my other uncle is a dentist, so the idea of being an artist did not sit well with them. A few years after graduating from college, I was in my mid-twenties without a full-time job that could support me or a family for the rest of our lives. This was something that they found problematic. My aunt and uncle, however, encouraged me. I remember them telling me that when they came from Cuba, they needed to find employment right away because they needed to support their children. Their jobs were not what they had wanted, but they weren't in a position where they had other options. They didn't have the luxury of deciding what they wanted to do. They said that I was not in the same position, so I should do what I wanted with my life. They were pretty much the only relatives who felt that way. That was important to me at the time."

[Gracia] "How about your parents? Have your parents at some point changed their view?"

[Rey] "Yes, I think the change began when I went to grad school with an assistantship. I didn't have to pay for anything. At that point, they realized that perhaps there was some worth in what I was doing. They saw that there was some financial value in it and consequently art seemed more like a viable career. I don't want you to get the wrong impression of my parents. They have always been very loving and caring, but they were very concerned about the decisions I had made. I realized early on that they would not be able to understand what I was doing or why I was doing it or how important it was to me. When I got a job—a full-time tenured job—they were finally able to relax and began to enjoy my accomplishments."

[Gracia] "In your career, let's say up to this point, had there been any markers, any major things that shifted, changed, or affected you dramatically? Was there anything that actually made you decide, 'This is what I want to do?'"

[Rey] "There are markers but, for the most part, they are not necessarily major ones. Along the way, as my skills as a painter have improved, I've been able to tie my intellectual and aesthetic concerns with the painting. I've found a sense of fulfillment that I haven't been able to find in anything else. There's times when I've left the studio, after twelve hours of painting, and I've felt that, although exhausted, this is what I should be doing my entire life and there is a sense of satisfaction that everything is coming together—everything, intellectually, aesthetically, technically. There's a sense of euphoria when that happens. It is a sense of confirmation that this is what I should be doing. It is not always a wonderful experience, however. Whenever I start a new project there is always some concern that I'm not going to be able to do as well as I want. I always try to make each painting better than the previous one. It can be a bit stressful at the beginning or when things are not going well with the painting. It haunts me until the issue is resolved in the work. Over the years, I have recognized that this is just part of the process and I have accepted it. There are also enough of those wonderful moments that keep me moving forward."

[Gracia] "You have now reached a point where you see things coming together; there is coherence in the work, you like it, you see that you are doing something that interests you and is both worthwhile and important. So, how do you see this work in the contemporary artistic scene? What is it that ties you to that scene? Are there things that separate you from it? How do you see your contribution, as it were, your role in the artistic world today?"

[Rey] "I think working artists who are aware of what's happening socially and/or artistically in their world and are producing work that addresses those issues are creating work that is reflective of contemporary society and consequently is contemporary art. When I start any project, I first think about the work as something that is personally significant and then in terms of how it fits into what I had done before (so that it's not redundant), how it fits into everything that I know about art history, contemporary art, and how it reflects what's going on in society. As a member of a social group, sometimes I need to analyze why it is important to me. These factors don't rule what I do, but they are important.

Often, the impulse or passion to make the work is so strong that other considerations take second place. My work has very little to do with what's 'popular' in contemporary art. There's so much happening at any given time in art that you really don't have to worry about what is mainstream. There's always a market. There's always some venues or alternative spaces that are willing to exhibit or support a direction in art that is reflective of what is happening in society."

[Gracia] "When you are involved in these creative processes which sometimes lead you to different paths, is the primary motivation here some idea you have? Is it some emotion? Is it the materials that you use? How do these things work together?"

[Rey] "Many of the projects come about without me realizing they are going to happen. Sometimes as part of the research for a project, I come across something that I never would have expected to find and a whole series of works comes out of it. A project or series of work can also occur after I've done all the research, I finished a series of paintings, I feel confident with what I've learned and then it's time to move on to learn something else and consequently that affects what the next body of work will be. A good example of this is the 'Balsa Series,' of which these two paintings here are examples (*Las Balsas IX* and *Balsas Artifacts: Cross and String*). I was doing research at the University of Miami's Cuban Archives Center and at the archives in the Key West Library. While exploring the area, I came across the Cuban Refugee Center which is on Stock Island, I believe. I'd heard of it before. I was very moved by the collection of balsas or rafts that were falling apart in the backyard. These were the remnants of attempts by Cubans to leave Cuba. Inside the refugee center was a collection of watches, compasses, small statues of the Caridad de Cobre and many other objects that were either donated by the Cubans who had successfully made the trip or found inside the deserted remains of rafts found in the open waters between Cuba and the Keys. At the time I was there, the collection wasn't well taken care of but that wasn't their main job. The Center provided support and emergency health services to the new immigrants. The Center has now become a modest museum of sorts and some of the rafts have been housed in a plane hangar outside of Miami. The first time I was there, the rafts were just falling apart because some were made with tar, Styrofoam, and rope. I was so moved by the sight of rafts and the need to document decaying remains of the vessels that I knew I had to do a series of paintings about them. I'd already heard of artists doing paintings and constructions of balsas for exhibitions, but I still wanted to do something different and emotional that captured what I felt that day. So as soon as I returned back to New York, I started the Balsa Series. I started them on plaster. It was important to me that they were shown with this dark interior so that they became almost like altar pieces and that they had their own housing. By creating this housing, these pieces could be exhibited in any space, gallery, or museum and they would have their own environment in which they would rest. By doing so, I didn't have to worry about whether the paintings would be in a bright interior or on different colored walls that would change the environment in which the paintings were viewed. It also was done so that it seems like the balsas are floating on the background. They're done in a very devotional manner, almost like *retablos* or *devotos*, which were paintings done, for the most part, by nonartists—devotional pieces—for saints, wishing for help or thanking them for their assistance. The thought of these everyday people creating these visual prayers to God or saints was a very important thing, tying together everyday experiences with a sense of spirituality. That's what I wanted to do with the work. I wanted to make it very spiritual, very devotional, without saying a great deal—putting a highlight on the piece, darkening up everything else—so that the absence of information would create a sense of silence when the work was exhibited and that, hopefully, would portray some of the emotional elements in the work. The other paintings concern the artifacts found inside the balsas. These were the objects that people who were leaving their country and their families had decided to bring with them. It became important for me to figure out the objects people would decide to bring with them. If I'm going to leave, what would I take with me? I could only take a handful of things from a country in which I grew up. What would I take? These objects were obviously significant to them so I thought it would be important to document what people would take to a different country when they were making this voyage. A lot of them would not survive."

[Gracia] ". . . there is a personal story here."

[Rey] "Yes, it happened many years before I did the 'Balsa Series.' Many of my relatives had come to the United States from Cuba on rafts. One of them was my grandmother who didn't survive the trip. So, it was something pretty important to me. It started me thinking about the whole idea of looking into Cuba and my culture, because, as I noticed that my relatives were passing away, I also noticed that my connection to that culture was also going with them. I thought it was time that I started to investigate the Cuban heritage that I had shunned away from for most of my life because I was spending most of the time trying to assimilate myself to American culture. Being Cuban wasn't that important. When my grandmother died, and later a few other relatives, I became much more involved in trying to find out about my culture—about the music, the religion, my family—and in doing so, my life became much more fulfilling. When I started to incorporate all this into my American culture, my work became more unified and I felt like I was finding my connection and perspective on the two cultures. So, I was working out that sense of identity through the work and through the research. Five years ago, I stopped doing work that was specifically about Cuba, because I felt that the void I had been experiencing was finally filled when I returned to Cuba for the first time after leaving there as a child. It was time to move on intellectually and emotionally. Like many things in my life, I find that what I do is cyclical. Throughout my career, I have repeatedly moved between realistic and abstract painting. As I have gotten older, the cycles have become longer between each of these changes. With the patience that age brings I have been able to concentrate more effort on the complexities of the subject matter that I did not or could not see when I was younger. Within this technical and aesthetic cycle, the interest in Cuba, that I had put aside, is now returning in the biological paintings of Cuba. The nature, the landscape, the fish, and the other elements of the country are working their way back into some of the new series of paintings and videos."

[Gracia] "This raises the question of identity that people are so concerned about these days in this country and in every country where there are groups of immigrants or minorities. Certain questions come up such as, for example, how do you feel when people describe you as a Cuban-American painter or artist? What do you think about this? Are you a Cuban-American painter, and in what sense are you and in what sense are you not? How comfortable are you with this kind of description? It's something that you'd use yourself?"

[Rey] "I think one needs to see the reality in the whole issue. First of all, I am Cuban American. I'm a painter. When I was doing work about Cuba and identity, it's hard to be upset when some people put you in a category that is reflective of your ethnicity and the work's subject matter. Ideally, as an artist, I want my work to be viewed universally. Because these problems aren't specific to only this culture and to this situation, it's something that's found in many cultures and with many individuals. I hope that this issue and the way I'm portraying it is universal and that different people can get something from the work. Hopefully, the feelings and emotions that I was talking about come through in the paintings. I hope that other people who aren't Cuban, who don't feel alienated, who haven't had the experience that I've had, can still relate to them. That's ideal. I want the work to be more than just in a category that's considered Cuban American. But, in reality, I can understand how it's put in that category. I hope that the work has a quality that transcends that type of classification. But, it would be unrealistic to feel slighted if it did not—and I'm not sure I am slighted. After all, I'm Cuban American and I'm proud of that and the work is about that, so if it's put in that category so be it."

[Gracia] "And, how do you feel with respect to other Latinos or Hispanics?"

[Rey] "I always feel connected to them, especially other Cubans, no matter where they're from or what generation they might be from. Because I feel like you're going through, or have gone through, similar situations so there's that connection but that does not mean, however, that I automatically have affinity toward all of their work. Just because they're Cuban American doesn't necessarily mean that I'm always going to feel connected to the work."

[Gracia] "Now let's shift a little and talk about your technique. Many of your paintings are made in the way the balsa series is made. How did you come to it? Why did you pick it up?"

[Rey] "I started by doing abstract work and actually shunned away from anything that was traditional, anything that had to do with painting, or using paint. I even used flour dough for some pieces. I used paraffin wax for others. The whole idea for using these mediums was that my work, at the time, had nothing to do with the tradition of painting. It was more about creating a certain texture or feeling and since there was no connection to the history of painting, I didn't want that relation in the work. I didn't feel that using paint was important. Then I started to do more realistic work and turned to issues dealing with Cuba, and I wanted the work to be very devotional. I wanted to incorporate the history of painting and how devotional work had been created in the past and so I started to incorporate the idea of using plaster as it had been used in frescos and the sense of connection it had to history. Then I began using traditional oil mediums to, again, make another connection to art history, and then again I used realism as another form of connection to the past. When I started using plaster, I wanted to come up with a process that was more reflective of our contemporary experience—something we have in our lives. So, I came up with a process that is less time consuming and more archival than frescos traditionally were. I've been using a MDO board which is a type of plywood. It has a lot of resins and alternating wood grain that keeps it from warping. Over the MDO, I put canvas, and then on top of the canvas, I add plaster—which is actually a form of plaster with some wood putty—and then that is mixed in with resin glues so that the paintings are much more likely to survive shipping and other circumstances that paintings go through in a professional career. The plaster and resin mixture does not absorb moisture like a fresco usually would. So, these elements help make the paintings much more likely to survive through many years of shipping and storage. I've been selective as to what I use to reflect a connection to the past and present in the work."

[Gracia] "In general do you favor darker colors? Some paintings are extremely dark—monochromatic almost: such as *Viñales*, *El Morro*, and *Isla de Pinos*. There's only a couple of colors in these, very muted."

[Rey] "The series of black-and-white landscapes that I did of Cuba is called 'Appropriated Memories.' The reason for the name is that I didn't have any memories of Cuba so I was using references from the 1800s. I wanted images that, for me, had little or no connection to Cuba's present political situation. I wanted to create a separation between the imagery that I was using and the reality of how things are now. I wanted to present—to concentrate on—the landscape as a symbol for a culture. And since it wasn't real for me, I wanted to make the work black and white. If the work is real and is something that I experienced, I generally try to paint it in color. Anything that is referenced but of which I have no memory of or real-life connection to—is painted in black and white to create that separation. The other reason that I selected that period— the late 1800s and early 1900s—was that I wanted to find black-and-white imagery that reflected those concerns. I could have gone into the mid-1900s and found color images but I wanted to work with the black and white and I wanted an untainted separation from the present. With respect to the fish paintings, some are very vivid and reflective of the American realist period of the 1830–'60s, when the discovery and documentation of the United States was popular. Large landscape paintings of different parts of the country captured the beauty of land that few had seen. They also did small realistic paintings and still lifes of their environments. That's what I wanted to do. I wanted to make these rediscovery paintings about our environments, nature and fish, because, in many ways, we've become disconnected from nature. Our lives are more about work and less about being connected to our environments. So I wanted to create a series that created this connection while paying attention to elements that were specific to a certain region. So, with these paintings, the color became more important because they identified a region: the colors of fish, the vegetation, those types of things. When doing underwater images, the light is much less intense. At times, I magnified the light so that when you're looking through these paintings it becomes almost voyeuristic; your attention is drawn to only certain parts of the work while the rest is darker. The edges are a bit blurry so that there is a soft transition between reality and the artwork. Hopefully it helps in making you feel like you're in these landscapes. Your eyes are not hopping all around the painting—it's not about the rest of the information in the painting, it's about the whole of the painting and about the emotion that you feel in the work. In some ways, it's reflective of the same concerns I had in the balsas where I'm putting most of the highlights and attention on certain parts, everything else is darker."

[Gracia] "Then it turns out that you're really an American painter in the American tradition. Because, this whole interest in biology, in nature, in the landscape, in the animals and so forth, it's been there at the beginning of American painting, hasn't it? So, you're really a part of that."

[Rey] "Yes. There's also a long tradition of naturalist painters/illustrators from Spain and France. They were the ones who first created visual documents of the Caribbean and parts of North America. I've also looked at a lot of Cuban painters and been intrigued by how they documented the landscape, fruits, and vegetation that were indigenous to the island. The same type of documentation happened in Mexico. I've always admired that type of work. In some ways I find that this work is almost separated from contemporary art because I'm going backwards; I'm documenting something that, as a contemporary artist, is very traditional, but the reason I'm doing it is that there's a contemporary need for it."

[Gracia] "I also wanted to ask you something about your inspiration. You did refer to particular factors that inspired you or gave you ideas but I see here, in your studio, all sorts of things. You have surrounded yourself with images of saints and all sorts of pictures. On this side you have pictures of fish, vegetation, and so on. So, how do you collect materials? You take pictures and then . . . ?

[Rey] "One of the things that I like about collecting and then putting the objects in the studio is that I enjoy coming into a workspace and feeling inspired. I think there's so much of my life that is filled with other responsibilities that I'm often disconnected from the art. When I come in here and I look at all of this—paintings from Cuba, references to Cuba in art history, naturalist illustrations of plants, religious iconography, Mexican landscape paintings, American photography of Native Americans, watercolors from contemporary naturalists, sketchbooks, the photographs that I've taken for future paintings—all these things help create a connection so that as soon as I walk in the studio, I feel like I'm in this very rich space with images and emotion. I walk into the studio and I feel connected to the work again and I can pick up where I left off. If I didn't have those references, I think the studio would just be a void. But now it's so rich that as soon as I walk in I'm ready to start working. I also play a lot of music and my most extensive collection is of Cuban music. It all helps me to connect."

[Gracia] "I think that at this point we need to ask you whether you want to say something else that occurs to you.

[Rey] "The only other thing that I want to say is that I have also started to do films and video. It's something that I've always wanted to do.

I've always been a big fan of films and how they portray reality and how accessible the medium is to the public. Mostly, through new technology with the computer and digital camcorders, I can do film editing in a manner that is accessible to somebody whose background might not be in film. This is something that I'm very interested in and have started to incorporate into installations with paintings so that the video footage of these environments works cohesively to make the work, again, more accessible to the audience.

[Gracia] "As in fact you have done at the exhibit at El Museo in Buffalo."

[Rey] "Yes. This type of installation is something that I've been thinking about for probably twenty years but haven't been able to do until recently. It's very exciting. This is a possibility for new work—and who knows what's going to happen with the work. I really never know. I know what might be happening within the next year or so but in the long run something else could happen."

[Gracia] "Incidentally, you have several paintings of Iceland. Can you tell me how it was that you came to choose Iceland?"

[Rey] "Iceland is one of those places that is not very popular. It's not a place that everybody wants to go to or has gone to. There is a sense of unfamiliarity to it. It also creates a nice contrast to Cuba and the work that I have done on my Cuba. I thought Iceland would be a perfect subject to include in an exhibition. Iceland is also known for its fisheries, and the salmon and arctic char runs, so I thought it was a great occasion to use to bring in my interest in biology."

[Gracia] "And you're a fisherman yourself."

[Rey] "I'm a fly fisherman and a guide—an Orvis-endorsed guide, and that was the other reason why I went to Iceland: being a fly fisherman and a guide, and because I also do some writing and some artwork that's published in fishing magazines. This is a whole new market that I've never had before; it's opened a lot of doors that might not have been opened before—people are inviting me to come to places around the world to do articles on their fisheries and to also do paintings about species that are indigenous to those areas. It's exciting to combine what I've been doing before with this new direction—integrating everything that I've studied in the past and that I've done in the past."

[Gracia] "I'd like to finish the interview with a vital question. Could you be, or have been, anything other than an artist?"

[Rey] "Before I became an artist I was thinking about biology because I was very intrigued with it and so I've come full circle. I have also been very interested in architecture. I have always thought that if I had another life, I'd like to be an architect; the whole idea of living inside your art and people living inside your art was very compelling. Although I'm sure that is a very idealistic interpretation of the field, but it's something that was of great interest to me. In hindsight, it's important to find a vocation that uncovers elements of yourself that you never knew were there or to develop skills that challenge you aesthetically and intellectually. Being an artist has done that, and now being a filmmaker is doing that also. I hope to continue to do these things. Being a teacher also challenges me all the time. These vocations have really made for a very fulfilling life.

[Gracia] "That's wonderful. Thank you very much, Alberto."

August 11, 2005
Interviewed in the artist's studio and in the Erie Museum of Art, during an exhibition of Rey's piscatorial and Icelandic paintings, filmed by Norma Gracia, transcribed by Paul Symington, and edited by Jorge J. E. Gracia.

The Artists' Work

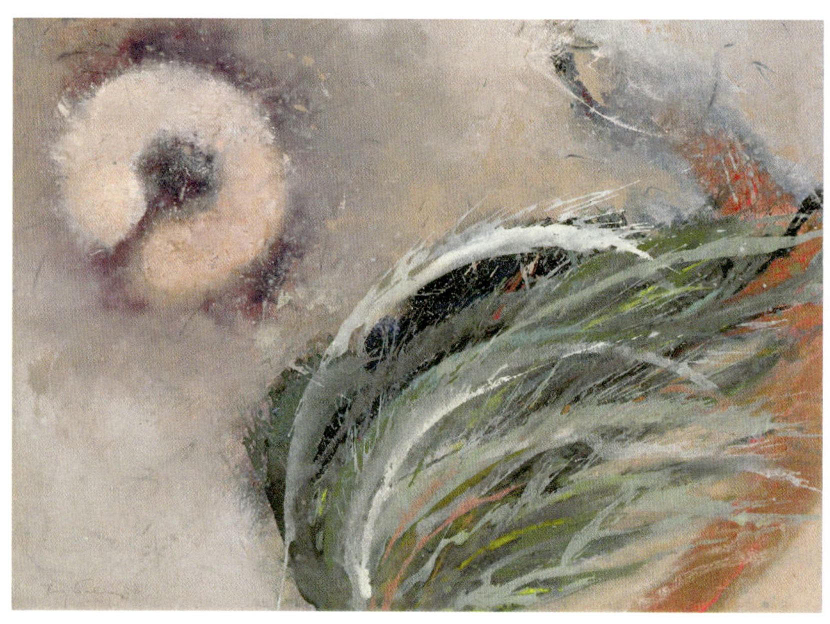

Baruj Salinas, *Flow Up*, Acrylic on canvas, 36' × 26", 1998.
Private collection.

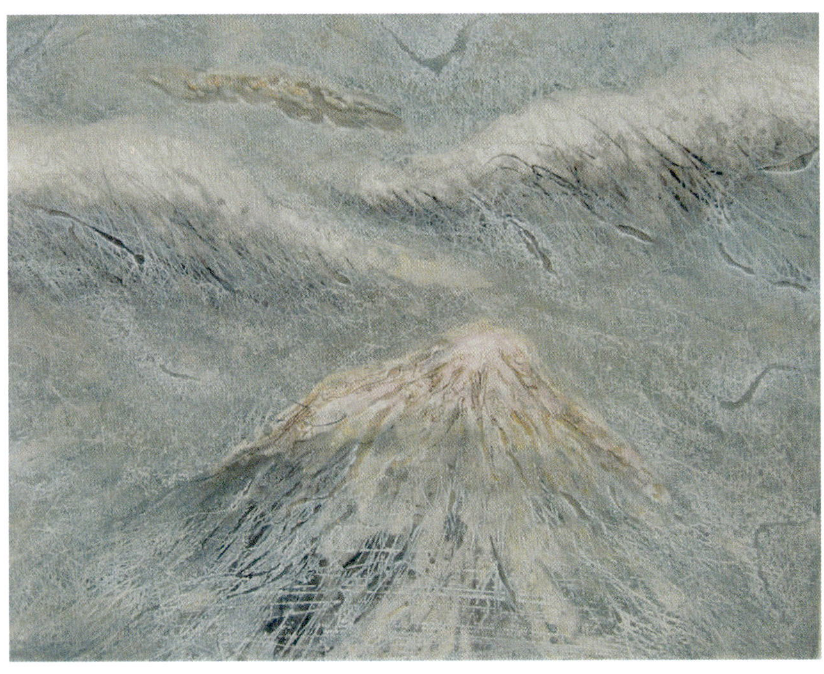

Baruj Salinas, *Fuji-San, Grabado 1(B)*, Color etching, 22" × 30", 1992.
Private collection.

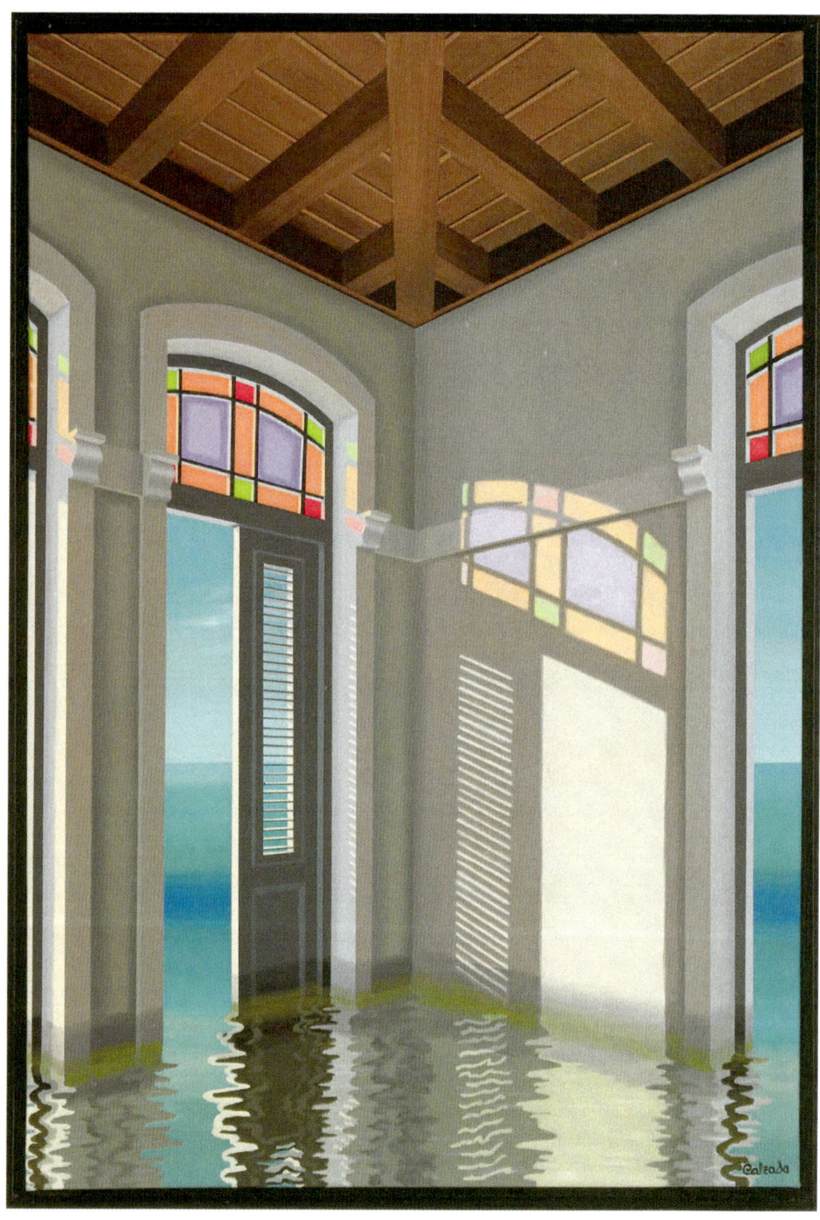

Humberto Calzada, *Island in Crisis*, Acrylic on canvas, 32" × 22", 2005. Private collection.

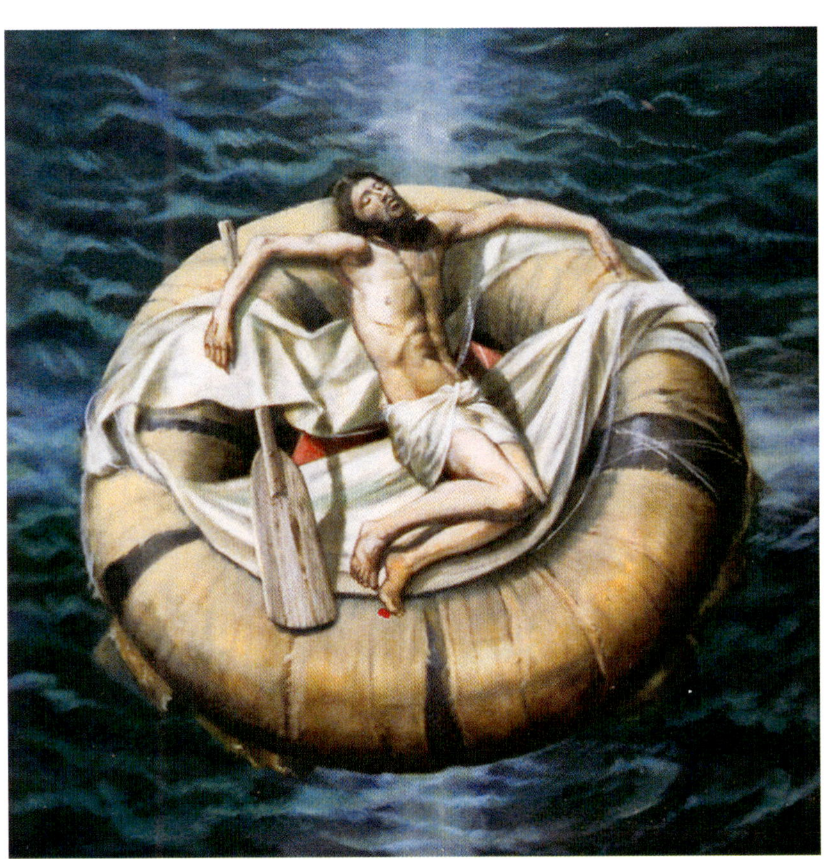

Emilio Falero, *Across*, Oil on canvas, 48" × 48", 2006.
Private collection.

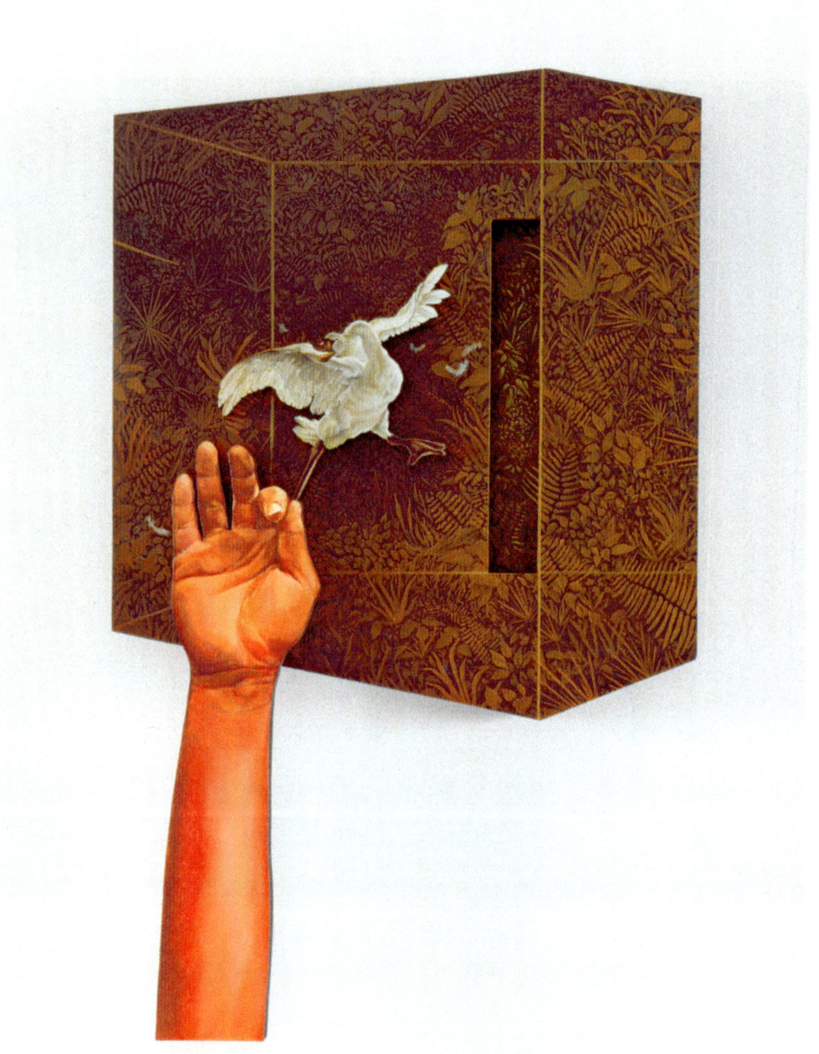

María Brito, *Self-portrait as a Swan*, Oil on wood, 30" × 37", 2001.
Private collection.

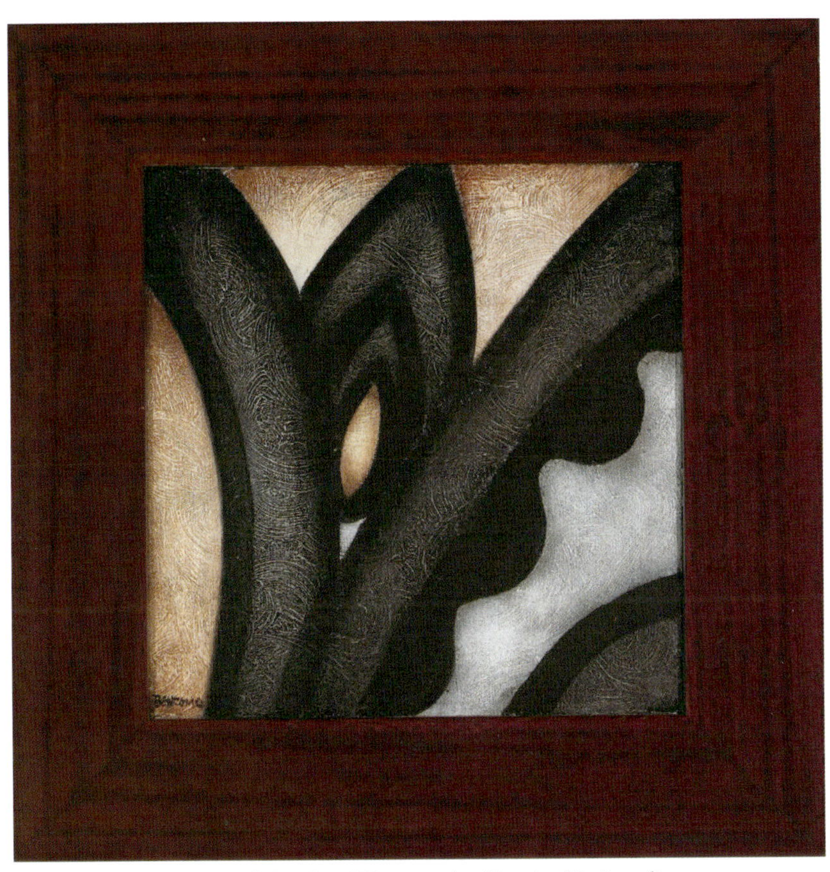

Mario Bencomo, *If Quebec Were in the Tropics II*, Acrylic on canvas, 12" × 12", 2006. Private collection.

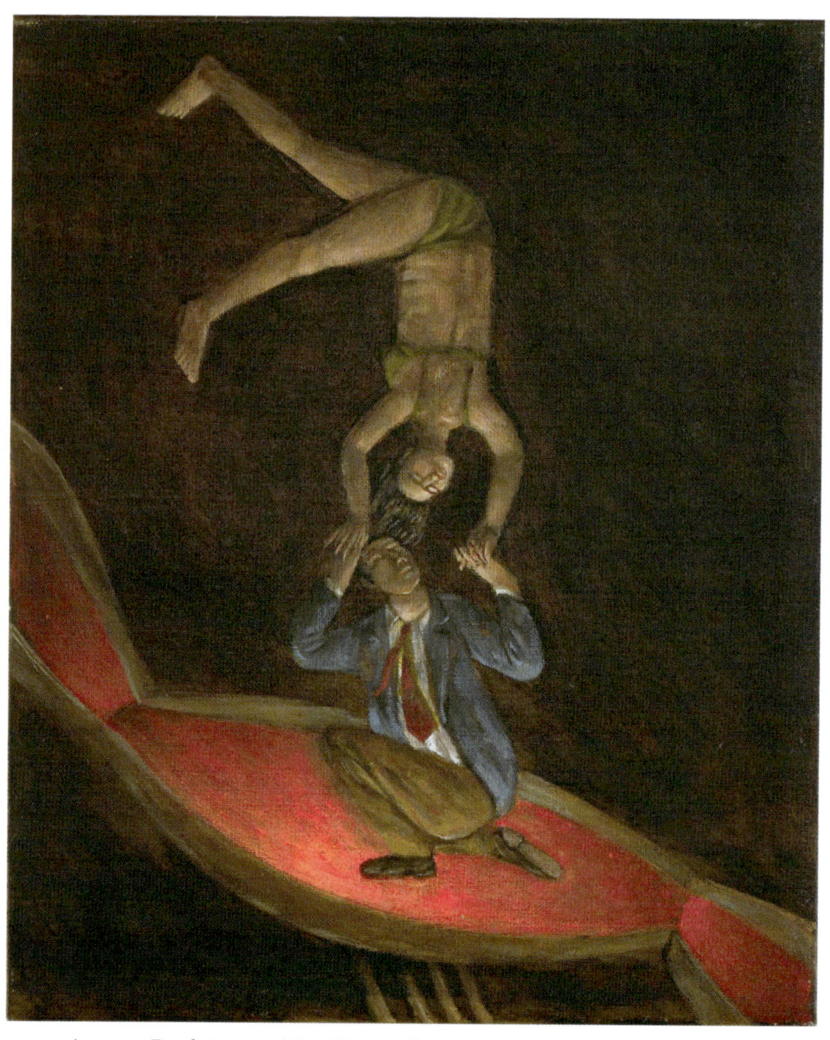

Arturo Rodríguez, *Untitled*, Oil on canvas, 20" × 24", 1997.
Private collection.

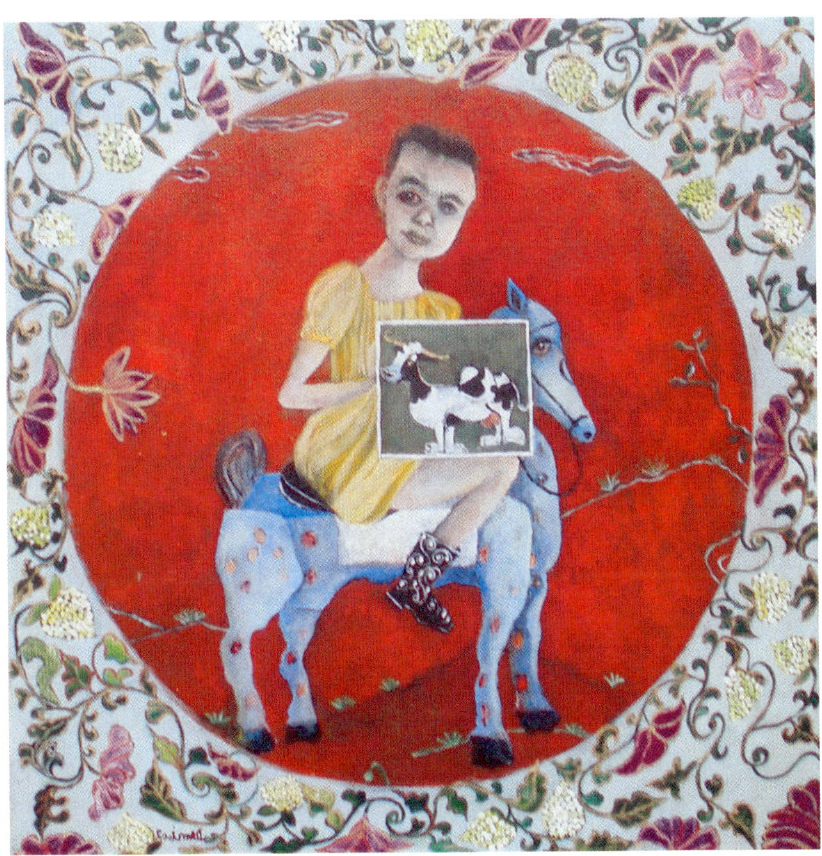

Demi, *An Artist's First Painting*, Acrylic on canvas, 24" × 24", 2005.
Private collection.

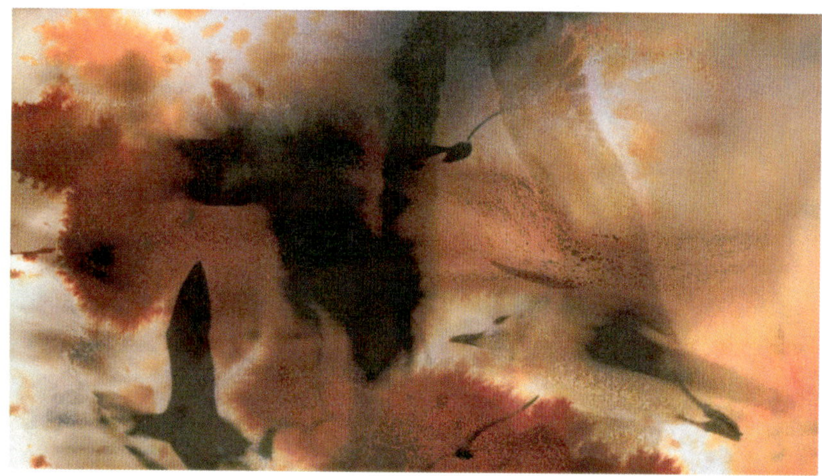

Juan Carlos Llera, *Fear of Flight*, Mixed media: computer generated print with painting, 33" × 59", 2004–2005. Private collection.

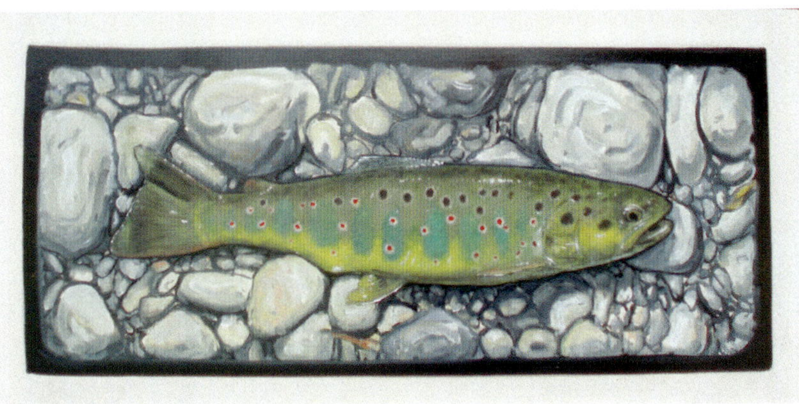

Alberto Rey, *Brown Trout, Homer Creek, Sardina, New York*, Oils on plaster, 15.5" × 33", 2004. Private collection.

Part II

The Writers

II THE WRITERS

Isabel Alvarez Borland

What does it mean to live in a language other than the one spoken during our childhood? Louis Begley, a Polish writer who came to the United States during his adolescence, tells us in a recent essay that during a book presentation in a U.S. bookstore, someone from the audience asked him to recall a poem from his infancy. He agreed with enthusiasm and began to recite, in Polish, a poem that his mother had taught him as a little boy. While Begley was reciting the poem, he was overcome by the horror that perhaps no one in the room would understand what he was saying and he feared he had lost his audience's interest and attention. Begley's anguish disappeared when he heard a chorus of Polish voices that echoed the poem that Begley thought was only his. In Begley's words, "I had made their past alive through my present" (*The Genius of Language*, p. 165).

Similar to Begley's experience, the works of the Cuban-American writers interviewed in this volume have also "made their past our present." All but one left their native country during their adolescence or preadolescence. Carlos Eire, Gustavo Pérez Firmat, Roberto Fernández, and Pablo Medina came from Cuba during the early sixties. Virgil Suárez arrived in the United States in the seventies. All of them share a sensibility or temperament which is based on the division or rupture with a childhood that took place in a different language and in another geography and culture. For these writers, the memory of a Cuban childhood is truly a verbal memory, a recalling based on language more than on any concrete reality. Their stories are told in a language of recovered memories even if their words appear in a language different than the one in which these memories occurred. On the other hand, for Ana Menéndez the idea of rupture stems from a different life experience. For ethnic Cuban writers such as Menéndez, the "borrowed" memories of her immigrant parents become central in her creative endeavor as she seeks to explore her Cuban roots. Born in the United States, the daughter of Cuban exiles and the youngest of those interviewed, Menéndez's work reminds us of the continuation and transformation of a literary tradition once it has departed its native soil.

The English narratives of 1959 created by Eire, Pérez Firmat, Medina, Fernández, and Suárez bring to the forefront issues of identity negotiation in a most explicit manner. Thus the predominance in this volume of interviews of writers belonging to the one-and-a-half generation who publish in English is intentional and responds to the objectives of our NEH project, which sought to explore how Cuban American intellectuals negotiated their identities through their creative and intellectual endeavors. Their interviews are arranged in a progression that ranges from those who have written in the autobiographical vein— poetry or memoir—to writers such as Roberto Fernández and Ana Menéndez, who are most interested in depicting the collective identity of the U.S. Cuban community in their short stories and novels. Unfortunately, due to the scope and objectives of this volume many Cuban-American writers of promise who today write and publish in Spanish could not be included.

What happens to a literature that changes cultures and languages but continues to insist on its Cuban essence? When we speak of the Cuban American artistic production we are in reality referring to writers who left their native country at very different stages in their lives and who are part of several migratory waves that have arrived from Cuba during the last forty-five years. A look at the novels and autobiographies of today's Cuban-American writers must take into account how the authorial voice positions itself in terms of Cuba—the native country—as well as the United States, as the writer's adopted land. Nevertheless, and in spite of the great differences among the perspectives and sensibilities of these writers it is history, memory, and culture that informs every one of their works.

Presently, Cuban writing outside Cuba is being created by a variety of generational and linguistic groups that reflect the migratory waves that have occurred since 1959: Camarioca in 1965, Mariel in 1980, and the exodus of the writers of the Período Especial in the 1990s. These consecutive yet different waves of immigration from Cuba to the United States have produced a unique pattern of exchange and renewal between the various generations of intellectuals in exile. While these exchanges have been quite fertile in creating an artistic renaissance of sorts, especially in the realm of music and the visual arts, the new voices coming from the island have also added complexity to the study of extraterritorial Cuban literature. Indeed, what we have at present are several generations of writers producing their works simultaneously in English and in Spanish and often from contrasting perspectives.

Even if the themes of exile and displacement seem to be a constant in the literature of the various groups, the perspective from which the story of diaspora is conceived and told varies considerably. For instance, the amount of time the authors lived in Cuba before coming to the United States becomes a barometer that determines the way the writers perceive their native country in their stories of exodus, as well as the manner in which they engage the United States as their adopted country. Such variations in perception and engagement toward the native and the adopted lands become evident if we compare the narratives of diaspora written by the first exiles with those of the ethnic writers of the third generation. If history drives the writing of the exiles, heritage becomes the main issue for the ethnic writer whose literature displays a need to explore the culture and language of their parents.

Ethnic Cuban Americans feel the need to leave a record of the story of a community split by history, a record that up to the last decade had remained untold. Cuban-American ethnic novels and stories join an already existing corpus of U.S. literature of Cuban heritage, not explicitly about the stories of the 1959, which is central in the appraisal of English literature of Cuban heritage in the United States. Since the early 1990s, ethnic Cuban Americans have begun to establish themselves as a significant writing presence in the United States. Led by Cristina García's pioneering *Dreaming in Cuban*, 1992, a plethora of novels by American writers of Cuban heritage has been published in the last ten years. Among the most recent, Ernesto Mestre (*The Lazarus Rumba*, 1999), Beatriz Rivera (*Playing with Light*, 2000), Andrea O. Herrera (*The Pearl of the Antilles*, 2001), and Ana Menéndez (*In Cuba I Was a German Shepherd*, 2001 and *Loving Che*, 2003). This body of writing joins the work of authors such as Pulitzer Prize winner Oscar Hijuelos (*Mambo Kings*, 1992) who lived in the United States prior to the 1959 exodus. The appearance of these works provides strong evidence of the fertile creativity of this growing body of American writers of Cuban heritage.

Between these two extremely different renditions of the Cuban story of 1959, are the narratives of those who came from Cuba as adolescents or preteens. Affected mostly by the Spanish memories of a Cuban infancy and by the perplexing fact of always living with these memories, their literature reveals the experience of self-fragmentation, a sensibility that was first expressed in the late seventies in the poetry and essays of Lourdes Casal and later in the anthology *Los atrevidos* edited by Carolina Hospital in 1989. The English works of the one-and-a-half generation turn toward the past, not to confront history or lament their loss as the first exiles had done, but rather to search for a way to balance the disparate elements of their existence such as their Cuban childhood and their American present. While works from older exiles such as G. Cabrera Infante's *View of Dawn in the Tropics* (1974) had tried to address and redress the injustices of official Cuban history, the questions asked by Cuban-American writers focus on the relationship between past and present and on the importance of re-creating an identity in the adopted country. If anger, despair, and sadness were the traits of the first exile expression, for the Cuban Americans who came from Cuba as adolescents, vacillation and ambivalence will be the prevailing emotions. The issue of English as a linguistic choice for the literature of this in-between generation is a question intimately linked to the individual writer's conception of his or her artistic identity. For these writers, the experience of exile is filled with tension and anxiety as they find themselves simultaneously inside and outside the experience they describe. To write about their exodus in the context of Castro's Cuba, Cuban Americans had to define their relationship to their homeland and simultaneously forge a new relationship between the self and the adopted country. Like many other exiles around the world, these writers endured a rupture between their present and their past selves and thus at first they had to learn to see and perceive their history and their reality from an outsider's perspective. The history challenged by the exiles has to be confronted by these second-generation writers in order to put it aside and in order to go on, even if this process is painful and at times fruitless.

It is therefore not surprising that four out of the six writers interviewed in this volume have published autobiographical memoirs in the last fifteen years: Pablo Medina's *Exiled Memories* (1990), Gustavo Pérez Firmat's *Next Year in Cuba* (1995), Virgil Suárez's *Spared Angola* (1997), and Carlos Eire's *Waiting for Snow in Havana* (2003). These bicultural memoirs evolve from a kind autobiographical style that responds to needs outside the mainstream tradition of American immigrant autobiography. Cuban-American autobiographical writing seeks not so much to call American society "home" as to redefine and expand just what being Cuban in America really means. Similar in some respects to other autobiographical narratives produced today by other ethnic immigrant writers, these texts propose a different image from what had been known traditionally as American immigrant autobiography. And, if an autobiography indicates a desire to examine origins in order to start anew, the use of English rather than Spanish also indicates the need to construct a new identity in English.

Writing in a language other than the language of birth becomes the means of regaining an identity or refashioning a new one, and in the case of the one-and-a-half generation writers, it also becomes a way to cope with change and with feelings of inadequacy. For these writers, movement from one language to another is experienced as a shift in identity as well and, in many cases, the protagonist's growth is a growth in the control of a certain language be it either English or Spanish. And even if the Cuba described in the autobiographical works of Suárez is not the same country recalled in the works of Eire, Medina, or Pérez Firmat, there are commonalities among these writers. For both Suárez and Eire, their native language remains frozen or trapped in their childhoods yet it is never forgotten as Spanish functions as a prologue to their English writings. On the other hand, the dilemma of identity is brought to a crisis as Pérez Firmat questions the presence of a core identity that can be expressed equally in the two competing languages. Pérez Firmat's Spanish is not frozen, and at times his native language seduces and simultaneously throws him off balance. Yet for others, such as Roberto Fernández it is the contrast between the immigrant generations and the Anglo and Latino ways of seeing the world that becomes a rich creative resource for his novels about the Cuban-American community in enclaves such as Miami and Belle Glade, Florida. Rather than focusing on the individual, the novels of Fernández and the stories of Ana Menéndez present a larger picture that addresses issues of acculturation and adaptation in today's dispersed Cuban-American communities. The two writers "borrow" the memories of the older generation in order to create their versions of their community in exile. Fernández's perspective is significant for it bridges the one-and-a-half generation and the vision of the younger Cuban ethnic writers such as Menéndez.

The Cuban-American writers interviewed in this volume have incorporated social and aesthetic aims into their fictions which have resulted in distinctive versions of conventional genres. The bicultural memoirs of Eire, Medina, Suárez, and Pérez Firmat and the fictions of community of Fernández and Menéndez have introduced techniques and contents which are the product of a merger of both the North American and Latin American literary traditions. English, as used by these writers, is the same yet it is different as it serves to validate the experiences of their group. By incorporating their Cuban selves into their English selves, the writing of these authors becomes enriched and therefore their ability to create magnified. If we could affirm in general terms that all human beings—bilingual or monolingual—experience an exile from their childhood, in the case of the bilingual and bicultural writer, his or her childhood encapsulates other exiles: geographical and linguistic. Finally, for all those represented in this volume Spanish is the language least utilized in their daily lives yet it becomes the creative impulse that nourishes all of their writings.

THINKING IN IMAGES

CARLOS EIRE

Carlos Eire was born in Havana in 1950 and left Cuba in 1961 at the age of eleven, part of the children transport known as the Peter Pan Operation in which 14,000 Cuban children were sent alone by their parents to the United States. After living in a series of orphanages and foster homes in Florida and Illinois, Carlos and his brother Toni were able to reunite with their mother in Chicago in 1965. His father, whom he never saw again, died in Cuba in 1976.

Waiting for Snow in Havana *is a childhood memoir that re-creates the first ten years of Carlos' life in Cuba, in particular the time before and after the 1959 Cuban Revolution. The boy's remembrances are those of a child who lives a protected and carefree existence in Havana and whose life is violently disrupted by history.* Waiting for Snow in Havana *is a narration of survival in many ways: the survival of an eleven-year-old child as well as the survival of an adult who needs to bring coherence to a life so violently changed by history. In the chapter we include, the parrot fish becomes a nostalgic image that blends senti-ments of beauty lost forever: "Something else to leave behind" (335). Eire's book won the 2003 National Book Award.*

An expert on religious reformations, faith, and spiritualism in modern Europe, Eire is the author of From Madrid to Purgatory: The Art and Craft of Dying in Sixteenth Century Spain *(1995) and* War Against the Idols: The Reformation of Worship From Erasmus to Calvin *(1986). He is the coauthor of* Jews, Christians, Muslims: A Comparative Introduction to Monotheistic Religions *(1997). He is currently the T. Lawrason Riggs Pro-fessor of History and Religious studies at Yale University where he has been a faculty member since 1996.*

INTERVIEW

Conducted by Isabel Alvarez Borland

[Alvarez Borland] "How did you become a writer, and how did you know that this is what you wanted to do?"

[Eire] "In my case, this is a tough question since I am really two different writers. I've been writing books and articles for most of my adult

121

life, but I did not become a 'real' writer until I wrote a book without footnotes. So I have to distinguish between the writer who published academic books and was known only by a handful of readers and the writer whose memoir earned the National Book Award and made it to the *New York Times* best-sellers list. The irony of it all is that the academic writer toiled for ten years a piece on each of his scholarly books, and sometimes for many months on a single article or essay, carrying out painstaking research, but the 'real' writer spent a mere four months producing a best-selling book, without putting much effort into it. And now it is only the writer who had fun who is called an 'author' or a 'writer' or even worse, his fourth book—the easy one—is often called his first book.

I suppose I knew I wanted to be a writer when I was in high school, especially after I had an essay published in the *Chicago Tribune* on the same day that the front page carried that amazing photograph of Earth taken by the Apollo astronauts as they orbited the Moon, in December 1968. By that time I knew I wanted to be a historian, and I knew that writing was an essential part of that profession. I also knew I enjoyed writing immensely. Of course, at that time I only saw myself as a potential college professor, not really as a potential *writer*. Once I entered graduate school and began to work on my dissertation, I knew exactly the kind of writer I would become. After all, graduate school is a boot camp where you are stripped of all ambitions save one—that of producing the perfect footnote—and where you are forced to accept a certain sort of mold and a certain kind of writing as your sole destiny.

I know exactly when I decided to become a 'real' writer. That moment was the night of April 28, in the year 2000, when I began to write *Kiss the Lizard, Jesus*, the book that would later be published as *Waiting for Snow in Havana*."

[Alvarez Borland] "Are there any significant literary markers you can share with us?"

[Eire] "As a scholar, there were the usual markers: great books of all sorts, which I hoped I could emulate some day. As a 'real' writer, the markers were odd, as one would expect for a Cuban boy who ended up in Illinois. First came Mark Twain, whom I read in third grade, in Havana. I have no idea if the Spanish translation was any good, but the story itself and the way it was told took me to another world. He was my first role model. Many times, as I played with my toy soldiers, I would make up stories on the spot and assign characters to them and act out elaborate stories. I will never forget the first day I amazed myself by coming up with a story that seemed to unfold inside my head as if someone else were writing it—a story that came alive on its own, as if I were merely a spectator rather than the writer. I don't remember what the plot was, or anything else about it, but it was a hell of a story, and my first real writing (without paper or ink). I had my first taste of what it means to create, and I am still trying to cope with that surprise."

[Alvarez Borland] "Are there any other writers—in addition to Twain—that were significant to you?"

[Eire] "My admiration for adventure story writers survived exile and stretched into high school. I preferred Jules Verne, Robert Louis Stevenson, and H. Rider Haggard, and just about any writer who could spin a good adventure yarn with memorable characters. And then there were the comic books I loved: Superman, Batman, Aquaman, Blackhawk, all a perfect blending of image and text. Then I was exposed to truly great writers and learned to appreciate good literature rather than good adventure tales. But all of these writers were English or North American: Shakespeare, Dickens, the Brontë sisters, Fitzgerald, Hemingway, Conrad . . . the usual list. I was especially awed by Shakespeare, and still am. And I read as much as I could, but given the fact that I decided to become a historian I spent far more time reading history than literature, all the way into graduate school. At school, José Martí was shoved down our throats constantly, but I never could warm up to him.

As I plunged deeper and deeper into the world of the sixteenth century in my dissertation, my recreational reading became as necessary for me as breathing itself. I took a great liking to Dickens, and read all of his novels, late at night. Out of the blue, right after I had finished *Our Mutual Friend*, someone suggested I read some detective novels, and I turned to Dashiell Hammett's *The Thin Man*. That was it. I was gone, enraptured by the hard-boiled prose and the nonstop action. *That's how I want to write*, I thought. I read all of Hammett, and thirsty for more hard-boiled prose, turned to Raymond Chandler. And that was that. I'd found it, at last: the perfect style. Though I loved the idea of finishing my dissertation, I really did not *love* writing it. But I really did love the idea of writing like Chandler, and began to write a detective novel as I put the finishing touches on my dissertation. And Chandler let me in on one big secret. In one of his letters, he responded to a reader who had asked him how he had come up with his unique style. His response became my credo: "copy shamelessly, and eventually you will find your own voice." Or something like that. So, the first paragraph of my first book, *War Against the Idols* (my rewritten dissertation) is a homage to Chandler— some might say a parody verging on plagiarism—in which I use hard-boiled prose to speak about the sixteenth century: a historian's rendition of the opening paragraph of Chandler's short story, *Red Wind*; no one has ever noticed. No one ever will, I bet."

[Alvarez Borland] "When did you discover Cuban literature?"

[Eire] "Needless to say, my Cuban teachers failed miserably when it came to introducing us to Cuban and Spanish literature. I did not discover Spanish language literature, or a Cuban writer until I was all done with graduate school. Traveling in Europe, I picked up copies of Guillermo Cabrera Infante's *Tres tristes tigres* and Gabriel García Márquez's *Cien años de soledad*. I spent much of the summer of 1980 reading those two books and they transformed me completely, not only in terms of what I learned about writing from them, but in terms of my very self. Until that point in my life I had never read anything in my own native language which was of any real literary merit. The two of them—different as they are—reawakened in me whatever was left of my Cuban and Spanish identity."

[Alvarez Borland] "In what ways did Cabrera Infante influence your development as a writer?"

[Eire] "As divine providence would have it, a year after reading *Tres tristes tigres*, I would get the chance to meet Cabrera Infante, when he came to teach for a semester at the University of Virginia, where I had landed a good job. Guillermo taught a seminar on his own works, in Spanish, for graduate students. I sat in the class, with his permission, and had the time of my life, hearing him speak for three hours once a week about his own work, weaving the autobiographical with the literary and philosophical, providing us all with an utterly transcendent and sometimes nearly psychotic dissection of the mystery of writing. I also got to serve as his chauffeur, driving him home after each seminar. He remained very aloof, and even made no attempt to disguise his distrust of me, or his contempt for me and for the subject I had chosen as my field of study ('Oye, chico, ¿Cómo es que te metistes a estudiar tal cosa como la religión?'). But I owe a lot to him, nonetheless. Sitting in that seminar and listening to him affected my writing in more ways than I can even imagine.

[Alvarez Borland] "What do you consider to be your main contribution so far?"

[Eire] "As a historian of late medieval and early modern European religious history, I have made one set of contributions. As the author of a memoir that was written as a novel and apparently does manage to read like a novel, I have no idea what my contribution is so far. It's way too early to tell, and I have no way of discerning such things anyway. As an outsider to the literary world, I have not yet learned how to think in its terms, and probably never will. All I know is that I have received several thousand letters and e-mails from readers, thanking me for writing that book. Some thank me for its literary merits. Some thank me for the storytelling. Some (all of them Cubans) thank me for having captured the past vividly. Some thank me for all of these things at once.

"The historian has tried to wrestle with a set of questions regarding the way in which we human beings imagine another dimension—the spiritual—and how we try to relate to that in our very physical and very painful mortal bodies, both as individuals and as societies. I am now working on miracles in the sixteenth and seventeenth century that most moderns would consider totally impossible: levitation and bilocation. It just so happens that the seventeenth century was a peak period for flying and historians seem not to care about that at all. Saints and witches flying all over the place, supposedly. What can we make of that? I have tried mightily to convince myself that working on subjects such as this will bring us all closer to understanding the great mystery of our existence. On some days I manage to believe it."

[Alvarez Borland] "Is your scholarly interest in bilocation related in any way to your bicultural identity?"

[Eire] "I suppose it might be, but I am not conscious of it. Up until about eight years ago I would not accept the fact that we all have blind spots and are unable to perceive some of the ideas and feelings that matter the most to us. Now I know better. In fact, I now think that it is precisely those 'invisible' ideas and feelings that rule our lives. They are as much a part of us as our own faces, and, like our faces, we can't see them without a mirror of some sort. So, yes, probably, but on the conscious level I am interested in bilocation for many other reasons, and chiefly because it is such an impossible miracle and so outrageously supernatural."

[Alvarez Borland] "Can you detect any change or evolution in your writing style(s)?"

[Eire] "My writing has changed in one very obvious way: the scholar who previously appealed to a few specialists and cognoscenti turned into a 'real' writer, with a real audience. I am convinced I simply began to use that other half of my brain that my training as a scholar had taught me to keep in a coma. I let go of discursive reasoning and embraced image and metaphor. One of the reasons I am interested in the subject of bilocation is that I often feel as if I do inhabit different places at the very same time."

[Alvarez Borland] "Could you elaborate on the differences between your scholarly and creative writing?

[Eire] "I write as two different people. Of course, the two of me are not totally different: it's not a Jekyll and Hyde sort of schizoid existence. But the scholar writes one way, and the 'real' writer in quite another way. The scholar's style—at least on the conscious level for that author—is one that seeks to combine elegance and utter simplicity. Get to the point, and be as precise and clear as possible, but do so with flair. In his heart of hearts, the scholar hopes he is also plugged into an ancient tradition, that

which takes religious claims very seriously as much more than wish fulfillment, perhaps even as closer to the truth than the empirical sciences.
The 'real' author fits into many traditions, but since he is largely ignorant
of what those traditions might be, he can't really say what they are. He
is certainly conscious of being simultaneously indebted to Augustine's
Confessions and Fellini's *Amarcord*, to Charles Simic's poems and Batman
comics, and to the ur-picaresque *Lazarillo de Tormes* and the faux-picaresque
Beavis and Butthead, but beyond that he has a very hard time pinpointing
what experts might conceive of as a tradition.

The 'real' writer's style is unique, or so he thinks, for it is something
totally new to him that developed over a long period of time in the
scholar's brain, but somehow managed to emerge fully formed in a great
and sudden rush. It's definitely hard-boiled at the core, but also immensely playful and lyrical. It's a style derived as much from film as from
other types of literature, with images at its center, with a structure that
is highly visual. The scholar became someone else in the summer of the
year 2000, and that someone else has not yet figured out how that happened, exactly, or why it took so long for it to happen. I don't think it's
necessary to go into much detail, since the change is so huge and abrupt.
If I had been able to publish my memoir as a novel, under a pseudonym,
as I fervently wished to do, I doubt that anyone, ever, would have been
able to identify me as the author of both *War Against the Idols* and *Waiting
for Snow in Havana*."

[Alvarez Borland] "How is your identity as a writer related to your
Cuban, American, Cuban-American, Hispanic, Latino identities?"

[Eire] "Ay, Dios mio. Tremenda pregunta. The author of *Waiting for
Snow in Havana* is definitely "Cuban-American," fully hyphenated. Since
he thinks in English, and even dreams in English, and can't even write a
decent sentence in Spanish, he can't ever be mistaken for a full, genuine
Cuban. But he definitely can't ever be mistaken for a farm boy from Iowa
either. As he says in his memoir, with a nod to Popeye, 'I yam what I
yam.' This means that he is not a Hispanic or a Latino either. I am proud
of being both a Cuban and an American. And I bristle when anyone asks
me to choose one or the other. I have never identified with the uselessly
broad identities of Hispanic or Latino, since I have never really felt I
shared much of a common identity with people from other Spanish-
speaking cultures, even when I've been called a spic. And since *Hispanic*
and *Latino* are most often conceived of in the United States as racial
identifiers—as a race distinct from white or black or Asian—I actually
loathe both of those terms. Now, suddenly, at the age of fifty-five I find
myself on the list of 'people of color' at Yale. How I wish I could smash
a chair over the head of the twisted jerk that came up with that awful,
racist terminology in the name of political correctness.

"The identity question is a paradoxical one for me. I don't care about it at all, and I care a lot. It irritates me, so I try to ignore it, and to pretend I don't care about it. The more I ignore it, the more it seems to irritate me. I hate being shoehorned into any kind of box or category, or reminded of what I am supposed to be or not be. The most irritating question that I keep being asked over and over again is how did I ever end up as a historian of late medieval and early modern Europe, and, even more shocking, how did I ever end up doing Swiss and German history. As if 'Hispanics' should not be interested in that, or, worse, as if they are incapable of doing something so far from their own culture. I am what I am. Nothing more. Nothing less. And I hate when anyone tries to link me to anything beyond that.

I was taught by my own family to think of myself first and foremost as Spanish, not as Cuban. Given the fact that my father believed he was the reincarnation of King Louis XVI and thousands of other individuals from all epochs and all parts of the globe, including the vanished continent of Atlantis, I was also taught to think of all things Cuban as an ephemeral glaze of sorts, like a thin coating of caramel or a wispy frost that quickly melts. Forbidden to listen to Cuban music in my own house as a child, forbidden to learn Cuban dances, forbidden to dance any kind of dance, or to engage in ill-bred *chusmerias* of any kind—like telling dirty jokes or keeping your shirt open beyond the collar button—constantly reminded that my entire family had only very recently arrived from Europe, and that we were outsiders on this weirdly Africanized island where Castilian Spanish was spoken with an uncouth accent, I never got the chance to be fully Cuban. Then I was whisked away to the North, and then the Very Far North for the remainder of my life. I never had a chance."

[Alvarez Borland] " 'I never got the chance to be fully Cuban.' . . . How Cuban do you feel?"

[Eire] "I feel as Cuban as an eleven-year-old Cuban boy who has lived the rest of his life apart from other Cubans and in very limited contact with Cuban culture. I can't assign percentages to my hyphenated Cuban-American self, like 50/50 or 35/65, or anything like that. But there is no denying that I am both at the same time, with equal intensity. I love having a complex identity. I also hate being forced to pinpoint which of my multiple identities is really 'me.' The idea that human beings can only be this or that (Cuban or American) is sheer nonsense. It is a lot like arguing that the human tongue is either for tasting or for speaking, but not both. Does the tongue have an identity crisis? Funny thing, the tongue is also a symbol for one's identity, as in the term 'mother tongue' for one's first language.

My day job remains my main identity: scholar and professor. Teaching is my business. Writing is my hobby, and I might as well do it in the basement, like some middle-aged insurance salesman who doesn't want the world to know that he plays with model trains. I have no contact with the literary scene at all: I read no book reviews; I don't follow the news about who wrote what or what so-and-so thinks; and I also read very few books that are outside of my work as a scholar. I have no time for that. I don't hang out with other writers. The scholarly writer in me is definitely some kind of Calvinist, maybe even a Swiss Calvinist. Nary a trace of Cuban in there, not even when writing the history of Spain. Not Hispanic or Latino either. He is simply a historian. His national, cultural, ethnic, or racial identity doesn't enter into any equation. I have spent all of my adult life living in places where there were very few other Cubans. Sometimes I lived in places where I was the only foreigner. On top of that, I have chosen a profession that makes me focus more on Western Europe than on any other part of the world. I am at home everywhere. I am at home nowhere. Sometimes when I search for a word in Spanish what I get is the German, or the French, or the Italian, or even the Latin. Every now and then it's all Greek to me, literally. *Kyrie Eleison*."

[Alvarez Borland] "*Waiting for Snow in Havana* has had both a particular and a universal appeal as a work of literature. Could you explain why this is so?"

[Eire] "We can never fully escape the particular culture in which we live, for it is the very matrix within which we think and act, the very structure of our thinking and being. An immigrant or a multicultural person may have a more complex matrix, but it is still a matrix with definite boundaries. In my case, this dialectic is right at the heart of *Waiting for Snow in Havana*. In fact, the dialectic was one of the very few things that I consciously chose to address on every page of the book. I had no outline, and no plan of any kind. I also did not rewrite anything. I simply sat down at my computer every night and wrote impulsively for four months straight. In other words, I had no preconceived notion of what this book would be when I began to write it and even as I wrote it. But I did have this one purpose in mind: to comment on the human condition through narrative, that is, to dwell on those aspects of my own life history that touch on the big questions that all humans ask, no matter where they live: questions of meaning about birth, death, love, suffering, joy, justice, truth, violence, sex, and so on. I did not have a list of topics either, but simply let the topics emerge from the narrative itself.

I also knew instinctively—and not because I had given it much forethought—that a child narrator would be able to comment on the universal through the particular in a much more effective way than an adult third-person narrator. Childhood is a very special place, a place in time rather than on the map, a universal place where all of us human beings experience the mystery of our existence with instinctive intuition. Yes, it's true that from the day we are born we learn to interpret existence through particular cultures, but the whole process of maturing from child to adult is a process of acculturation, a process wherein we gradually shed our universal, instinctive self and develop in its place a particular culturally conditioned self. Childhood also has a certain universality to it, as a very special period in everyone's life, a period of intense learning and of playing games, and of struggling to make sense of things."

[Alvarez Borland] "Are you conscious of a goal when you begin to write a novel or a poem?"

[Eire] "When I write as a 'real' writer rather than as a scholar, more often than not what is going on in my head is much closer to a film than to a book. Maybe even closer to comics than books. I think in images and the words flow from them. The images always come first. Films have made perhaps even more of an impact on me and my writing than books, but that's a whole other story. I always have goal when I start any project, scholarly or not. But I only have the vaguest notion of what to do, exactly. I simply sit down at the computer and let the inspiration flow. I guess this means I only have an overall goal when I begin a project. I let the details sort themselves out as I write."

[Alvarez Borland] "Did you consciously work with memories when writing *Waiting for Snow in Havana*?"

[Eire] "A memoir is nothing but memories. In my case, I did no research at all. I consulted no one else. I made it a point not to check my memories against anyone else's. I wanted this book to come straight from memory. As I wrote I relived my childhood, and I got the chance to make sense of it as a middle-aged man. It was the most fun I have ever had. Even more fun than the original experiences, for the pain was dulled considerably by the barrier of time. I realize now that the memory I ransacked was a highly emotional place and that the events I chose to relate were those that touched intensely on deep emotions."

[Alvarez Borland] "For whom do you write?"

[Eire] "I wrote *Waiting for Snow* with no particular audience in mind, other than an amorphous one: non-Cubans who know little about Cuba or who wrongly idealize the Revolution. It was a great shock and a surprise to discover that Cubans love the book and identify with it. But it has yet to appear in Spanish. I suspect that those readers who pick it up in Spanish may have a different reaction to it, since its sensibilities are mixed and not one hundred percent Cuban. A lot of the humor might be lost in translation, figuratively as well as literally. But that is only a guess on my part.

On another level, I was also conscious of this dialectic with a certain sense of vengeance and no small measure of anger: I was writing as a

Cuban about Cuba to expose all non-Cubans (and especially North Americans and Europeans) to the truth about that Cuba that existed before Fidel came along and to the fact that the worst thing about the Revolution was the way in which it sought to steal everyone's soul. In other words, I wanted to place every non-Cuban reader under my skin, as much as possible, so that they could experience the reality of the Cuban Revolution as Cubans. This sense of purpose stemmed from my own experience: from the countless times I've had to put up with inane questions about Cuba ('Oh, you mean you really had toilets, just like we do?') and offensive little lectures on the glories of the Revolution ('Oh, but you didn't have to leave Cuba; you left because you are very selfish person and a right-wing wacko who couldn't stand the fact that the Revolution drove out a corrupt oligarchy, redistributed property justly, and established free education and health care, and wiped out all poverty and disease.'). I knew the only way to get across to North Americans and Europeans, whom I imagined as my audience, was to think and speak as most of them do and to make them feel the same sense of outrage I have felt throughout my life about the cretins who ruined my native land and tried to steal my soul. I wanted to let them know that I and every other Cuban are not inferior to them in any way, and that we deserve to enjoy the same kind of freedom."

[Alvarez Borland] "What has been your experience with the U.S. publishing houses and the politics of publishing in this country?"

[Eire] "The politics of publishing in the U.S. are very complex and hard for me to explain. All I know is that I have a very fat folder full of rejection letters, and that it was very hard to get my first book published. The memoir was a snap: I sold the first draft within three weeks of having finished it. I don't think there is a bias against writers from Spanish-speaking cultures, but I do think there is some skepticism about the appeal any 'Hispanic' author who writes about 'Hispanics' might have outside of the ethnic market they make up. Since I can't write in Spanish, I really don't have much of a choice.

My own experience leads me to think that there is more political interference in the Spanish language publishing business than in the English one. Otherwise, why is it that *Waiting for Snow* has already been published in Dutch, German, Finnish, Czech, Portuguese, and Polish, but has yet to appear in Spanish? I know for a fact that every major publishing house in Spain not only passed up the book, but that they did so without even reading it, never even letting it through the door, even after it won the National Book Award. I suspect it has a lot to do with the fact that it is viewed as politically incorrect. Same thing for Latin America. The assumption being made is that every Cuban exile is not only a moron, but a selfish monster and a fascist."

[Alvarez Borland] "Could you expand a bit more on your story of immigration and assimilation?"

[Eire] "My desire to be many things at once probably stems from the fact that as I was growing up in Cuba no one in my family wanted to admit we were Cubans and no one had a romantic attachment to the island. Even my father, a third-generation Cuban, never tired of expressing his disdain for Cuban culture. I also learned to hate my own country at a very early age because of Batista and all of his crimes against his own people, and then to hate it even more for producing something as monstrous as Fidel Castro and his so-called Revolution.

So, when I arrived in the U.S. I was more than happy to adapt quickly. Finally, I was living in a decent place, with genuine freedom. The fact that I was at the very bottom of the heap economically and socially did not bother me one bit, because I knew that would just be a temporary status. (Little did I know that by choosing an academic career I would never rise very far from the bottom.) My American foster family made me even more eager to shed my skin, so to speak. They were so wonderfully generous and loving, and so unable to speak Spanish. It was sink or swim, but I didn't see it as something bad. On the contrary, I loved the idea of becoming someone else, of gaining a new identity. Then, after nine months with this wonderful family I went to live in a foster home for Cuban boys, run by a Cuban couple that was childless. Eight to twelve boys in a two-bedroom house in a Miami slum. And half the boys are juvenile delinquents, and very violent. And the Cuban house parents are cold and aloof, and even cruel. We are fed only one meal per day and get seventy-five cents per week allowance. I couldn't wait to get out of there and that stifling environment, which also happened to be a very Cuban environment.

Then I moved up north to Bloomington, Illinois, to live with my uncle, who had been relocated there. We were the only Hispanics in town, and one of the very few foreign families. My immersion in American culture became nearly total, even though my uncle and aunt spoke Spanish at home. The questions about my Cuban identity that I got in school from the other kids were always most unpleasant: always displaying their ignorance and their feelings of superiority. 'You had toilets in Cuba?' 'You had televisions?' 'You had schools?' 'You had clothes?' Most of them were very surprised to find out I hadn't grown up in a grass hut, wearing loincloths.

Whatever I had in me that was Cuban, I shed. I worked hard to get rid of my accent too, to ensure that no one would be able to pinpoint what I was and ask me stupid questions that reminded me constantly of a negative image that had nothing to do with my real self. Then I moved to Chicago to live with my mom, and I ended up at a public high school that was full of kids from all over the world, all races and religions and ethnic backgrounds, and I was like a drop of wine dropped into the ocean. Better yet: a drop of water in the American melting pot. I picked an American Jewish girlfriend. Then I picked a career that took me away from Cuban communities. And the career also brought me in constant contact with extremely well-educated idiots who would always tell me how wonderful the Cuban Revolution was and how selfish and stupid all Cuban exiles were for fleeing such a paradise. For twenty-seven years (1973–2000) I lived in total isolation from Cuban culture, and in total denial of my Cuban identity. Forgetting was the key to my survival. Then, along came Elian. . . . and something in me snapped completely. What I hadn't realized during all those years of isolation is that you can never forget who you were as a child. And it took one Cuban boy to make me aware of this."

[Alvarez Borland] "As an immigrant writer do you see yourself as expanding or redefining who we are as Americans? As Cubans? Could writing in English about a context which is Cuban change the nature or perception of the English language itself?"

[Eire] "Any time you expose the reading public to an immigrant story you are expanding the collective mind-set beyond established boundaries. I know for a fact that writing in English about my Cuban boyhood has affected many readers' perceptions of the English language. I have letters and e-mails to prove it. Several perceptive readers have told me that I have given English a Cuban voice; others have said that I have given Cubans an English voice. It works both ways, I think."

[Alvarez Borland] "What is your relationship to English? To Spanish? Is being bilingual an asset to your writing?"

[Eire] "Being bilingual has been an asset. But I am also fluent in five other languages besides English and Spanish. That helps even more, for my exposure to those other tongues has given me multiple perspectives on the miracle of language and the power of words. German has been immensely helpful, for it has laid bare to me the root meaning of many English words in a way that English alone could not. My favorite German word is *handschuh*, which means glove. It is a very simple concept, turned into a word: hand = hand; *schuh* = shoe, from *schutzen*, to protect. My second favorite German word is *staubzauger*, or vacuum cleaner: *staub* = dust; *zauger* = sucker, from *zaugen*, or to suck. One of the key pieces of advice I took from Zinsser's book *On Writing Well* was this: if you have a choice between English words with Latin roots or Anglo-Saxon roots, always pick the Germanic one, for it packs a greater punch. *Flapping* always trumps *undulating*. This rule of thumb is correct about nine times out of ten. Knowing German has given me the opportunity to find the Germanic words more easily and to understand their root meanings more clearly.

English is the language in which I think, dream, pray, and count, and imagine. It's my language now and it has been my principal tongue since the age of twelve. Spanish is a stunted dwarf with magical powers. I can't write or speak Spanish without making a fool of myself. I read it with no difficulty at all, but I can't communicate with it very effectively. This is because I need to think in English first and to translate as I read or speak. Quite often, nothing comes out. Blank. Quite often I manage to get something out, but it's all twisted and ugly. But certain words in Spanish get to the core of my soul as no English word can."

[Alvarez Borland] " 'But certain words in Spanish get to the core of my soul as no English word can.' This is quite a fascinating assertion from someone who says he cannot write a word of Spanish. Can you explain?"

[Eire] "When I speak Spanish I think in English and translate very quickly. When I write in Spanish, same thing, only harder, for when the words appear on the page I can see how awful it is. At least when I speak I am blind to my errors. But this doesn't mean that I cannot appreciate Spanish. Beautiful Spanish is still beautiful—and I am sometimes moved by it in a very special way. Some words in Spanish seem to have an added emotional depth to them. I suppose if I took the time to reflect on them, I might discern how they acquired that emotional depth. But I don't have the time, and I just let those words surprise me, time and time again. This is what I think is going on: Again, it's the power of childhood over the rest of one's life. Some words are learned in that very special, very emotionally charged environment of childhood and they carry with them in one's memory whatever the emotional baggage may be. *Frijoles* means more than beans. It means a steaming hot plate of rice and beans and also a nice breaded steak served to you by your mom, back when you were surrounded by all your family. It also means a certain routine, a certain dining room, certain episodes. In my case it means the day that my grandmother's pressure cooker exploded and her entire kitchen was covered in *frijoles negros*. It also means Americans trying to pronounce the word, and always sounding very scatological: 'free-hole-ass.' It is a word that carries all the comforts of home and is also a reminder of everything you lost. Someday maybe I could compile a dictionary of my emotional words: *timbiriche, lija, aguacate, embolia, almohada, escaparate, cucaracha, enano, muela, mula, malanga*.

January 2006

WHAT SOUNDS GOOD ALSO RINGS TRUE

———————————————————————————————————GUSTAVO PÉREZ FIRMAT

Born in Havana in 1949, Gustavo Pérez Firmat arrived in Miami in 1960 when he was eleven years old. A sense of unresolved contradiction colors all of Pérez Firmat's writing, a body of work that spans across several genres: the memoir, the novel, poetry, and literary criticism. In El año que viene estamos en Cuba, *the 1997 Spanish translation of his 1995 memoir* Next Year in Cuba, *Gustavo writes of his reasons for writing an autobiographical work: "Me he demorado demasiados años en aprender que hay continuidades que trascienden tiempo y lugar y lenguaje. Soy quien fui: el niño cubano es el padre del hombre americano. No puedo entenderme si no respeto a ese niño, si no le devuelvo el lugar que le corresponde. No es cuestión de reducir fracciones sino de integrarlas." It is precisely the need to integrate the fractions of his identity that informs the totality of Gustavo's published works.*

Pérez Firmat is the author of several scholarly works among them Literature and Liminality *(1986),* The Cuban Condition *(1989) and* Tongue Ties *(2003). His poetry has appeared in collections such as* Carolina Cuban *(1986),* Equivocaciones *(1989), and* Bilingual Blues *(1995).* Life on the Hyphen *(1994), an examination of Cuban culture in the United States during the first half of the twentieth century, served to create what is today the field of Cuban-American studies.* Cincuenta lecciones de exilio y desexilio *(2000), a collection of vignettes, re-creates the tensions produced when two languages are alive and in conflict within the same author. His most recent creative work is* Scar Tissue *(2005), a book of poems about illness, healing, and exile. In 2004, Pérez Firmat was elected to the American Academy of Arts and Sciences. He teaches at Columbia University where he is David Feinson Professor of Humanities.*

INTERVIEW

Conducted by Isabel Alvarez Borland

[Alvarez Borland] "How did you become a writer? Can you tell us how and when this happened?"

[Pérez Firmat] "I became a writer the night—actually early morning—when my son was born: *creación* as *procreación*. I used to have a notebook (a real notebook, with little sheets of lined paper: this was in the age before the *hada cibernética* touched our lives with her memory stick) where I wrote new words, quotations I liked, the titles of books I wanted to read; and so while Rosa was in labor I began scribbling what became my first poem (I use the term loosely), 'Carolina Cuban,' where I wonder what sort of Cubans my children would be. Everything I have written since then is a long, sometimes inventive, sometimes tedious footnote (or *futanota*, as we say in my classes) to that birthing poem. If I were not a father, I would not write poems. I also think that ultimately everything I've written has been written for them, David and Miriam: *por y para ellos*, then."

[Alvarez Borland] "Tell us about your literary road. What are important markers? Did some people play important roles?"

[Pérez Firmat] "When I was a freshman at Miami-Dade Community College, I took a survey of Spanish literature with a bitter little man appropriately named Dr. Funke, who made it clear that teaching at a community college was beneath him. The class was boring, a lifeless recitation of names, dates, titles. Except for one afternoon, when Dr. Funke was reading a poem by Gustavo Adolfo Bécquer, the nineteenth-century Spanish poet, about the loneliness of a corpse that stays alone in a funeral parlor after all the mourners have left. As he read the poem, Dr. Funke began to get teary-eyed. When he reached the last line, he could barely speak. By way of apology, he explained that he had a son who had passed away when he was our age and that this poem reminded him of his son. I found out two things that day: that Bécquer's poem is about the loneliness of the living, not the dead; and that literature gives expression to experiences that would otherwise remain namelessly painful. Although I didn't know it at the time, this incident may be the reason I became a writer—and a professor."

[Alvarez Borland] "Was the work of others significant to you?"

[Pérez Firmat] "Since I make a living by teaching literature, I have to read for my classes and the literature I teach finds its way into what I write. A few years ago I published a novella called *Anything but Love*. Some time later I was teaching *El túnel*, a book by Ernesto Sábato that I had taught many times before, and was surprised by all the echoes of *Anything but Love* in *El túnel* (actually the other way around). But I'm not the sort of writer who reads all the time. I'd rather write than read and I'd rather watch ESPN than write. Growing up in Miami—a boutique rather than a book city—I read hardly at all. The nuns in the parochial school I attended used to punish me by making me come in on Saturday mornings to read. I had to sit in the library for two hours. The only thing I remember reading was a biography of John Paul Jones, and I'm not sure how much that pushed me down the literary road."

[Alvarez Borland] "Who are the writers that you admire most?"

[Pérez Firmat] "Some of the ones whose work I have envied and (perhaps) learned from throughout the years: Jorge Mañach, John Updike, A. E. Housman, Borges, Henry James, Jane Austen, Scott Fitzgerald, Lezama Lima, Cabrera Infante, Alejandra Pizarnik, Roberto Fernández, Virgil Suárez, Christopher Morley. As I write the names that pop into my head, I realize what an arbitrary, chaotic list this is! Even more chaotic if you add the nonliterary influences, which may have left a deeper mark: American song lyricists from the 1930s and 1940s; Cuban and American comedians like Leopoldo Fernández, Guillermo Álvarez Guedes, Henny Youngman, Alan King. And many other people whom I remember and don't remember. I'm the sum total of my influences—plus the five percent that belongs only to me."

[Alvarez Borland] "How do you see your work in the contemporary literary scene? Do you consider yourself in the mainstream, at the margins, elsewhere?"

[Pérez Firmat] "I'm a marginal figure but, as you know, the margins are everywhere. I like being *al margen* but not *marginado*, out of sight but not out of the way."

[Alvarez Borland] "What do you consider to be your main contribution so far? Is this a matter of style, ideas, or something else?"

[Pérez Firmat] "A contribution is what I make to the March of Dimes. I don't think of my books as contributions. I don't write them to contribute to anything except my own shaky peace of mind. Is a man who goes out in the middle of the street, takes his clothes off and screams, 'Look at me! Look at me!' making a contribution? Because that's what I do."

[Alvarez Borland] "How do you explain this acute need for attention?"

[Pérez Firmat] "I don't."

[Alvarez Borland] "How would you describe your style of writing? How has it changed throughout your career? If you were going to pick a tradition where your work fits, which would it be?"

[Pérez Firmat] "When the MS of *Next Year in Cuba* was being copyedited, my editor said to me that I was a 'writer's writer'—which sounds like a compliment but actually wasn't. He meant that I was too taken with words and (thus) wrote too many sentences, which he proceeded to cut. I also remember that one of Raymond Carver's students once asked Carver whether he (the student) should become a writer. Carver answered with a simple, complicated question: 'Do you like sentences? I like sentences. I like words. I even like paragraphs. If you like something, you spend time with it. If you spend time with it, you get to know it. Once you get to know it, it tells you little secrets.' Someone once also called me a 'master of linguistic play'—which wasn't entirely a compliment either. I don't make an effort to play with words. Sometimes I make an effort *not* to play with words because when I play with words I have the sneaking suspicion that the words are playing with me. But manipulating language is pleasurable and offers a kind of release. Plus, time flies when you're making puns."

[Alvarez Borland] "Indeed your works—both scholarly and creative—have shown an increased interest in language, a need to 'zoom in' into sentences, words, even syllables. This obsession became most explicit in your *Cincuenta lecciones de exilio y desexilio*, a book which details your relationship to Spanish and English. How does this special relationship you seem to have with language affect your creative process?"

[Pérez Firmat] "Like others, I tend to write by ear. Somehow (and the 'how' is a mystery to me) you come up with a sentence that sounds good, and then you realize that it also conveys what you wanted to say—that what sounds good also rings true—or that it conveys something different but perhaps just as pertinent as what you wanted to say. Sense then follows sound. I'm hopelessly, helplessly phonocentric, perhaps because I come from a country where all the men sooner or later go deaf (while the women, on the other hand, get louder and louder, perhaps so that their deaf husbands can hear them).

One more thing: wordplay is much more frequent than one would think because it encompasses a lot more than wordplay. It includes phrase- and sentence- and paragraph-play. Ultimately it's language-play, which is the same as language use. Take Nabokov's statement: 'I'm as American as April in Arizona.' What is it about this sentence that makes it memorable? First, it varies on 'as American as apple pie,' a variation made pointed by the near homophony of 'apple' and 'April.' Second, there's the alliteration of American/April/Arizona. Third, and best of all, 'Arizona' is not even an 'American' word because it sounds Spanish—a compound put together from 'zona árida'—but apparently is of Amerindian origin. So is this wordplay? To me it's just a good sentence: cunning rather than punning."

[Alvarez Borland] "Do you find it easier to use this type of play in English than in Spanish?"

[Pérez Firmat] "Yes. For one thing, Spanish has no homophones. For another—the complementary phenomenon—it also has no 'homographs.' As that great linguist Ricky Ricardo once pointed out, in Spanish words that look the same sound the same and words that sound the same look the same. In English, as he explains, 'bough,' ' cough,' and 'through' look the same but sound different; and 'bough' and 'cow' look different but sound the same. Ricky's conclusion: 'Crazy language!' The other reason may be personal. Perhaps I feel freer to fool around in English because it's not my mother or father's tongue. Although I don't mind writing English with an accent, I try not to write Spanish with an accent. But as you say, in *Cincuenta lecciones de exilio y desexilio*, which is all in Spanish, there's a fair amount of what might be regarded as wordplay."

[Alvarez Borland] "Are there periods or stages in your literary development? Major changes in direction or style?"

[Pérez Firmat] "I've gone from 'early Gustavo' to 'late Gustavo' and somehow skipped the 'mature Gustavo.' Since I'm a late-bloomer baby-boomer, my 'early' period includes stuff I wrote in my thirties and forties—the poems in *Carolina Cuban, Equivocaciones* and *Bilingual Blues*; *Next Year in Cuba*; *The Cuban Condition, Life on the Hyphen*. The 'late Gustavo' (not to be confused, *plis*, with the dead Gustavo) would include what I've written since—*Anything but Love*; the Spanish version of *Life on the Hyphen*, which is called *Vidas en vilo*; *Cincuenta lecciones de exilio y desexilio*; *Tongue Ties, Scar Tissue*; and whatever I'm writing now. The early Gustavo was a manic man; the late Gustavo is a melancholy baby."

[Alvarez Borland] "Would you describe your work as Cuban, American, Cuban American, Hispanic, Latino? How is your identity as a writer related to these ethnic categories?"

[Pérez Firmat] "To begin with, my definition of a Cuban American writer is a Cuban who writes in English. And so I don't think of myself as an American or a Cuban or a Cuban-American or a Latino writer, but rather as a Cuban who sometimes writes in English and at other times writes in Spanish. And it's always the language I'm not writing in that is my home. I can't write in English without missing the Spanish that is missing, and I can't write in Spanish without missing the English that is missing. These are the sorts of 'tongue ties' I've tried to unravel in a recent book. Also, maybe one shouldn't confuse nationality with literary citizenship. Even though George Santayana was not American, he said: 'It is an as American writer that I am to be counted, if I'm to be counted at all.' So here was a Spanish man who was an American writer."

[Alvarez Borland] " 'And it's always the language I'm not writing in that is my home.' Your remark is important if we think of *Anything but Love* and *Cincuenta lecciones de exilio y desexilio*, two books that appeared in the same year. In addition to being in different languages, these books are so different that they could have been written by two different people. Your creative writing in English, it seems to me, is much more direct, at times bitter, while your Spanish writing seems more melancholy, more heartfelt. Any validity to my impressions?"

[Pérez Firmat] "Well, but bitterness can be heartfelt, no? Still, it does seem as if those two books were written by different people, and in some sense they were. My 'I' and my 'yo' don't sound the same. I'm not even sure how well they know, or like, each other. So in English, as you point out, I tend to be louder, more abrasive; while in Spanish I tend to be quieter, more melancholy. I write 'I' and hear '¡Aye!' I write 'yo' and read 'y/o.' It's an amazing thing, the English-language 'I': capitalized, singular, erect, almost like an exclamation mark. To translate it properly into Spanish we'd have to write: ¡YO! Santayana has a poem that begins, 'I would I might forget that I am I.' That's how I feel sometimes. The problem is that Santayana's sentence says 'I' four times."

[Alvarez Borland] "Critics often say that valuable works of literature are universal. Yet, they also claim that they have to come from particular experiences, and fit within a tradition. How does your creative work resonate with the experiences of others?"

[Pérez Firmat] "I don't know about "universal," but sometimes experiences or incidents one thinks of as private or idiosincratic turn out not to be. In *Next Year in Cuba* I write about the word *hollín*, soot. In Cuba our backyard—actually a tiled *patio*—always seemed to be covered with a fine film of *hollín*. In the book I say that *hollín* is a word that I haven't heard or spoken in twenty-five years, but one that evokes for me large chunks of my childhood. After the book was published, several people wrote to say that this word was important to them too, that *hollín* for them also was some sort of Cuban fairy dust or grimy madeleine. So here I thought that my attachment to *hollín* was a personal quirk, and it turns out that others feel about *hollín* as strongly as I do."

[Alvarez Borland] "Does your work arise from what you see in the world, or from what you feel inside? Are these related to your experiences of exile?"

[Pérez Firmat] "Edward Hopper was asked once what he was after in a painting of sunlight hitting a wall. He replied: I was after myself. Which means that looking out can be a way of looking in."

[Alvarez Borland] "I remember that when you published *Next Year in Cuba* you were made aware that your book resonated with many Cuban Americans. Could you share with us some of the responses from your readers?"

[Pérez Firmat] "My favorite one came from a man named Emilio, who lived in Union City. His letter was handwritten in uneven block letters on a lined yellow sheet. It said:

'As I sit in my basement smoking a (PG) cigar and reading the last few pages of this beautiful book, I can't help but write you a letter of appreciation. I am full of emotions that I wish I could put down on this letter, but with only a high school diploma is hard for me to do, and very little experience writing letters, so excuse me. While I read this book, I think is me [*sic*] writing the words in it because our feelings are so much alike, it blows my mind. I'm 36 years old came from (la provincia de Santa Clara) Cuba in 1969 with my sister, mother, father. Now married to an American-Italian wife who speaks Spanish as well as I do for 11 years. A son named Guillermo 10 yrs (does not like that name so is Willie) and a daughter named Sophia 8 yrs old. Smoking a cigar, reading your book, with my son next to me, looking at the USC vs Notre Dame football game, and drinking a glass of homemade wine with tears in my eyes. My son asks what is wrong, so I explain and go thru my famous speech about CUBA. And he listens and understands.' "

[Alvarez Borland] "Do you consciously work with memories?"

[Pérez Firmat] "Well, everybody 'works' with memories, whether you are a writer or not. It's what makes you believe in the coherence, the continuity of your life. As for me, as I say in *Next Year in Cuba* and other places, when I grow nostalgic, it's not for the Havana of my childhood but for the Miami of my adolescence. I have very fond memories of the early years in Miami, hard as they were. Cuba seemed so close then. And the only people in my family who weren't alive were those who hadn't been born yet. Now things are different. Now most of the people in my family who are still alive are those who hadn't been born when we came to the United States. And Cuba seems far, far away. A couple of years ago during Nochebuena I realized that I was the oldest Cuban in the house. This sent me into a depression that hasn't quite lifted yet."

[Alvarez Borland] "Are you aware of how your art modifies your memories? For instance, in *Next Year in Cuba*, did you consciously fictionalize some events in order to make them more interesting to the reader?"

[Pérez Firmat] "No, I tried to tell the truth. But of course I didn't. After the book came out, I kept getting angry calls from family members wanting to set me straight about things that they thought I had gotten wrong. My mother, who didn't like the book at all, even threatened to write her own version: 'Lo que Gustavito no dijo.' "

[Alvarez Borland] "You mentioned before your new collection of poems, *Scar Tissue*, which is and will be out by the time this interview is published. Could you tell us a little about the why and what of it?"

[Pérez Firmat] "A few years ago two things happened that changed my life, were my life susceptible to changing: my father passed away in Miami after waiting for forty years to return to some mysterious place he called Cuba, and I was diagnosed with prostate cancer, a disease that he also had. Because the two events occurred within a couple of months of each other, they bundled together in my mind and out came *Scar Tissue*, a sticky sequel to *Next Year in Cuba* and *Life on the Hyphen*, where I write about enduring illness in a foreign language, about coping with losses of various sorts (*de padre, de patria y de próstata*), and generally about the hurt inside the hyphen. (It turns out that the hyphen was a scar all along.)

In *Scar Tissue*—my informal title is *'Knife on the Hyphen'*—I write about prostate cancer, a common but unliterary disease, with the same candor and even ardor with which others have written about breast cancer or AIDS. Kafka says somewhere that a book should be the ax for the frozen sea inside us. After the surgeons took a scalpel to my belly, I took an ax to my *entrañas*. What was left was Scar Tissue."

[Alvarez Borland] "How do you begin to write a novel or a poem? Does it have to do with particular experiences?"

[Pérez Firmat] "I write when I get into one of my moods. What may be inspiration in others is agitation in me. Except for *Next Year in Cuba*, which was written with a plan, my other books (not the criticism, the 'creative' writing) came about, if not by accident, by chance. Since I'm blessed with a bad memory, I keep journals to remember what happened—who did what to whom and for what reason—and books like *Anything but Love, Cincuenta lecciones de exilio y desexilio* or *Scar Tissue*, as well as all of the poems, began as journal entries. You begin jotting things down haphazardly and after a while you realize that these sentences or paragraphs are going somewhere, that they have or can be given some sort of shape and purpose. Then you stop scribbling in your journal and begin writing a poem or a book."

[Alvarez Borland] "How does having a contemporary audience matter to a writer? Who are your readers? For whom do you write?"

[Pérez Firmat] "Since you are one of my readers, why don't you tell me who *you* are? I said before that everything I've written has in some way been meant to be read by my children. That's true, but it doesn't mean that what I write isn't meant to be read by others as well. It's like this interview. I'm addressing you, Isabel, but I'm also speaking to others—and among those others: myself. Jorge Guillén once said: 'No se escribe para, se escribe porque.' Poorly translated: 'One doesn't write "for," one writes "because." ' When you write 'because,' you're writing for yourself, because there's something you need to say, or to say again, regardless of whether anybody is listening. My impression, or my prejudice, is that the best books are the ones written as if nobody is listening."

[Alvarez Borland] "What is your opinion of literary critics? If you had money to spare, would you give a damn about what critics and audiences think of your work?"

[Pérez Firmat] "I'm fortunate in that I don't make a living from writing, and so I have less incentive to pay attention to what the critics say (but, only in English does one 'pay' attention; in Spanish we 'lend' it—*prestamos atención*—which seems to me more equitable). Also, critics come in different flavors: newspaper critics (plain vanilla), academic critics (chocolate fudge), friends and family (passion fruit). In any event, I have a tacit pact with my real or ideal readers: I don't have to please you; you don't have to read me. This way I can write what I want and they can choose not to lend me their ears. And nobody pays."

[Alvarez Borland] "Could you be, or have been, anything else but a writer?"

[Pérez Firmat] "I could have been—what is more, *should* have been—anything but a writer. That's why one of my books is called *Equivocaciones*—because I'm a writer not by *vocación* but by *equivocación:* it's not a vocation but a mistake, a kind of geographical accident. Growing up, I never wanted to be a writer or a professor. Growing old, I still don't want to be a writer or a professor. But exile turns us into other people, makes or remakes or unmakes us into who we are not. And once the undoing is done, it can't be redone. So I'm sitting here in front of my *desordenadora* drinking a dirty martini and writing that I should not have been a writer."

[Alvarez Borland] "What is your relationship to English? To Spanish? How Cuban do you feel? Is being bilingual an asset to your writing?"

[Pérez Firmat] "Others will disagree, but for me bilingualism is a liability: *una suma que resta.* I have often wished I could not choose whether to write in English or Spanish. Then words would only fail me in one language. Then I would not have to translate myself to myself. Then my 'I' would not haunt my 'yo.' One person, one language. One person, one house. One person, one country. As old-fashioned as this sounds, this is how things should be. (I mean, how I wish things were for me.)"

[Alvarez Borland] "It seems that writers who alternate between languages in their public writing have a story to tell about each language, and yet each language brings about different aspects of your feelings about your own life."

[Pérez Firmat] "Como decía más arriba, el inglés me conoce alegre mientras que el español me conoce triste. Tal vez ésa sea la verdadera razón por la que juego con palabras más en uno que en otro. El español es la lengua de la ausencia, de la pérdida: la voz de mi padre, que ya no existe. En cambio, el inglés es el idioma de la convivencia, de la cotidianidad, el que uso para hablar con mis hijos y mi esposa. El otro día me di cuenta de que la única persona en mi familia con quien todavía hablo en español es mi madre. Pero hace veinte años no había nadie en mi familia con quien no hablaba en español. Y de aquí a cinco o diez años no habrá nadie en mi familia con quien no hable en inglés. Estas cosas afectan la relación de uno con sus lenguas. Si una persona a quien uno quiere—un padre, una madre—habla cierto idioma, ese idioma también habla por ella. Por lo tanto, acudir a ese idioma en su ausencia se convierte en un acto de recordación, de recuperación, en una manera de dialogar con él o ella. Ahora mismo, hablando contigo en español, también estoy conversando con mi padre. O más bien, como en el poema de Florit, conversando 'a' mi padre, ya que él no puede contestarme."

[Alvarez Borland] "Why did you just switch to Spanish? Is there a core inside yourself that remains unchanged no matter what dictionary you reach for?"

[Pérez Firmat] "Yes, there must be a core or *corazón* that doesn't change. *Soy quien fui, hace años, para siempre.* But how can I get there from here without resorting to one language or the other, which turns core into encore, the speechless *corazón* into a wordy *coraza?* It may be that I go back and forth between Spanish and English to trick my languages into transparency, to sneak up on them before they put up their wall of words or *pantalla de palabras.* If I can open a crack between Spanish and English, then perhaps the core/*corazón* can peek out through it. Not that anybody should care, though. My core may be even less interesting than my *coraza.*"

[Alvarez Borland] "What distinguishes Cuban Americans from other Latino writers?"

[Pérez Firmat] "Perhaps it's more interesting to think about what they have in common—the English language, for example. Cuban-American literature, like Latino literature, is becoming or has become an English-only zone. And yet these mostly anglophone writers have not stopped pining for their *patria grande* or *chica,* for Havana or Little Havana, for Sagua or La Sagüesera, but in a language that makes those places more distant. Longing for Cuba or things Cuban in the language of Cuba makes sense; longing for Cuba in the language of America is a little odd, and yet I and others do it all the time. Odder still, often the nostalgia is directed at the Spanish language itself. This longing for Spanish in English is one of the features that joins Cuban-American literature to Puerto Rican or Chicano literature. Latino literature, whatever its ethnicity, is full of English-language love songs to Spanish, ballads that are also valedictories. The Latino writer carries a torch he or she can't lose for the language she or he has lost. Sandra Cisneros has a wonderful poem that begins, 'Make love to me in Spanish, / not with that other tongue.' Okay, fine; but if we both know Spanish, why are you telling me this in English? And what is 'that other tongue' if not the language in which the poem is written?"

[Alvarez Borland] "So why do you think she says it in English?"

[Pérez Firmat] "Because she wouldn't know how to say it in Spanish. The speaker's attachment to Spanish is sentimental rather than practical: a 'tongue tie' rather than a linguistic habit. But this does not make her attachment any less strong or genuine. When she asks to be loved in Spanish, she's looking for a secret self—someone she used to be or maybe someone she never was. In New World chronicles of discovery, translators are called *lenguas*, the body part standing for the whole person. Something like this happens here: her lover is her *lengua*, and her *lengua* names her, tells her who she would like to be. Except that the self she desires exists in and through a language that neither she nor her lover inhabit. Which is why, although the poem is called 'Dulzura,' it leaves a sour taste on the tongue."

November 2005

A BARATAN EXPERIENCE

— PABLO MEDINA

Pablo Medina was born in 1948 and came to the United States from Cuba in 1960 at the age of twelve. If asked about personal identity, Pablo Medina would first and foremost identify himself as a writer. For him ethnic labels are used and misused in order to classify writers and literatures: "When I became a writer and started publishing my work . . . I was called a Hispanic-American writer or a Cuban-American one, or occasionally, a Latino writer. . . . I had the distinct impression that I was somehow being manipulated. I wanted to be known simply as a writer, a good writer preferably, and all other labels seemed to detract from and diffuse that ambition." Medina's novels and poetry are proof that he has lived up to his desire to be seen as a writer first and foremost. And yet, his novels and poetry offer us subtle evocations of the lost world of life before the Cuban Revolution and present us with the many faces of the melancholy of dislocation.

Medina is the author of a memoir, Exiled Memories: A Cuban Childhood *(1991), the first in a series of autobiographical accounts that have been published since the 1990s by Cuban-American writers of Medina's generation. He has published three novels:* The Marks of Birth *(1994),* The Return of Felix Nogara *(2000), and* The Cigar Roller *(2005), and several volumes of poetry:* Pork Rind and Cuban Songs *(1975),* Arching into the Afterlife *(1990),* The Floating Island *(1999), and* Points of Balance/Puntos de apoyo *(2002). Medina is the recipient of a Cintas Foundation Fellowship, an NEA grant, a Woodrow Wilson–Lila Wallace Fellowship, and grants from the New Jersey and Pennsylvania State Arts Councils. He is on the faculty at the Warren Wilson MFA Program for Writers and teaches writing and literature at the New School University, where he also serves as Director of Lang College's Writing Program.*

INTERVIEW

Conducted by Isabel Alvarez Borland

[Alvarez Borland] "How did you become a writer?"

[Medina] "According to my grandmother (the family mythifier), she once found me making pictographic symbols on the wall of the bedroom with the feces that spilled out of the sides of my diaper. It was then that

145

my grandmother concluded that I would be a *literato*, or a man of letters. I became no such thing but a writer, a man of words and of sentences."

[Alvarez Borland] "Interesting you should mention your grandmother since in your first novel, *The Marks of Birth*, the figure of the grandmother becomes a writer within the text and an important teller of the story of exile. How do you see the impact of the first exile generation on your own writing?"

[Medina] "I am part of the first exile generation, don't forget. I came at the age of twelve, with enough Cuban cultural baggage to identify myself (as an individual, not a writer, since I didn't consider myself such at the time) as fully Cuban. Also keep in mind that I came to the United States (New York, to be specific), having attended two bilingual schools in Havana, Cathedral School in Vedado and Ruston Academy in Biltmore. That story is told in my 1990 memoir, *Exiled Memories: A Cuban Childhood*, first essay."

[Alvarez Borland] "Well, the first exiles were our parents and their parents, we—you and me—came along with them as teens. I wanted to know what impact, if any, did your elders have on your writing about the story of the Cuban exile."

[Medina] "My grandmother was one of those people who encountered, engaged, and understood the world through stories, that is, by transforming actual experience into imaginary landscapes. Her stories ranged from the banal to the profound, and they were often didactic, but that did not diminish their charm and their extraordinary wisdom. In her voice I heard unintentional echoes of Cervantes. When I read *One Hundred Years of Solitude* as an apprentice writer, I heard echoes of her voice in that text. All those echoes running together formed a Möbius strip of sorts—Cervantes, my grandmother, and García Márquez running together until I couldn't tell where one ended and the other began.

Neither of my grandmothers could tell me any stories about exile because they came three years after us, along with my great-grandmother, who told me many stories about the family dating back to the War of Independence (The Spanish American War for the uninitiated). None of the stories had to do with exile but several had to do with displacement from Pinar del Río to Havana and with economic struggle, which the family suffered until the late 1940s when they achieved a modicum of comfort."

[Alvarez Borland] "Could you elaborate a bit more about the story behind *The Marks of Birth*?"

[Medina] "The story in *Marks of Birth* might be construed as a story that illustrates the Cuban exile experience but it is first and foremost a literary form called a novel, subject to certain demands and reflective of that aesthetic object called the Novel, with a tradition dating at least as far back as Cervantes. It is there where I want to dwell and those issues (of form, of aesthetics) that I want to discuss. Be aware that I am not writing sociology but literature and that the story of Cuban exiles (my own story and that of others) interests me only insofar as it provides raw material for literature. I bring up the distinction because it seems to me that literary critics have fallen into the intellectual aberration of considering literature in light of certain extraliterary values borrowed mostly from the social sciences—sociology, psychology, et cetera. I keep in mind what Freud once said: "Everywhere I go I find that a poet has been there before me."

[Alvarez Borland] "*Exiled Memories*, the memoir you mentioned earlier, led the way for many other memoirs about the story of the exile of our generation such as Gustavo Pérez Firmat's *Next Year in Cuba*, Virgil Suárez's *Spared Angola*, and most recently Carlos Eire's *Waiting for Snow in Havana*. What about the making of that memory book?"

[Medina] "I wasn't interested in leading the way. I just wanted to write down stories I had experienced directly or had heard from the different family members, mostly women, who surrounded me when I was growing up. I was le petit prince, *un príncipe enano*, to use Martí's phrase, among adult women. They coddled me, spoiled me rotten. I loved every minute of it."

[Alvarez Borland] "What are your literary allegiances—is your work influenced by writers within the Cuban tradition?"

[Medina] "My literary allegiances have not been so much to Cuban or North American literature per se, but to Western literature. I am as close to the work of Italo Calvino and Mark Twain as I am to the work of Lezama or Cabrera Infante. I must additionally clarify that, except for the work of Martí and Juan Clemente Zenea, I was not aware of Cuban literature at the age of twelve. Yet, I was reading Twain and Hemingway and European writers I will bring up in due time."

[Alvarez Borland] "How did you know you wanted to be a writer?"

[Medina] "I didn't know. Let's just say that I couldn't find anything else I liked to do. Believe me, if that had been the case I would not be a writer but a fireman or a doctor or a *rumbero*."

[Alvarez Borland] "Are there important markers in your writing life?"

[Medina] "There are many markers, significant and not. I remember my Tata holding me close to her, her huge breasts all but smothering me. I remember reading Martí and Rafael Pombo and the *Thousand and One Nights* (with all the racy parts taken out). I remember Jules Verne and Emilio Salgari and Mark Twain. I remember watching as my great-great-grandmother was disinterred. Some of the hair was still attached to the skull. I remember walking into their bedroom as my aunt and uncle were making love. I tried to keep a straight face and asked, 'Where is my cousin?' "

[Alvarez Borland] "It is interesting that you should mention episodes that remain in your memory as markers. Do traumatic episodes play an important role in your imaginary as a writer?"

[Medina] "There you go borrowing a term from psychology—'trauma.' My life experiences stand alongside my literary experiences. Seeing my great-great grandmother's skull remains in my memory as a marker, it is true, but no more vivid than reading about Captain Nemo, a man whose moral outrage led him to become a misanthrope, in *Twenty Thousand Leagues Under the Sea,* or reading about the invisible man in H. G. Wells's novel. Or am I remembering now Claude Reins's masterful characterization in the movie, a talking picture in the fullest sense of the word? Mr. Reins couldn't be seen but he could be heard. Knowing this, look at the principal characters in all three of my novels. Antón García Turner, Félix Nogara, and Amadeo Terra (especially Amadeo) are all struggling to be noticed in some fashion. But then this is the work you should be doing and I should merely be commenting on. As Robert Rauschenberg once said, 'You can't be a bird and an ornithologist at the same time.' "

[Alvarez Borland] "Antón, Félix, and Amadeo—all three characters seem to reflect a little of the different stages in the life of the Pablo Medina I have known. Any truth to this?"

[Medina] "That might be the case with Antón and Félix. I haven't reached Amadeo's age so I cannot say for sure. Let's talk again when I'm in my late seventies."

[Alvarez Borland] "Fair enough. Antón, Félix, and Amadeo are characters conceived in very different ways. While Antón seems drawn from an almost minimalist perspective, Amadeo is quite the opposite. If you were going to pick a tradition where your work fits, which would it be?"

[Medina] "Magico-Imagist-Baroque-Minimalist-Meta-Super-Realism."

[Alvarez Borland] "Your answer lends itself to commentary regarding the different styles exhibited in your novels. For instance, your first novel seemed to have been written within the tradition of *Realismo Mágico.* On the other hand, *The Cigar Roller* seems to go back to a more mimetic way of narrating and brings to my mind the main character of Fuentes's *Artemio Cruz.* Could you speak a little about the trajectory or the changes in your style of writing in terms of the fiction you have published?

[Medina] "I was not trying to be truthful here but elusive. I am the last person to know the truth about my writing. I frankly don't worry much about what my style is. I would hope it is individual, stamped with my own voice rather than someone else's. As I wrote *The Cigar Roller* I was reading and rereading Rulfo's *Pedro Páramo,* one of the great Latin

American novels of all time. That book influenced me as much as it influenced Carlos Fuentes as he wrote *The Death of Artemio Cruz*."

[Alvarez Borland] "As a writer, how do you relate to the ethnic labels and designations such as Cuban, American, Cuban American, Hispanic or Latino?"

[Medina] "I am a writer who was born in Cuba. To say Cuban American is a redundancy. All Cubans are Americans in the geographic sense. In addition, Cuban culture was thoroughly influenced, before 1959, by the culture to the north. Besides, the label may have a sociocultural value, though this is arguable, but little literary or aesthetic value."

[Alvarez Borland] "And yet, novels such as *The Return of Felix Nogara* are imbued with the Cuban American story or experience. The same can be said of the silent character named Anton in *The Marks of Birth*. Don't you think that a literature of exile such as yours creates its own aesthetic?"

[Medina] "You call it a Cuban American experience, which you are free to do as we live in a free society. I call it a Baratan experience. You wander into dangerous territory here. Don Quixote derives his identity from reading books of chivalry; in other words, his sense of self is derived from his readings, not from his life experiences. Analogously, Félix Nogara's sense of self is derived from reading too much history and politics. Only after he abandons these at the end of the book does he gain a sense of self in reality rather than from illusion. The book begins and ends in Barata (derived from Barataria, which is the island Don Quixote promises Sancho). But I am doing too much of the work that literary critics, who have forsaken close textual reading in favor of grandiose ideas of identity and culture, should be doing."

[Alvarez Borland] "Obviously the cultural turn prevalent today in literary criticism doesn't excite you. Are there any critics you value?"

[Medina] "What critics? The only critics I value are inside my head. Sometimes there are hordes of them in there screaming; sometimes there is only one. On occasion they fall asleep. Once I thought I had killed them all but I was dreaming."

[Alvarez Borland] "Do you consider your work in the mainstream, at the margins, elsewhere?"

[Medina] "I am having trouble answering this question because I don't know where I stand. I don't want to say that I am at the margins simply because it is the romantic thing for a writer to say. The fact is that I have a good job, I am happily married, and, judging from outward appearances, I sit squarely in the mainstream. Yet I also feel that I must stand apart in order to observe and record."

I am both an innie and an outie, though if I were a gambling man I would wager that all writers are innies in that they must internalize their experiences before they can write about them. Some of my experiences have to do with exile; others not. For example, while in Guatemala years ago, some of my friends and I were riding around the countryside and we came upon a corpse on the side of the road. Its face was covered with flies and its penis was sticking straight up in the air. I have not written about that until now. I imagine I have not yet fully internalized it. Another time I was in a plane trying to land in Phoenix, Arizona, when we hit bad weather. The plane started shaking violently. The shaking seemed to go on forever and people started screaming. Next to me was a beautiful woman who was as distressed as I was. We held each other's hands until the plane landed. We didn't say anything to each other and I never saw her again. If the plane had crashed they would have found us hand in hand and people would have reached all manner of incorrect conclusions about it. My wife might have even divorced me posthumously (after cashing in my life insurance policy). In reality, the woman and I were just scared."

[Alvarez Borland] "Would you say that isolated intense experiences such as these will find their way into your poetry somehow?"

[Medina] "If these experiences make it into anything it will be a novel or story, but, I hope, not in a sensationalistic way. My poetry lately seems to tell its own story, go its own way, and that is fine by me."

[Alvarez Borland] "Which brings to mind that beautiful bilingual collection of poems entitled *Points of Balance/Puntos de apoyo* that you have recently published. Can you tell us how it came about?"

[Medina] "What I attempted to do in *Points of Balance/Puntos de apoyo*, was to establish a linguistic interplay, pairing poems that are not translations, but, rather, reflections of each other. As one critic has written, the result is 'a dynamic dialogue between two moods with each pairing, the mood shifting after every poem, and, true to the demand of the form, shifting within the poem itself.' The form he refers to is the fulcrum, or *fulcro* in Spanish, which I developed. It is a six-line poem divided into unrhymed couplets with a syntactic/semantic shift in the middle couplet, combining the dialectic of the sonnet with the imagistic power of the haiku. I hate to disappoint but the most intense experience I felt was developing and working with the form itself."

[Alvarez Borland] "What could you tell us about the creative impulse behind this work?"

[Medina] "The poems in *Points of Balance/Puntos de apoyo* represent a span of eight years. Their spark was a moment of panic, the result of working too intensely on the novel *The Return of Felix Nogara* and feeling that I would never write another poem in my life. I put aside the novel and wrote the first *fulcrum* in English. A few hours later I wrote one in Spanish. I was so engrossed in what I was doing that I didn't know what language I was working in. It was a very exciting moment for me: not to

know, not to care what language I was using when everything I had done
to that point had been predicated by the conscious choice of one language
or another. The process of writing the poems that are now included in
Points of Balance/Puntos de apoyo slowed down as it had to, but I continued
working with the form until I had enough to collect into a book—sixty-
four in English and sixty-four in Spanish—and to conform to the number
of hexagrams in the *I-ching*, a text that had a seminal influence in the
composition of the *fulcrums*. I should clarify that the hexagram is a six-
line figure, the result of the casting of coins or sticks, which is used in
Taoist philosophy as a guide to ethical behavior."

[Alvarez Borland] " 'I was so engrossed in what I was doing that I
didn't know what language I was working in.' Your remark is very interesting to me in terms of the creative process of a bilingual writer such as
yourself. What is your relationship to English? To Spanish? Is being
bilingual an asset to your writing?"

[Medina] "We are engaged to be married. We are engaged to be
married. I am a bigamist. I am a Cuban who happens to be a writer. Being
bilingual is an asset to me as a human being."

[Alvarez Borland] "How does having a contemporary audience matter
to a writer?"

[Medina] "Is there any other kind of audience? Without a contem-
porary audience a writer has no readers. I don't know who my readers are.
I would hope not all of them are academics. With apologies to John
Donne, I write for thee."

[Alvarez Borland] "What are the politics of publishing in the U.S.?
Are publishing houses looking for ideal American Dream stories? I should
note that you have published with very reputable editorial houses
but many of your fellow Cuban American writers have had trouble getting their works into print. What are your thoughts on the U.S. publishing world?"

[Medina] "Now that my work is gaining some acceptance, publishing
is not as important as it once was. I am not so hungry for it. Getting money
for what I write is important as a measure of acceptance. It's nice to have
the additional income. I don't know what you mean by the politics of
publishing in the U.S. Some publishing houses are looking for American
dream stories, and so they are not interested in what I do. Other houses are
interested in serious literature and I have had the good fortune of publishing with some of the best—Farrar Straus & Giroux, Persea Books, and
Grove Press. Fewer presses are interested in serious poetry. My most recent
poetry publisher, Four Way Books, is one of those few."

[Alvarez Borland] "The past couple of years have been extremely productive for your work. Could you explain any extraordinary circumstances

that might have made it so? Could you provide us with details regarding the story behind your most recent novel, *The Cigar Roller*?"

[Medina] "I have been no more productive the last couple of years than I've ever been. It's just that a number of publications have coincided in 2005, making it appear that I was more productive than ever. Remember that books take time to write. More specifically, I have been researching *Cigar Roller* for upwards of ten years. The actual writing took a year and a half. As I said, I began to do research on the Cuban community in Ybor City about ten years ago. I initially thought I would write a social history of the place, since there are few books, most of them academic and therefore not the most exciting reading, about that extraordinary place. But I am not a social historian and felt I lacked the will to become one. Then I thought I would do a historical novel and began working on one but gave up on that because it bored me. I wrote most of *The Cigar Roller* during a very intense period while I was in the White Mountains of New Hampshire during my sabbatical year. In the midst of the cold, darkness, and isolation of the place (I was living on a mountaintop, completely alone), I faced many issues about myself as a Cuban and as a man that had lain dormant until then, and they all became incorporated into Amadeo Terra, a master cigar roller who has suffered a severe stroke that has completely paralyzed him. Lying in a hospital bed unable to move or speak he has no option but to face his limitations as a human being before death drops its blanket on him. Character took over. I began to see the novel as an exploration of the human condition. The history is still there but remains in the background, the foreground being occupied by Amadeo's internal life. On another level, I wanted to write a novel that was a poem. I liberated myself from the demands of chronology and causality and wrote much as memory appears, disjointed, uncertain, and spontaneous, subject less to the passage of time than to the spark of emotions and the experiential triggers that dominate it. For Amadeo these were primarily fear and regret. He could have been any nationality, but he was a Cuban, and a "cigar roller" at that. It is worthy of note that the book has now appeared in Spanish in Mexico as *El forjador de puros*. I originally wanted it titled *El torcedor de tabacos*, which would be the appropriate Cuban way to translate "cigar roller," but the Mexican editor and translator convinced me that Mexicans wouldn't know what *torcedor* meant. So I accepted their recommendation and am now glad I did. The book might be less Cuban but is certainly more Hispanic than *The Cigar Roller*, written totally in English."

[Alvarez Borland] "What distinguishes Cuban Americans from other Latino writers?"

[Medina] "What distinguishes Cubans from other Latin Americans, writers or not, in the U.S., is that they insist on defining themselves within the context of exile, not of immigration. This is the case even with the new generation of Cuban writers such as the novelist and short story writer Ana Menéndez and the poet Richard Blanco, whose experience of exile is secondhand, through their families' memories. The first was born in the United States and the second came inside his mother's womb, yet exile suffuses their work."

[Alvarez Borland] "Did your recent visit to Cuba have any impact on what you have written since? Would you think it necessary from a creative standpoint that a writer make such a journey as a kind of recovery of a childhood spent not only in a different language but also in a different space?"

[Medina] "The visit to Cuba changed me as a person. I saw firsthand the ruins of my memory. I came back numb, not knowing which end was up. But the trip confirmed for me several things: first, my parents were absolutely right in bringing us out of there when they did; second, socialism is one of the greatest insults to the human spirit that has ever been devised; third, I was totally justified in feeling blue all these years; fourth, childhood goes away naturally or forcefully, but it goes away, and all you can do is try to shape your life in the light of the present, not the past. Fifth, exile is an incurable disease. Once you have it, it stays with you forever. These issues may be evident in my writing, but it is for me to know and you to find out."

January 2006

WRITING WITHOUT MASKS

——————————————————— VIRGIL SUÁREZ

Virgil Suárez was born in Havana in 1962. His family left Cuba for Spain in 1970 when he was eight years old. Four years later, the family moved permanently to the United States. Suárez is the author of a celebrated memoir, Spared Angola: Memories from a Cuban-American Childhood *(1997). The poems and vignettes that make up this narrative constitute a vivid personal recollection of a time in Cuba that has seldom been recorded in English. There is no idealized nostalgia in Suárez's remembrances, rather the adult looks back at his early years in Cuba and often narrates sordid or traumatic instances that marked his childhood: his father's depressive behavior caused by the events of the Revolution, and the poverty and scarcities all had to endure during the first decade of the Revolution. Suárez's memories do not seek to idealize the past—merely to record it. And while there is clearly a healing impulse in the writing down of his childhood memories, for him the healing occurs in writing about these difficult episodes so that they can be erased from his mind.*

Suárez has published several short story and poetry collections among them In the Republic of Longing *(1999), and the most recent,* 90 Miles: Selected and New *(2005). Virgil's poems are lyrics that also tell a story, a manner of writing between genres that is typical of his poetic style. The author has published four novels:* Latin Jazz *(1990);* The Cutter *(1991);* Havana Thursdays *(1995); and* Going Under *(1996), and is editor of several Cuban-American anthologies such as* Iguana Dreams *(1994) and* Little Havana Blues *(1996). Suárez is Professor of creative writing at Florida State University in Tallahassee, and teaches at the MFA program at Bennington College. He is the recipient of fellowships from the NEA and the State of Florida Arts Council.*

INTERVIEW

Conducted by Isabel Alvarez Borland

[Alvarez Borland] "How did you become a writer?"

[Suárez] "I knew I wanted to have a creative outlet of some sort early on in my life, maybe when I was eight or so. My paternal grandmother Isabel was still alive, and she lived with us in Havana. She read

154

me stories from the Harvard Edition of *One-Thousand-and-One Arabian Nights*. There were other classics she knew too, like *The Count of Monte Christo*, *The Three Musketeers*, and possibly, if I remember correctly, *The Hunchback of Notre Dame*—lots of French writers, classics. I heard stories, and I was captivated by them, and the inflections (and tonality) in the voices of the speakers. It was a time in Cuba in the late sixties when the whole world revolved around stories, what one heard, what one saw. They were perilous and delicious times for a child. I did not begin writing until later, after we had traveled to Madrid and even later on to Los Angeles. I must have been fourteen or so. I knew I wanted to write; I knew I had something to say, to tell. I began writing formally in high school after reading American writers the likes of Saul Below, Nathaniel West, and Fitzgerald. To this day, I still reread *The Great Gatsby*. But no one had a more profound impact on my writing than John Steinbeck and Edgar Allan Poe. Those two writers in particular I dissected and studied for many years: Steinbeck for the prose and Poe for the sound and the rhythm of words. I was sixteen or seventeen when I finally started to keep a notebook and wrote my poems in it. But I had already started writing my 'impressions.' ”

[Alvarez Borland] “Tell us about your literary road. What are important markers? Did some people play important roles?”

[Suárez] “My literary road has been straightforward, I think, and in many ways charmed by angels. I stumbled upon a few good teachers who helped me write better all the while I learned English. When I first started to write, I started in English. I think I did it as a way to not only learn the language formally, but to have fun with it so I wouldn't get bored. I had several high school and college teachers help me along the way, among them Enrique Alvarado, Joel Goldstock, John Duran, and later in college Elliot Fried, John Herman, and Charles Stetler to name a few. In graduate school, I continued to write both novels and poetry, though the poetry I never showed to anybody. I was a closet poet until the mid-eighties when I started sending my poems out to literary magazines.”

[Alvarez Borland] “Why a 'closet poet' . . . can you elaborate? And why did you not write in Spanish?”

[Suárez] “I considered my poetry too private and personal to ever want to show it to anyone. Plus a lot of it was derivative from my reading of Borges, Paz, and Neruda. The biggest influence on my poetry, as I said earlier, was Edgar Allan Poe and, of course, José Martí. Both are masters of sound and narration in their poetry. Their work made a huge impact on me. But I still felt, even while I was still in college, that poetry was simply too personal and private for me to ever show it to anyone, and God knows I didn't want to sacrifice my work in the Writing Workshops.

I did not write in Spanish because I did not want anyone in my family or circle of friends to know. In some warped way (and it worked) I figured that, if I wrote in English, the people I cared about would not be able to understand what I wrote and therefore not realize I was writing about them. It was a simple plan, and it worked."

[Alvarez Borland] "Do you consider yourself in the mainstream, at the margins, elsewhere?"

[Suárez] "I always work from the margins out, meaning that I write solely about matters that pertain to my life as a Cuban American, a Cuban really living in exile. My work has been informed by this and nothing more. This is my human condition. I care not in the least to write about other things. This has consumed so far forty-four years of my life. Why begin on some other unknown journey?"

[Alvarez Borland] " 'A Cuban really living in exile,' and yet you indicate English as your first and only writing language. Is this a contradiction? How do you think your feelings of exile differed from those of your father?"

[Suárez] "I think this is an important psychological moment for me because perhaps I write in English precisely because it was not my father's language. He hated the way it sounded and I've always been enamored of the idea that since I had chosen never to please my father with the choices I made in my life (i.e., become a poet and not a dentist, etc.) that this is an important reason for my decision to write exclusively in English. I also didn't want people in my family snooping around with my stuff, my journals, and my diary. My father's feelings on being exiled are not mine in that he wanted closure in his life. I never want closure in mine. I love chaos because I've been a child of it. I love the fact that nothing stays the same and everything is always in constant flux. As a writer, I see the beauty in such things. I also write in English because I've wanted not to be a part of a Cuban literature continuum. I wanted— and I don't know if my colleagues who write in English feel this way— for the language to be a reminder to future generations of readers that the reason some of us wrote in English was that we had been aborted from our place of birth. By circumstance, and not by choice. The life of an exile is chaos; I always like to emphasize this aspect of the Cuban-American experience."

[Alvarez Borland] "What do you consider to be your main contribution so far?"

[Suárez] "I don't necessarily like my old work, but there are pieces that were groundbreaking for me as I developed into the writing I am doing today. I consider novels such as *The Cutter* and *Latin Jazz* to have been important markers because of what they taught me about writing.

I no longer write novels because they are too hard to sustain at a time when I feel I owe nothing to my life as a writer. *Spared Angola: Memories from a Cuban-American Childhood* (1997) is still my favorite book because with it I learned to write without masks, naked, so to speak, and to hone my voice so that I could tell my story without having to summon fictional techniques. My poetry is what keeps me focused these days. I still write a story and essay once in a while, but it is poetry that maintains my interest."

[Alvarez Borland] "*Spared Angola* is a book that has a peculiar structure as it tells the story of your childhood in Cuba through poems and vignettes that have a chronology of their own. This kind of structure has a profound effect on the reader as it forces us to connect these traumatic episodes through association rather than continuity. Do you think you might try working within this mix of genres again?"

[Suárez] "I wanted that book to be a type of collage, a pastiche of emotional moments in my life. I wanted to make the reader feel a bit uneasy about reading these fragments and vignettes and feel the hopelessness of such a condition. I have, in fact, written a second volume of these recollections titled *Infinite Refuge* (2002)."

[Alvarez Borland] "As I read your recent poetry in anthologies such as *In the Republic of Longing*, as well as the poetry of *90 Miles*, I notice that most of the poems are narratives that tell ministories that could be conveyed in vignettes rather than in poems. Can you elaborate on your choice of poetic forms?"

[Suárez] "That is precisely the observation that I make to myself every day. I want to write a poem, yes, but I mostly want the poem to narrate a story. My poems are seldom lyrical because I have to keep my eye on what I want the poem to capture and say. So often I cannot divorce myself from the nature of the story. I use the best I can summon of language to help me preserve a narrative memory of the textures, the sensory materials of my life. I often see myself there, as a child, remembering what it felt like to eat a mango, or slice open a papaya and see its dark seedlings . . ."

[Alvarez Borland] "How would you describe your style of writing? Has it changed throughout your career?"

[Suárez] "My style is direct, cinematic. It relies heavily upon scene and dramatic tension. I borrow from my own life, and in my poetry, I simply speak of those things I've lived through and remember. As I mentioned earlier, John Steinbeck was a big influence on my voice and my style. So was Nathaniel West. Direct, simple, declarative, sentences. I never send the reader to the dictionary, and I like that."

[Alvarez Borland] "Are there periods or stages in your literary development?"

[Suárez] *"Spared Angola: Memories From a Cuban American Childhood* was groundbreaking because I learned the value of spinning my own life and childhood through memory. I found my voice with that book, my internal, logical voice, the one that speaks without fear, without reservations. *'Sin pelos en la lengua,'* as my father would say."

[Alvarez Borland] "Would you describe your work as Cuban, American, Cuban American, Hispanic, Latino? How is your identity as a writer related to these ethnic categories?"

[Suárez] "This is not something I ponder all the time, but I am a Cuban-American writer. I write about what matters to me in my life, my condition. And that condition has always been one of exile, of being an outcast, of being different. It is how I see and perceive the world. I don't think of myself as a victim of circumstance. I think of myself as being part of a chosen few who learned to deal with being a gypsy in the world. I believe that whatever you call me cannot be ignored, homogenized, mainstreamed, et cetera. I belong only to my time and to my history."

[Alvarez Borland] "Would you say that your feelings of 'being different' were centered on the issue of language? Can you expand on your sense of being 'a gypsy in the world'?"

[Suárez] "See, I think I was not meant to be a writer. Had I not had to leave the country of my birth, I think I would have still been a creative person, perhaps a painter or a sculptor, but I would have ended up doing something different, maybe farmed or done something mechanical in nature. Repair broken things . . . but fate had her hands in it, so I became a writer because, once plunged into exile, I've not been able to avoid the feeling of not 'fitting' in, of not being part of any one group, or place. My life has been movement, my life has been change. I am a prince of instability. I ebb and flow at random, and I like this. Perhaps I say I like this because I am not totally aware of what I will derive from such changes, which is more writing, more stories. But I remember being terrified as a child when I would hear that people were leaving, or that we were leaving (and we did) and that there was the chance of no returns. I felt this was adventure of the highest order, adventure with a terminal risk. You can't go home again, so true, but then I don't want to go home. The road is home for me. It's the place where I can peer from at the things that hide in the shadows or which are flooded in the light. I think it is the exact same place we all stand as we decide to become good or evil. I like the idea of being in the middle and have no moral qualms about being able to be both."

[Alvarez Borland] "How is your writing related to your experiences of exile?"

[Suárez] "All of my work, including the most recent collection of poems, *90 Miles: Selected and New,* deals strictly with my life as an exile.

Personal experience distilled through a witness's heart and mind. Simply put, I write about what I've witnessed and what I have lived through, and that is the condition of my exile, of the exile of my people, of their struggle to survive and prevail against all obstacles and odds. I think of characters such as Julian Campos in *The Cutter* and how he was a close rendition of my father as a young man. I think of Diego Carranza in *Latin Jazz* and how he resembles the young man I was growing up in Los Angeles in the seventies and eighties. I've been around the Cuban exiled community all of my life. I know what it feels like. I know the longing and the deprivation. I think of other writers I admire such as Gustavo Pérez Firmat, Roberto G. Fernández, Elías Miguel Muñoz, Matías Montes Huidobro (who writes in Spanish only) and even Reinaldo Arenas, who left Cuba in 1980, much later than any of us 'exiles.' It's the same condition being repeated, played out through different characters, written by different people, but it essentially boils down to the essence of being cast out of the garden. What to do now? Well, that's life. That's the life road. It's a journey of the grandest order, and you better be ready for it."

[Alvarez Borland] "Do you consciously work with memories?"

[Suárez] "I deal mostly with those memories of my Cuban childhood that took place between 1962–1972. It seems to me that I could never exhaust those memories. They have informed most of my work, which now spans almost twenty books of prose and poetry."

[Alvarez Borland] "What about the fact that these memories took place in Spanish. Do you equate the language of childhood—Spanish—with childhood itself?"

[Suárez] "This is a good question, but writing about them in English gives me a necessary distance. It provides the filter and the lens so that I can play out my omniscient voice. I can think about a memory from different angles, but yes, sometimes when I hear my parents speaking, I hear them in Spanish."

[Alvarez Borland] "How do you begin to write a novel or a poem? Are you conscious of a goal when you set to work?"

[Suárez] "I write every day Monday through Thursday, sometimes up to ten hours a day. Even on those days when I have other responsibilities, the objective is to write as much as I can. I compose my rants and chants, as I call my first drafts, in the morning, and then I revise them as need be during the week. I revise always after lunch, this way if the work is truly boring, I can convince myself to begin again the next day. As I said earlier, I no longer write novels because they don't matter to me as much anymore. I don't think I have anything that cannot be said in a poem or in a short story. My life has been lived, as Nadine Gordimer calls it, in the flash of a firefly. This is the work of the story and poem, not of the novel. I'm glad I wrote my novels while I was young and had the energy. Now I simply have enough energy to write poetry, stories, and essays. Shorter pieces that give me almost an instant gratification I like. Perhaps the charge that I write too much is true, but I guess I've always mistook my addiction for my discipline."

[Alvarez Borland] "How does having a contemporary audience matter to you as a writer? For whom do you write?"

[Suárez] "I never worry about audience. My audience is insignificant to me. I write about the important things that matter to me, and if they matter to someone else, then that is fine as well."

[Alvarez Borland] "What is your opinion of literary critics?"

[Suárez] "I think critics have a place, but there's also a difference between a literary critic/scholar and a newspaper hack. The scholars usually end up mattering in the long run, whereas the journalist/book reviewer is a slut for time and space. A newspaper book reviewer will destroy a book in a sentence or two. I think there's something morally corrupt (some people claim jealousy) about being able to destroy something in less time than it took to create. Maybe I'm just too much of an idealist."

[Alvarez Borland] "Could you be, or have been, anything else but a writer?"

[Suárez] "You bet. To this day I still pretend I am a chef, a sculpture artist, a mechanic, a porn star. I've never been anything but a writer, but I want to be something other. That's the problem, as my mother says, I've been educated and therefore rendered useless. I think the older I get the more I agree with that assessment. I am useless as a person. I can't fix anything; I don't have any saleable skills, nothing. I live inside my head."

[Alvarez Borland] "What is your relationship to English? To Spanish? Is being bilingual an asset to your writing?"

[Suárez] "English is the language of barking dogs, that's what my father always called it. In this way it is also a beautiful language, if you happen to like barking dogs, which I do. I've never been able to retain any of its rules, but I love it for that reason. It is always a new language to me because I am constantly learning it or remembering how I learned it. It's always exciting and unexpected. I live and fuck in English. Spanish is the foreign language to me, though it is the language of my roots. I feel very Cuban, but Cuban in English. I feel like a Hollywood myth, but I like it. I like feeling like a hologram. I like being bilingual because I am a juggler at heart. I like speaking in as many tongues as I can muster, pass the mustard sil vous plaiz!"

[Alvarez Borland] " 'I feel very Cuban, but Cuban in English.' I certainly like that. Do you mean that your own particular brand of English could itself convey a Cuban rhythm of sorts?"

[Suárez] "Certainly, and again, those of us who write in English are leaving a record of our place at the table here in the United States. I am very proud of my heritage, my lot in life. I would not change it for anything else. I am who I am and it's not only because I've eaten a lot of spinach too. Cuba is in my blood. I make love to my wife in Cuban, but never in Spanish. Actually I don't talk while I'm making love, I sing Barbarito Diez and Trio Matamoros songs: '*Sabrosona es la negra del solar, tan sabrosona y tan buena . . . or la mujer de Antonio camina asi . . .*' What can I say? I am a sucker for the two cultures of which I am a product!"

[Alvarez Borland] "Are publishing houses looking for ideal American Dream stories? How does your story differ from theirs?"

[Suárez] "I used to worry about publication and about publishers, but I no longer do. I don't really care about who they are or what they do in part because these days I only publish strictly in literary magazines. My publishers have been very good to me, though. And it has been a blessing to work with editors who themselves are poets. This is not the case with New York publishers and their editors. They are anything but people who know how to read and/or communicate. I think most are great drinkers. And they drink so they can pretend they are good lovers, but even that is yet another failure to them. New York has too much of a stranglehold of what they want to publish and who writes. They stereotype everyone and that's why they would never understand what someone like me is trying to say and or write about."

[Alvarez Borland] "Could you be more specific on your own experience with the NY publishing world?"

[Suárez] "Sure. After the first two novels, everyone wanted to know if I would write something other, something else, something about not being Cuban, or Cuban-American. I couldn't do that. What, me, write about my trip West on Route 66? I mean, I would love to write that, but it will again reflect my Cuban self on that road. I remember talking to an agent once who told me that she could not represent me because I wrote about Havana like one of her other clients, and so it would be a clear conflict of interest. Imagine that. I just got tired of people without any sort of literary background telling me what stories they would like me to write. At the end of the day, I simply wanted a bit more control over my work. Books are not (or should not) be written by editorial boards or committee. That's my take on it."

[Alvarez Borland] "As an immigrant writer do you see yourself as expanding or redefining who we are as Americans? As Cubans?"

[Suárez] "I don't think about this much. I'm not out to change the world, or anybody's mind, but I do want to add my voice to the record.

And that record is of someone who's had to live in exile all his life. I know the nature of the beast, Martí said, because I have lived in its entrails . . . I love that. But my heart belongs to that little island in the middle of the Caribbean."

[Alvarez Borland] "What is your relationship to those writers who came from Cuba with established reputations?"

[Suárez] "I've read them and respect those Cuban writers who came with established reputations, but they seem foreign to me. I stopped reading them in Spanish many years ago, and they don't serve me well in translation. It's always best to read Lezama Lima, Carpentier, Sarduy, Arenas, et al when one is young, and then spend one's life trying to reinvent what they've said."

[Alvarez Borland] "What about the writers of your own generation?"

[Suárez] "I think I turn to the usual suspects that are not only inspirations to me, but people I consider my friends: Roberto G. Fernández, Gustavo Pérez Firmat, Adrian Castro, Richard Blanco, and many others. Poets, fiction writers, writers who do it all well like Ricardo Pau-Llosa."

[Alvarez Borland] "What distinguishes Cuban Americans from other Latino writers?"

[Suárez] "Other than the fact that we are politically powerful and savvy, not much. Cubans and Cuban Americans have to realize that we are, in the eyes of Anglos, all the same. We are one nerve-wrecking, Desi Arnaz Lucy I'm HOME, muchomachoman, Latin lover, hot-tempered hot tamales . . . All you have to do is look at how Hollywood continues to image us. How they have blurred the lines between all Latinos. There's nothing to do but set the record straight, you know, and show them through our writing that 'Latinos' are very diverse, that we are different people, and that we come from different places. But the truth is that as Latinos we will take over this country in the next twenty-five years. We'll see how the Anglos like playing this crazy game called democracy our way, where there's no more white spaces to fill with white flight."

[Alvarez Borland] " 'True assimilation begins with the Third genera-tion.' Do you agree or disagree? Is this important to your own writing?"

[Suárez] "Sure, I see it in my daughters, with my daughters. They are as American as Apple Pie. They will reconnect with Cuba the first time they set foot there. I don't think I want to loose my vantage point and succumb to total and complete assimilation. In my dictionary 'assimi-lation' looks too much like the crappy little town I live up here in North Florida. Too much facade and not enough substance!"

[Alvarez Borland] "Is there anything else that should be said about your work?"

[Suárez] "This is what will be written on my gravestone: BELIEVE IN POETRY, BUT DON'T FORGET TO LIVE!"

November 2005

ESCAPING THE HUMORS

———————————————————————— ROBERTO FERNÁNDEZ

"Este país trastorna a la gente," says Titina, a talk show hostess and one of the many characters that appear in Roberto Fernández's most recent novel En la ocho y la doce. *The author has never put words he believes more deeply in a character's mouth. Fernández's parodic portrayal of how a minority community reacts to displacement provides a critical perspective that differs widely from the other members of his generation who appear in this volume. In his works, Roberto has traced a collective biography of the Cuban community in exile in Miami, and in other Florida locations such as Belle Glade, Florida. No longer safely protected in Little Havana, Roberto's characters have to live up to their homelessness and to their fate as immigrants. And whether the author chooses English or Spanish as the language of his publications, all of his novels challenge idealized notions of community by depicting the tensions of life after exile, in particular the conflicts between the first generation and their American-born children.*

Born in Sagua la Grande, Cuba in 1951, Fernández arrived in the United States when he was ten years old. He has been writing and publishing creatively since the mid-1970s. Between 1975 and 1985, the author began his career publishing several short story anthologies in Spanish such as Cuentos sin rumbo *(1975) and* La montaña rusa *(1985). In 1982, he published a collection of related vignettes under the title* La vida es un special. *In the 1990s, Roberto switched to English with* Raining Backwards *(1988), and* Holy Radishes! *(1995).* En la ocho y la doce *(2001), Fernández's most recent novel, he returns once again to the language of his childhood. Roberto is the recipient of a Cintas Fellowship and of an Artist Fellowship from the Division of Cultural Affairs in Florida. He is a professor of Spanish at Florida State University in Tallahassee.*

INTERVIEW

Conducted by Isabel Alvarez Borland

[Alvarez Borland] "Roberto, could you pinpoint a moment in time when you decided to become a writer?"

[Fernández] "I started writing to escape the humors. This happened in a class as the professor proceeded to dip his index finger in a Vics vapor rub bottle and stick the vaporized index in his nostrils, ear, and cleaned it with his mouth while making all sorts of gasping sounds. This was a three times a week ritual and since his lectures were so incoherent, I pretended I was taking notes. He suffered from sinusitis. The name of this congested muse will not be revealed."

[Alvarez Borland] "You have been publishing fiction since 1975, longer than any member of your Cuban American generation. Can you comment on *Cuentos sin rumbo* and *La montaña rusa*, short story collections that mark the beginnings of your writing career?"

[Fernández] "In *La montaña rusa*, the most salient feature is the parody of an arts and literature contest within the novel. In order to win, the participants had to convey the most vitriolic anticommunist perspective. I had fun writing the short stories and poetry for the contest, and sketching some real bad art. Actually, the winning pieces in poetry and art were done by prominent scholars who I commissioned when they were obscure and not the beacons they are today. In *Cuentos sin rumbo*, my very first collection, what prevails are tales with a surprise ending and a touch of the whimsical."

[Alvarez Borland] "Who are the writers that have inspired you the most and how have they helped to develop your own style?"

[Fernández] "Cabrera Infante, Kurt Vonnegut, Gustavo Pérez Firmat (the bilingual bard), Celia Cruz (the guarachera from the Orient), Rene Touzet, Mario Fernández-Porta, Garcilaso de la Vega, El Cid, George Washington. The influence of Cabrera Infante in my works is in the structure and in the dialogue. I especially like the vignette in *Three Trapped Tigers* about the two girls under the truck and the attention that came to them at the expense of their eavesdropping on the fondling couple. My story, 'It's not Easy,' is influenced by that situation and by the idea that in order to stay in the limelight, your tale keeps changing until it becomes a myth. Mirta's myth about Eloy trying to rape her in *Raining Backwards* is also influenced by the idea of what we would do in order to get attention. In regard to Pérez Firmat, what I write and what Gustavo, the poet, writes are in many respects theme and variations on the Cuban-American condition. Our literature is an echo, a sounding board that reflects the ethos of that community. He is the master of the bilingual pun. The rest that I have mentioned here are my intertextual collaborators, or perhaps victims. In my fiction have used bolero lines from Touzet and Fernández-Porta's 'Tu y las nubes,' lines from the songs of Celia Cruz, field correspondence from Washington, scenes from El Cid, and the poetry of Garcilaso de la Vega, among others."

[Alvarez Borland] "The above list shows a lack of regard for hierarchies of any kind and a mixing of categories that is also reflected in your fiction. Some of your stories sometimes mix figures such as patriot José Martí and Miami talk show hostess Cristina Saralegui, for example. Can you elaborate on this irreverent penchant for mixing historical and cultural categories?"

[Fernández] "Actually, I have included Joe Martty and Titina, which are facsimiles of the originals and, as with all copies, it's not the same as the original. Cultural symbols either historical or from pop culture are subject to debunking. The whole of humanity could be debunked by nuclear conflicts. And that is why: 'I cultivated a white rose in June as in January for the friendly friend that gives me his frank hand . . .' "

[Alvarez Borland] "This last quote is a literal translation of a José Martí poem. What can you tell us about this technique of yours which relies on the literal translation of Spanish into English? Would you say your 'special' kind of English requires a bilingual reader?"

[Fernández] "In *Raining Backwards* there is a tongue brigade that forces upon the populace the usage of English. The revenge lies in producing an English that is veiled because it is based on literal translations from Spanish. For instance, the menu from the restaurant 'Friends of the Sea' in *Raining Backwards* reads: 'Shrimp at the little garlic,' 'Saw at the Oven,' 'Pulp in its own ink,' 'Flour with moorish crabs,' 'Seafood sprinkle' . . . such a list demands a knowledge of both Spanish and English in order to make any sense of it."

[Alvarez Borland] "Which language do you prefer for your writing?"

[Fernández] "I take pleasure writing and playing with both languages. Particularly, I enjoy bilingual puns. More than code switching, I rely on literal translations such as we have been discussing."

[Alvarez Borland] "Do you think that your version of the English language changes the perception of that language for the English speaker?"

[Fernández] "I think it does influence the language. At some level, it expands the Spanish vocabulary of the English reader if you don't explain the Spanish word in italics that you have used in the text. Let's say it condiments the language."

[Alvarez Borland] " 'It expands the Spanish vocabulary of the English reader.' Can you explain further? Are you interested in "interpreting" or mediating Cuban culture to the monolingual reader?"

[Fernández] "I'm not interested in interpreting. There are many others that do that. I'm more of a tribal writer."

[Alvarez Borland] "Do you consider your work at the margins or elsewhere?"

[Fernández] "Depending on the label, I could consider myself at the margins of mainstream of some mainstreams or at the epicenter of some very small margins."

[Alvarez Borland] "Explain this idea of 'labels' and your position within them."

[Fernández] "The idea of labels is the result of this country's obsession with categorizing. The writer doesn't ask for the label. We are given one. Am I pretending to be the 'crazy goat' with your question?"

[Alvarez Borland] "No. I can usually understand 'crazy goats' as long as they were born in Sagua la Grande. Which brings me to the younger Cuban Americans and their understanding of your work. Can you comment on the warm reception you have received from your Miami readers, in particular the younger Cuban Americans? What aspect of your writings do you think appeals to the younger set?"

[Fernández] "What appeals to them is that they recognize their grandparents and other relatives in my fiction. It is familiar territory, and they can identify with it."

[Alvarez Borland] "Why do you write?"

[Fernández] "To leave constancy of a people in transition, a community that lived in a time warp in order to survive, through parody and satire. *Raining Backwards* is a good example of a portrait of a community in the process of becoming something else."

[Alvarez Borland] "Yes, *Raining Backwards* could be considered your best-known work to date. Can you tell us about how you went about creating such a marvelous portrait of types, themes, and situations of Cuban Americans in 'transition'?"

[Fernández] "The kernel for *Raining Backwards* was the story by the same title. I started writing the rest of the novel in West Palm Beach and continued in Florence, Italy. Thus the Italian allusions in the novel which, to date, no one has pointed out. As far as the theme, it was easy to see that we were a community in the midst of transforming itself with all the dislocations it produces, and with the chaos of such an ebullient mixture."

[Alvarez Borland] "Most of your writings seem to favor a fragmentary structure that draws its meaning through accumulation and refuses any type of chronology. Why do you feel it is important to create this sense of dislocation in the reader?"

[Fernández] "My style is fragmented like life itself or like memories with multiple voices. My latest stories are first person narratives. I write in a postmodern vein, I suppose. From my earliest works to my most recent [*En la ocho y la doce*], I have relied on interconnected vignettes as my structural technique. In my latest works, though, I have preferred the first-person, straight-line narrative. I am referring to recent stories such as 'Encrucijada,' 'The Augustflower,' 'It's not Easy,' and others."

[Alvarez Borland] "Indeed your most recent use of the first-person point of view such as in 'The Augustflower' seems to make your narrative less chaotic than your earlier writings. In that short story the main narrator seems to want to clarify issues for the reader more than I had noticed in your earlier works. Are you seeking a more orderly narrative line these days?"

[Fernández] "I do not know for sure. The project that I'm working on now, *Angry Letters to Former Lovers* [working title] is a combination of the epistolary, interpolated vignettes and the intervention of insects that kill their mates."

[Alvarez Borland] "Sounds pretty cruel to me. Perhaps such a naturalistic bent would require a bit more authorial guidance?"

[Fernández] "The death of the insects is normal and merciful. The bickers of angry humans are normal and merciless."

[Alvarez Borland] "Earlier in this interview you indicated that you were writing about a community 'in transition.' It seems to me that many of your stories are about the solutions that your characters invent in order to cope with the challenges of exile and immigration. Most of these coping mechanisms involve a fantasy or double life for your characters such as we witness with Nellie in *Holy Radishes!*, Mirta in *Raining Backwards*, as well as many others characters who appear in all of your works. Could you elaborate on your handling of this theme?"

[Fernández] "In *Raining Backwards* myth creation is the defense mechanism many characters use to cope with their new reality. This mechanism is a universal response to deal with situations that are not understood. In *Holy Radishes!*, Nellie's escape from both the island and the peninsula is through mythical Mondovi. (Actually, Mondovi does exist). Nellie is neither happy in Xawa nor in Belle Glade, her dream is elsewhere. The character of a recent story, 'It's not Easy,' uses simulacrum to escape his reality. He takes his cues from the news and imitates the facial expressions of the suffering displaced Albanian Kosovars so that his friends will commiserate with him because his wife has left him."

[Alvarez Borland] "It is interesting that while many of your contemporaries have written Cuban American memory books (i.e. Eire, Medina, Suárez, Perez Firmat) you have never attempted to write about yourself. Could you tell us why?"

[Fernández] "In many ways, my writings arise from the experiences of others, and probably the reason for the multiple voices and perspectives in *Raining Backwards*. I write fiction and use parody and satire. I don't think those are a good match with the genre of the memoir. I guess, my contemporaries feared the millennium."

[Alvarez Borland] "Since you are able to remember and have your own memories of Cuba and of your departure, why do you resort in your fiction to examining the issues of your parents' generation as well as those of the younger generation rather than those of your own? Is it too painful to think of what you went through?"

[Fernández] "My trauma is very light compared to what others have experienced. In Cuba, I was either meant to be a great surgeon or a genius at interspecies adaptive behaviors. I was performing heart transplants on lizards, and had to leave behind three patients in the freezer. I had also succeeded in convincing a turkey hen to nest on forty duck's eggs. The problem was the trauma caused to the hen when the ducklings went for a swim at the nearby pond. I was about to solve that problem. There is the trauma of the career of a budding scientist cut short by political upheavals."

[Alvarez Borland] "Can you tell us about your creative process? Where do your ideas come from? When you are writing, do you work consciously with memories?"

[Fernández] "I work with borrowed and distorted memories. *Raining Backwards* is filled with distorted memories. In *En la ocho y la doce* and *La montaña rusa*, I also worked with distorted self-perceptions and memories with plenty of cobwebs. And, in the story 'Encrucijada,' the narrative revolves around a returning exile suffering from Alzheimer's. My inspiration could come from a line of dialogue I am overhearing which triggers an image. I have no set goal when I begin. The image takes me to the goal."

[Alvarez Borland] "But is it really the image or the language that takes you there? It seems to me—as I read you—that you capture the Cuban-American speech to perfection and that you reproduce in your writing expressions I had never heard for years but which always ring true. Could you expand on this?"

[Fernández] "I studied dialectology. My antenna goes up when it comes to dialogue reproduction. I take pleasure in reproducing popular speech. Especially, when the people deny that they don't 'speak that way.' Take the Spanish word for coal, 'carbon,' for instance. A Cuban criticizing Puerto Rican diction would tell him or her: 'You don't say "calbón," you say "cabbón." ' It is the case of the kettle calling the pot black."

[Alvarez Borland] "How Cuban do you feel?"

[Fernández] "I am an exile from Cuban Miami—a place that is fast disappearing. I started publishing in English when Gloria Estefan started to sing in English. I took my cue from Gloria. Mainly, I started to publish in English so that I could reach a new generation of Cuban-Americans, and to reach a wider audience. My most recent novel, *En la ocho y la doce* was published in Spanish at the request of the publishing house."

[Alvarez Borland] "Does it worry you that Cuban Miami, as you indicate, is on its way out?"

[Fernández] "It is always good to go back 'where everybody knows your name,' and that is the case of Miami for us. Loosing the capital of our mythical land would be traumatic."

[Alvarez Borland] "What is the relationship between your work and the work of your generation? Of the older writers? The younger ones?"

[Fernández] "I relate to the works of my own generation and enjoy the output of younger writers. I am a fan of the works of Gustavo Pérez-Firmat, Virgil Suárez, Achy Obejas, and Ana Menéndez. I totally relate to the playful aspects of Gustavo's poetry and prose—his puns, linguistics riddles, the counterpoint between English and Spanish, his CubaNo and AmericaNo. I also relate to Virgil's characters' search for meaning in a sea of emptiness, successful but at what prize. Menéndez's *In Cuba I Was a German Shepherd* captures the nostalgia of the older generation. Obejas's quest to belong, to find her Jewish identity in *Days of Awe* has mythical proportions. I think all of us have many things in common."

[Alvarez Borland] "In your opinion, what characterizes Cuban-American writing?"

[Fernández] "The use of borrowed memories and displaced nostalgia."

[Alvarez Borland] "When you mention 'displaced nostalgia' I think immediately of Nellie, in *Holy Radishes!* Could you explain what you mean by 'displaced' in this case?"

[Fernández] "In Nellie's case, she feels nostalgic for a place she has never seen, a mythical land she has never visited. 'A land where you don't have to remember what you don't want to remember.' Many young Cuban Americans feel nostalgic for the mythical land of their grandparents, a place they have never visited either."

[Alvarez Borland] "Who is your audience?"

[Fernández] "My audience are Cuban Americans of a certain generation, I believe, and captive Latino literature university students."

[Alvarez Borland] "Do you feel that writing helps you exorcise your demons?"

[Fernández] "I enjoy being a writer. It flushes your mind. I am sure it must prevent cluttering. If I hadn't decanted all the images from life during 'the exile years,' I don't know where I would be."

[Alvarez Borland] "Do you wish your literature to be recognized as Cuban American? as Latino? As something else?"

[Fernández] "As Cuban-American, mestizo literature. The label that is applied to my works does not really concern me. I'm included in the anthology of the *Cuban Short Story of the Twentieth Century* and also in the *Biographical Dictionary of Southern Literature*. Go figure that one out."

[Alvarez Borland] "What are your thoughts on the assimilation of Cuban Americans to the U.S. mainstream?"

[Fernández] "It all depends on where they live. I know Cuban Americans as a whole are much more assimilated than we would like to admit and it bothers us when we are still perceived as 'the other' after so many years in this country. For instance, a few weeks ago, a friend and I were asked by the manager of a hotel in western New York State if we were vacationing from Cuba and for how long we were staying in the U.S. We both were baffled and hurt."

[Alvarez Borland] "Many of the episodes of *Raining Backwards* and *En la ocho* play with the idea of involuntary cross-contamination. I recall vividly how Mr. Olsen ate a *boniato* dish and actually liked it in spite of his hatred for the Cuban neighbor that had cooked the dish. There are other episodes of this kind in your fiction. What are your thoughts on this process of 'natural' assimilation?"

[Fernández] "It's the inevitable process of mutual assimilation. First you start eating their food, and then they marry your children, much to yours or their chagrin. Has this happened to you or your spouse?"

[Alvarez Borland] "Indeed it has. My husband has become a great cook of Cuban dishes and makes the best *vaca frita* I have ever eaten. Still and all, I have not managed to like peanut butter sandwiches.

In which ways does your work depart from the traditional 'American Dream' story as it depicts the tensions among the various Latino groups within the Miami and greater Miami region?"

[Fernández] "My works depart from the American dream in the sense that many of the characters have already a dreamland that they inhabit. Many Latinos view Cubans in the United States as a privileged group when it comes to immigration, and thus there are tensions. 'The Augustflower' is precisely about that notion of privilege."

[Alvarez Borland] "You have said somewhere that '*Raining Backwards* is like a happy funeral, a New Orleans–style funeral about a culture. Not about a culture being assimilated, but a culture turning into something totally different.' It seems to me this comment could apply to all of your works and also relates to the presence of humor in your writings. Could you care to comment on any aspect of your quote?"

[Fernández] "Humor is the weapon of the disfranchised. The Cuban Miami of the sixties, seventies, and eighties revolved around nostalgia, political upheavals, and the myth of how special we were in the world, but it lacked a mirror for the community to see the face of that reality. Through the humor in parody and satire, I have tried to present such a mirror."

[Alvarez Borland] "Do you wish to be read and published in Cuba? Have you done this already? What about traveling there?"

[Fernández] "I have been read in Cuba to some extent, and some day, I would be curious to visit where I was born, Sagua-on-Deep River.

It was a tranquil land, a bucolic town on the river shore. The river rivaled the Amazon in its depth. It flooded the farmlands once a year making the cotton fields so productive. I still remember the gothic spires, and the streets covered with soot, black particles from the sugar mills, sticking to the blades of grass, trees, roofs, and sidewalks."

[Alvarez Borland] "Indeed Roberto. How well I remember those gothic spires of our lovely hometown!"

[Alvarez Borland] "You seem to work slowly and deliberately compared to other writers."

[Fernández] "It must be the influence of painter, Emilio Falero. He has a beautiful painting featuring the gothic spire of Sagua and a tropical Ruth holding a bundle of sugar cane. I used to go to Emilio's apartment and watch him paint Ruth as I wrote parts of *Holy Radishes!* and waited for Ramón Guerrero to drop by. The three of us used to pick up my daughter Tatiana from school. We were a source of great embarrassment for her. It took Emilio eighteen years to finish this painting."

July 2006

CROSSING THE CREST OF FORGETTING

ANA MENÉNDEZ

Ana Menéndez's interview is quite different from the others in this volume not only because she writes from the perspective of a different generation, but also because she opted to reflect on her craft as a way of introducing herself to her readers. The daughter of Cuban exiles who settled in Los Angeles in the early 1960s, Menéndez was born in the United States in 1970. Ana saw Cuba for the first time in 1997.

In 2001, Menéndez published, In Cuba I Was a German Shepherd, _a collection of stories that has been translated into eight languages and whose title story was awarded the Pushcart Prize for short fiction. All eleven stories in this volume examine different perspectives into the nature of exile. In 2003, she published_ Loving Che, _a first novel. Menéndez's latest work presents us with a protagonist that imagines for herself a love affair with Che Guevara inspired by the photographs of the_ comandante _available in newspapers and magazines._ Loving Che _invites the reader to consider the effects of truth and illusion in the construction of the personal story or memoir. Here Menéndez takes advantage of Guevara's status as a pop icon, and uses the images of this overly recognized public figure as a prop within the story of her novel. Through all of her creative work, Menéndez comments beyond the Cuban story and reflects her own experience as a writer, a sometimes frustrated collector working with the borrowed memories of her parents. Ana Menéndez is a graduate of the NYU creative writing program where she was a_ New York Times _Fellow. Currently she resides in Miami and works as a journalist for the_ Miami Herald.

INTERVIEW

Conducted by Isabel Alvarez Borland

[Alvarez Borland] "Ana, how did you become a writer?

[Menéndez] "I never aspired to be a "writer," only to write. I'm still learning to do both, though sometimes I rather fear I've become far more expert at imitating the first. In the last year, I began a new novel, one unrelated to Cuba, at the same time that I started a new job as a columnist for the _Miami Herald._ Your questions arrived in the middle of this time and taunted me throughout. In their own strange way, they reflected the crisis of writing and nerve that I am still struggling through. To paraphrase Henry James: I work in the dark, I do what I can, I give what I have."

[Alvarez Borland] "How would you explain your craft to others?"

[Menéndez] "In the beginning, the alphabet was magic. Bowl shards found near Athens and dating back to 680 B.C. are decorated with letters, and archeologists have concluded that probably the whole alphabet ran clockwise around the bowl's perimeter—for beauty as well as protection. It was a time when writing, as a gift from the gods, was considered spiritually powerful. Egyptian rock writing has been discovered along the road network that once linked the ancient Nile cities. It was an early form of graffiti, and it was somber work. The writers, probably army recruits traversing the difficult terrain, would scratch out their names and titles on the rock and end with a reference to a god. The inscription itself was thought to be something of a talisman, a magical appeal to the ages, as well as a public and permanent reminder that one individual, by this particular name, had passed through this site—had existed! The name and the prayer would be seen by generations of travelers, enhancing the condition of the soul in the afterlife. Persian and Chinese scribes perfumed their inks with herbs and fragrant oils, in a show of respect, perhaps, not just for the scribes themselves, but for the material, for the reader, and above all for the divine nature of the script. It is easy to forget, from long association, that the alphabet is a human invention (quite different from language, which is almost as much a part of our physiology as the ability to see or process information, or digest food—something mysteriously given us). And the alphabet's invention was revolutionary—comparable perhaps only to the invention of the wheel—for it gave our human thoughts a new permanence, traced the until-then unseen face of language. In the beginning, its power must have been nearly overwhelming.

Even before there was widespread writing, there was storytelling. When memory served as record, the stories had to be easy to remember. So Homer created his metered epics about wars and wandering heroes and Herodotus embroidered his histories with fanciful, unforgettable stories about virgins and epic journeys and a king who was so lucky that when he cast his great ring into the ocean as a sign of humility, it returned to him inside the belly of a great fish. So we now are the inheritors of these two great traditions—storytelling and writing. To us today they seem inseparable, but it is good to remember their individual natures, each of them descended, in their own way, from the divine, which is another way of saying, from our image of the divine self. Language is a strong natural force, wrote the poet Víctor Hernández Cruz, and one should be prepared to deal with its psychic powers. The psychologist Wolfgang Koehler believed that memory was the indispensable human attribute, the gift that allowed us to thrive as a species. The animal, he suggested, has no memory of the day before and therefore can never learn. Oliver Sacks, though, in a series of essays on deafness, suggests that the truly indispensable human ability is language, for without it, there is no thought, no way of ordering experience. Somehow both views speak to our twin legacies of storytelling and writing—one roaring out of the seemingly infinitely expandable realm of imagination and the other tied down, boxed and ordered upon the written page. Surely the creative mind of the prealphabet storyteller differed remarkably from ours, for he wrote, as it were, on an endless but invisible surface. We are conscious now of our written selves, of the way words look on a page, of the way they're ordered and of the special linear quality of the thoughts they express. *Ulysses*, Borges said, could only have come after a long tradition of storytelling—a tradition that has become almost inseparable from the writing one."

[Alvarez Borland] "Why do you write?"

[Menéndez] "The surrealists used to ask similarly stunned writers, Why do you write? Every writer must answer this for himself—otherwise he is groping in the dark with a head full of fancy words. Do you write for fame? For money? For glory? There are so many better ways to go about achieving all those. Immortality? Madness? Because it's expected of you? God help us—to teach a lesson, make a point? The world falls apart, man is cruel, children die of hunger . . . and there you sit at a desk and . . . write? Why? 'All writers,' wrote George Orwell, 'are vain, selfish and lazy, and at the very bottom of their motives there lies a mystery.' He compared writing a book to a long bout of a painful illness. 'One would never undertake such a thing if one were not driven on by some demon whom one can neither resist nor understand.'

" 'I write because I don't know,' wrote the sly Portuguese poet Fernando Pessoa. Later, in the same book, he says, 'To write is to forget. Literature is the most agreeable way of ignoring life.' And finally: 'Perhaps the novel is a more perfect life and reality, which God creates through us. Perhaps we live only to create it. It seems that civilizations exist only to produce art and literature; words are what speak for them and remain.'

"Perhaps, too, art, the process of creating, is a sort of wakeful dreaming, as essential to life and sanity as the worlds we dream with our eyes closed. We know, through science, that human beings deprived of dreaming eventually go mad."

[Alvarez Borland] "What keeps you writing?"

[Menéndez] "Simply because when I have managed to make it work, when I have written something worthwhile, it is a delight to read it back to myself. I write for the pleasure of it, and for the pleasure it gives me to imagine that others might receive similar pleasure. Of course, as pleasures go, it's one of the difficult ones. It's this, I think, that keeps me writing. If writing were easy, if it were an automatic pleasure button, I would have long ago grown bored with it."

[Alvarez Borland] "When did you decide to become a writer?"

[Menéndez] "Because it's the only way I have of ordering experience. When I say I never aspired to be a 'writer' what I mean is that nothing of the title particularly appealed to me. But I always knew I wanted to tell stories. Again for the pleasure of it but also because telling stories helped transform memory into something I might hold and shape. Since I was very little, I loved to tell stories, especially funny ones that would make the other children laugh. Usually the stories were about my family, something my parents or my sister had done the night before and that I would then embellish for laughs. When I was about fourteen, I got it in my head that I wanted a summer job. My mother steadfastly refused. I persisted and persisted until I managed to wear her down long enough at the mall to go up to the manager of the Original Cookie Company and ask him if he was hiring. He looked me over and said that yes, he was! Then he took me to a remote part of the mall and interviewed me for a very, very long time, going over cookie-making procedures in great detail. By the time we walked back to the cookie store, my mother and grandmother had put on a tremendous show. They'd hauled out mall security and were screaming at the girls behind the counter. When they saw us, my mother immediately set upon the store manager: 'Where did you take her? Where? What kind of procedures are these? You should be ashamed of yourself.' And on and on and on, the whole Cuban show. I was absolutely mortified and I cried all the way home. I'd never been so angry at my mother. Then a strange thing happened. The next day at school, as was my usual habit, I began to tell the story at lunch. By the end of it, I had everyone in stitches. And I learned then the incredible power of stories to transform, not just others, but experience itself, even the world. One day, I had been mortified in my despair, the world unfair and out to keep me down. The next, the world was made over and an embarrassing experience recast. And all because of storytelling—the only tools I'd needed were words. It was a powerful lesson that I didn't grasp until many years later. But if I had to pick a point where I said, yes, I'm going to write, that was it."

[Alvarez Borland] "Which genre are you currently working on? Do you feel that the short story is your preferred medium? Do you write poetry? Are you working on a second novel?"

[Menéndez] "I'm working on a second novel now and hope to finish it in a few months. I do want to return to the short story. At the Book Fair this weekend, I had the pleasure of introducing a panel featuring Deborah Eisenberg, John Dufresne and Mary Gordon. And I can't tell you what a thrill it was and how much it made me pine for the short form."

[Alvarez Borland] "Do you see any links between the stories in your anthology *In Cuba I Was a German Shepherd* and *Loving Che*, your recent novel? I can think of links between the daughter in the short story *Her Mother's House* and the daughter in *Loving Che*. Was that story the seed of the novel? Will you return to the short story as a creative medium? Have you ever written poetry?"

[Menéndez] "My uncle, Dionisio Martinez is a poet and I would never dare compete with him in that department. Yes, I think the parallels between *Her Mother's House* and *Loving Che* are valid; both stories deal not just with the disconnect with history but that disconnect (and desire to repair that) within our own relationships. My own mother is very loving and steady, but she also has a very enigmatic quality to her; I've always had the sense that I will never really know her. This is not said as any kind of criticism. In fact, I don't think it's possible to ever "know" other people. Most of us scarcely know ourselves."

[Alvarez Borland] "How important is the role of fantasy in *Loving Che*? Could you discuss this question in terms of Teresa, the mother protagonist in that novel? How do you see invention as playing a consoling role to the first exile generation? How does the idea of coping with exile relate to your own generation vis a vis that of your parents?"

[Menéndez] "I suppose in a way Teresa's story is all about the sustaining power of fantasy. Growing up, that's all that Cuba was for me— a fantasy land. As I got older, I realize that, in large measure, that's all it was for my parents as well. This is not to diminish what they went through or the magnitude of their loss. But they were both very young— in their late teens and early twenties—when they left and as I've gotten older I've come to understand that many of their ideas about the island carry not only the rosy touch of nostalgia but the flattened understanding of youth."

[Alvarez Borland] "How does the idea of creating contexts for existing photos play into the figure of Guevara as pop icon in your novel? Why Guevara as the choice for Teresa's affair? Why not Castro himself? In this novel Che is really a repository of someone's fantasies . . . could he have been anyone else?"

[Menéndez] "I think you answer the question perfectly—because Guevara is the pop icon (as I've said before you don't see hip teenagers walking around with photos of the decrepit Fidel on their T-shirts). If it were a different novel, I suppose he could have been James Dean or Marilyn Monroe or some other beauty who lived fast and died young. I do think that when we pine after these kinds of people we are pining after a simpler time of our own youth."

[Alvarez Borland] "*Loving Che* explores the idea of the personal history and the role or right of inventing our personal histories. You are one of the few Cuban American writers who has not written a memoir. Is this a conscious choice?"

[Menéndez] "Oh my God! I'm only thirty-six. What on earth would I write a memoir about? Actually, my family probably offers plenty of material for a strange memoir. But I wouldn't dare, not now. In the meantime, I much prefer to invent."

[Alvarez Borland] "The idea of memory and invention permeates *Loving Che.* Teresa needs to invent and create a personal story in order to pass it on to her daughter. Can memory exist without invention? Can we trust memory?"

[Menéndez] "Memory is the first storyteller. We can "trust" it, but at our peril. I think if my parents or my grandmother were to write a memoir it would be filled with just about the same level of fantasy, give or take a few bearded men."

[Alvarez Borland] "I have completed writing an article on the photograph as aesthetic device in *Loving Che* and G. Cabrera Infante's *View of Dawn in the Tropics* (1974). Could you elaborate on how the photograph was useful to you in your novel?"

[Menéndez] "This is amazing. In fact, *View of Dawn in the Tropics* was my main model as I was writing *Loving Che.* I adore that book. I think I had read it in Miami when I was younger. But when I was living in India, I came across it in a bookstore and read it again and it just floored me. I know that people complain that it was just a bunch of outtakes. For me, it was a revelation—literature stripped down to its emotional essence. I have so much admiration for that book. When I was writing I also read a lot of photography books and, of course, Susan Sontag's well-known *On Photography.* At first I only described the photos, in the manner of GCI. Then, after reading Sontag and Barthes on the death inherent in the photograph, I realized I had to include them. A funny aside, my father read the draft of the novel in one sitting and, the following morning, he said to me: 'Chica, la verdad que me gustó la novela. Pero es necesario tener tantas fotos de ese hijo de puta?' "

[Alvarez Borland] "Why is the older generation in exile so important in your writing? If you wrote your story how would it relate to theirs?"

[Menéndez] "Good question. I'd never really thought of it that way, but I suppose you're right. Maybe I just needed to exorcize those ancients before I could get on with my own story. In fact, this novel I'm working on now begins in a very autobiographical vein. It eventually veers off into total invention, but it is interesting (I hadn't thought of this until your question) that it took two books before I could get down to my "own" story. Of course, the novel has nothing at all to do with Cuba."

February 2006

The Writers' Works

CARLOS EIRE

TREINTA Y CINCO

It was a miracle. It had to be. You can't doubt what you see. If this wasn't a miracle, then nothing else could be.

The color of the sea was changing, as if some giant brush were being applied from beneath. Or was it from above? I stared long and hard at the wild cloud-shaped rainbow in the water. There were splashes of tangerine in there too, little bits of sunset at midday, along with splashes of blood red hibiscus blossoms.

And it *moved*. The colored cloud inside the water kept moving to and fro, twisting and turning with great speed.

It was the most extraordinary thing I had ever seen, and perhaps the most beautiful. I stood there on the dock of a formerly private beach club, under the sun and the clouds, transfixed. I thought surely this was a vision sent directly from heaven—one that spoke to me without scaring me to death. All the visions I'd heard until then had been frightening: Jesus and Mary and the saints appearing to children and giving them messages that none of the adults around them would believe. I'd heard of statues in churches moving, or breathing, or talking. I'd also seen a very scary movie about a boy named Marcelino who struck up a friendship with a crucifix that came alive. The Italian priests across the street had screened that movie outdoors one night, but none of us kids dared to put our hands in front of the camera for that one, much less a middle finger. Talk about scary! The thought of Jesus coming to life on his cross and speaking to me seemed worse than Frankenstein, Wolf Man, Dracula, the Mummy, and the Creature from the Black Lagoon put together.

Twenty years later, in Lugo, not far from where my grandparents had been born, I would almost end up locked into a chapel with a similar crucifix for an entire night. The sacristan didn't see me and locked the gates while I was looking at the altarpiece. The thought of spending the whole night in there with a life-size crucifix, in total darkness, was too much for me to bear. I started yelling for someone to open the gate and get me out. My Spanish cousins laughed for days about that.

I explained to them that I had a fear of bleeding Christ figures, but that only made them laugh harder. They're probably still laughing. "Watch out, don't run into a bleeding Christ on the way," one of them said to me as I boarded a train bound for Madrid.

But this fast-moving storm of shapes and colors within the turquoise water was a good miracle. It moved and moved without stopping. Sometimes it split into two and the halves circled around to form a whole again. And in the meantime, as the halves danced with each other, the contrast between the cloud and the turquoise sea grew even more intense.

Truth, beauty, goodness, and eternity were out there dancing with the sharks and all the other creatures that feed upon one another—and sometimes upon humans—with sharp teeth or stinging venom. Love was there too, unencumbered by self-centeredness, possessiveness, doubts, or jealousy. Trouble-free love, squirming inside a wondrous sea—a sea already too beautiful to take in.

Was this a farewell vision of everything that was beautiful in my birthplace, all wrapped into one?

This was so much nicer than Window Jesus or Eye Jesus coming to life. This was grace, pure grace, out there, embodied amidst the sharks.

I don't know how long I stood there, or what I said. I had the strangest sensation of not having my feet planted on the ground. Then my brother and my friends Rafael and Manuel showed up. Eugenio was already beyond the horizon, in the United States. We all wondered out loud as to what it could be, and what *El Alocado* might have said.

Tony called out to our dad, and he came over, accompanied by Ernesto. With all of his years of experience in this life and in previous ones, Louis XVI, too, was stumped.

"That is truly amazing. *Que maravilla!*"

The miracle was not just for me, for sure. That made it even nicer.

Our noise attracted several other people.

"Parrot fish. It's a whole school of them," said the man behind me. "Hundreds and hundreds of them. Maybe thousands. I've never seen that many all at once." He explained to us all how parrot fish swam in groups and how they swarmed sometimes.

I thought of the shark pool at the aquarium and the parrot fish we had rescued. We went back about once a week, just to see him. Of course, each time we went we also stared at the shark pool. It kept getting more and more crowded.

And the diving board never shut up about Ernesto. Never. "Do it now. Push him in. Sneak up on him from behind. You'll feel so much better after you do it. Push him in, Now!"

We all stood there on that dock, watching the miracle unfold for a long, long time. It was as if we were glued to the dock and aloft at the same time. Ernesto stood there too, totally silent.

Eventually, the miracle vanished just as it had arrived. The colors moved farther and farther away, towards the horizon, northwards, riding the Gulf Stream, towards the United States. And then, suddenly, we could no longer see them.

Something else to leave behind, I thought

No amount of wishing on our part brought them back that day or any other day, and no memory has ever come close to the real thing. After staring at the sea for a while, we went home to await the *desengaño* that was sure to follow.

From *Waiting for Snow in Havana: Confessions of a Cuban Boy* (New York: Free Press, 2003), pp. 335–37.

FIRE IN MAY

for Rolando Pérez

The house is mine this morning.
No one around to mock my fire
unless I tell her, and I won't
before the fire is history
and I am warm and imperturbable.

Crackling like an autumn,
the fire consumes the summer day.
I am one, it makes two,
the only breathing things
in the chilly house.

Because I come from a country
where the trees are always on fire,
Because sons grow up and go
away and never leave you,
Because fathers grow old and go

away and never leave you.
Because mayhem is in me,
Because brothers blaze inside me,
Because I feel like midnight
when it's ten o'clock in the morning,

It has taken me two lifetimes,
several decades, many people,
to learn what a roaring fire
in May can do against the morning,
against the almost empty house.

TRISTEZA DE MAMÁ

for Isabel Álvarez Borland

It's not that she has grown smaller, stooped.
It's not that she forgets things, fiddles
endlessly or can't raise her arms without flinching.

It's not her tender stomach, bare cupboards,
squalid little house. It's not my brother's troubles
or my sister's divorce. It's not that she no longer

has a husband to nurse and lose sleep over
or that she's outlived everyone she knew
in Cuba or that her children move to towns

whose names she cannot pronounce. When I was young
and unyielding, she squeezed kindness from me
by likening her mother to a candle—*una velita*—

that was flickering out and didn't know why,
Now she's the candle that ignores the killing
breeze. She doesn't know she could outlive me too.

Weighing her down like useless wings,
it's what she doesn't know that grieves her.
Every Sunday she asks, not quite mechanically,

how I am. I say "fine" and change the subject.
The unspoken is a hurt between us. So much love
tucked away inside pleasantries and small talk,

so little chance, now, to tell her what she needs
to know. I thought my silence would spare her,
but silence spares only those who want sparing

to begin with. For the rest, Mami among them,
silence like mine wounds deeper than any knowledge.
Next time she calls, perhaps I'll tell her.

From *Scar Tissue: A Memoir* (Tempe, AR: Bilingual Press, 2005), pp. 57, 75.

DRIVING HOME

The tapestry of autumn flashes by.
The barns are silent as etchings.
The meadows glisten in the rain.
What happened to summer
and the red-haired girl who kissed me?
I was sure then everything worked,
daisies and wildcarrot in the sun,
waves of high grass lapping my kidneys.
I am driving home
and the day is darkening,
clouds touching the far hills.
An old man in suspenders
hammers on a fence despite the rain.
Despite the rain a smell
takes me years ago to childhood,
aguacero, carretera,
my father home at last
from mending fences.

From *The Floating Island* (Buffalo, NY: White Pine Press, 1999), p. 100.

RITES OF SPRING

Rain, cold morning,
a mother dead, a father aging:

numbers like steps,
numbers like wakings,

a slight green tint to the trees,
the growing tenderness of branches.

RUSSIAN DOLL

Every wall is an eye,
every eye is a wall.

I have only myself tonight
in a language inside a language

about the white sky falling
and the black earth.

MIRAGE

I move from one language
to another, I dive
from a pool of water
to a pool of dreams,
from the fire of words
to the shadow beyond them.

Pablo Medina

THE POET AS AN OLD MAN

He suffered from wisdom,
clipped wings, then became

moving stone, reluctant
fish hook, a sentence

like a missing tooth
the ascension of ablatives.

From *Points of Balance* (New York: Four Way Books, 2005), pp. 79, 55, 5, and 103.

THE SEED COLLECTOR

My father, for all the years he lived in exile,
spent afternoons, after he arrived from work,

slicing open pomegranates, *guayaba, mangos* . . .
eating of their meaty pulp, then saving the seeds.

He dried them on napkins held down by rocks
on the brick fence post, or he placed them

in plates and left them to dry in the wind
by the open kitchen window. Once I asked

what he was doing with all these seeds, and he
spoke of the rarer fruits we didn't have here

in Los Angeles, the *guanabana*, the *mamey*
mamoncillo, and *caimito* . . . fruit I remember

eating back in my Cuban childhood, but never
again, and he missed them, he said. *Las extraño.*

He dried the seeds of bonnet peppers, red,
green, *ají decachucha,* tomato seeds, habanero

chilis . . . seeds like teeth in the sun. Why
so many? And he'd stick a hand deep in his

pockets and show me a handful of them,
these seeds like gold crumbs in his hands—

He scattered them everywhere as he walked,
on people's yards, in his own, on the medians,

sidewalks, open fields, vacant lots. His mission
was to plant these seeds along his path, a memory

of his days in Cuba, our days in paradise, he said
and walked out of the house toward the setting sun.

From *90 miles: Selected and New Poems* (Pittsburgh: University of Pittsburgh Press,
2005), pp. 107–108.

THE TROUBLE WITH FROGS

It's irrational, I know, like the fear of flying
     or high places,

but irresistible nonetheless, for frogs hide
     in the luscious green

of the plantain's fronds. There, they nest
     and call out

for nuptial visitations. Become invisible against
     the corrugated tin

of the outhouse at my grandmother's house,
     then jump . . .

The neighborhood kids catch them and put them
     down my shirt

and in my pants. Who understands the terror
     of this cold and clammy

thing moving against the skin? All the time the child
     thinks there is no return

from such fear. At night beyond the mosquito net,
     they call out.

From Havana to Tallahassee,
     frogs have evolved

into this fear of a childhood not lived,
     not remembered,

but out there, in the distance, they call; they beckon
     no matter how far I travel,

I cannot escape this trouble with frogs.
     All I can do

is embrace the fact that they are there,
    like the past,

calling out, beckoning for the mind to leap.

From *In the Republic of Longing* (Tempe, AR: Bilingual Press, 1999), p. 85.

NELLIE

Nellie was glad she hadn't burned herself this time. She unplugged the sizzling iron, put the starch underneath the kitchen sink, and began folding the freshly ironed clothes. She began placing the garments in two worn suitcases which rested open-mouthed at the foot of the bed. The luggage was spotted with faded stickers, echoes of long-ago sojourns—a faceless bullfighter battling half a bull, a Tower of Pisa which no longer leaned, and a Beefeater beheaded by time. First she packed the underwear, then her blouses, followed by skirts, shirts, and slacks. On top, she carefully placed her favorite and only remaining evening gown, a royal-blue dress with brocades, pearls, and sequins. Though the dress had not felt the warmth of her flesh or heard the music and laughter of a ball room for some time, Nellie brought it out to look at it for a moment when she ironed each day. She covered the clothes with moth balls, impregnating the house with the stench of time. Then, with a suddenness born out of her small hope, she slammed the suitcase shut and with a series of vigorous kicks made the luggage disappear underneath the bed.

She licked her index finger and flicked the iron, making sure it could be stored inside the closet without risking a fire. Delfina had warned her when she was a child to be careful of fire. At the time, Delfina had been trying to light a blaze under a kettle of water to boil Nellie's father's soiled shirts while Nellie, contentedly sucking on a mango, and always the observant child, watched her.

"See the fire, little girl?" Delfina asked. "In your path there is something charred by flames. Beware of anything that burns!"

Though the two years her family had spent in the bungalow seemed like twenty, Nellie could not bring herself to unpack their bags. Her daily routine of ironing and repacking helped to keep her faith from being snuffed out altogether. She hoped that this was not lasting, not permanent.

* * *

It was hot for January. Nellie took the cardboard fan she had found on her doorstep and escaped to the porch, where it was cooler. The front of the fan depicted a Scandinavian Christ resting by a riverbank shaded by tall beech trees, and holding a black sheep in his lap. On the back, a holy message was written in incipient Spanish: PESCADOR ARRE

PIENTA DIOS ENOHADO CON USTED VEN Y TIEMPLO
PRIMERO VIVO LLAMAR REVEREND Y AMIGO AUGUSTUS B.
FENDER. OLE! SE HABLA PEQUENO ESPANOL. (FISHERMAN,
REPENT! GOD MAD WITH YOU. COME AND I SCREW FIRST
LIVING. CALL REVEREND AND FRIEND AUGUSTUS B.
FENDER. OLE! A SMALL SPANISH IS SPOKEN.) Nellie wiped the
rocking chair with a rag that hung from her left pocket and smelled of
garlic, then sat down. She started to fan and rock herself in perfect syn-
chrony. Her gaze was lost in the cane fields that surrounded the house
and stretched beyond the horizon. Her eyes became cloudy remembering
Rigoletto, attired in a light red sweater. His memory grew smaller and
smaller until it became a tiny glowing speck on the edge of her mind.

Nellie remained on the porch with her eyes fixed on the fields until
she heard the clanking and whirring of old bicycles approaching. School
was out for the day and her children, happy to be free, were coming
home. She hurried to supervise the cola-fueling operation and lament her
fate to the children. After Nelson Jr. and María-Chiara had left, burping
with satisfaction, she turned on the television, an old RCA whose picture
faded in and out every five minutes, and began watching *Donna Reed*, her
favorite show. The set did its best to produce a vision of family life, but
the fuzzy picture soon became a downpour of tiny gray dots. It forced
Nellie to rely on her ears to follow the plot. As best as she could tell,
Donna and Dr. Stone were planning a trip to Europe. Donna wanted to
go to Paris and her husband to London. In the last scenes the couple was
in the midst of an argument. They suddenly hushed because Jeff and
Mary had come home from school. Donna dried her tears with her apron
and Dr. Alex Stone welcomed the kids with a big smile.

The theme music signaled that the show was over for today and that
her husband, Nelson, would arrive in an hour. He worked as a stocker for
Rosser and Dunlap Trucks and Rigs. It was the first real job he had found
after arriving from Xawa; he held on to it, happily stagnant despite having
once been the head of his father's vast business empire. For Nelson, his
new environment was a labyrinth from which he didn't want to escape.
He was frozen like a pre-Cambrian bug in a drop of amber.

Nellie, wearing her flaps, padded into the kitchen to prepare dinner.
She walked in as if facing a firing squad. A note from Nelson was held
in place on the refrigerator door by a magnet in the shape of an angry
green worm holding an M-19 on its right shoulder and a tricolor flag
with a lone star in its left. The note suggested: "After placing the pots,
pans, and skillets on the burners, make sure to turn the burners on."
Nellie usually forgot that final detail.

From *Holy Radishes!* (Houston, TX: Arte Público Press, 1995), pp. 7–9.

TRAVELING FOOLS

All the men on my father's side of the family have been mad in one way or another. There was my great uncle Panchito, who joined the communist party in 1934 when it was a nothing party of dreamers only to quit in 1965 when the party officially denied him permission to fly to the moon. He could have turned all those years of underground meetings and patriotic songs into something, he could have cashed in and finally helped his family. Instead, he spent the last years of his life writing angry letters to the Ministry for Travel and Culture, arguing that if the Russians could send a flea bitten dog to space, certainly the Cubans ought to be able to send a loyal party monkey to the moon. His latter letters were scrupulously ignored. And he ended up dying in a rented room in his niece's apartment, fighting her until the last for the right to his homemade rum. In the end, the party would not even allow him to be buried in the Patriot's cemetery.

There was a cousin named Severino who hanged himself from a banyan one Spring morning after a passing traveler told him there was buried treasure on the other side of the mountain. Severino, who had never even traveled beyond the swamp. As a boy he had been happy to sit out by a stream for hours and launch paper boats, waiting until one disappeared downstream before sending out the next one. The passing traveler was never seen or spoken of again until many years later, miners discovered a silver vein hard against the mountain. The townspeople, in an act of remembering common to those times, named the mine after Severino. And, most recently, there was my grandfather Solomon, who, as an exile in Miami, one cool winter morning began digging a tunnel beneath the azaleas with the intention of surfacing someday in Havana.

The first two stories have been passed down through the family and I can't vouch for the truth in them. The last one I saw with my own eyes and can tell you that nothing can match the image of a shirtless old man with a dream. He had it all planned out, my grandfather did, for he was a man who took great pride in logic and the scientific method. Before he even began to dig, he filled a great many notebooks with figures that explained precisely how many shovels of dirt it would take, how wide the hole should be, and how many years would have to pass before he finally broke through the sand on the other side.

I was only eight years old then, but sometimes after school I helped him dig. My grandfather had barely made it under the property line when his project ended abruptly. It seems the Americans on the block had called the police to say the old man next door was digging what appeared to be a mass grave. It took some days to sort out the complications that followed. But my grandfather never recovered from his disappointment. He sunk into a deep sadness that didn't lift even after my father, also prone to making mathematical calculations, pointed out a mistake in his figures and said that it actually would have taken 16,742 years to dig to Havana.

But perhaps the most tragically brilliant of this mad lineage was Matias Padron, a third great-cousin of my father's through marriage by way of his mother. The family connection is tenuous, I know. But I feel a certain pride in claiming Matias, for his story has passed into the island lore of Cuba; his story is also our story.

Matias, so it is told, was not a very big man. This is also true of most of the men on my father's side of the family. But unlike most of the men, who tend to make up in width for what they lack in height, Matias was slightly built all around. He was, it is well known, even smaller and thinner than his wife, who scandalously abused her advantage to keep Matias timid and soft-spoken at home. Matias didn't seem to mind this and often played along good-naturedly, now and then repeating a favorite phrase he had heard about the greatness of a man being measured not from the ground to his head, but from the distance of his head to God. The literal-minded took this to be an even greater disadvantage. But Matias knew what he was talking about.

Since he had turned 18, Matias had been running the post office in Santiago de Cuba. By the time he was forty years old, he had browsed twenty-two Christmas catalogs from El Encanto, leafed through dozens of Bohemias and read several hundred letters of love, the great majority of which were not between husbands and wives. But the task that took up most of his time and the one, that by all accounts, he adored above all the others, was predicting the weather. In those years, the postmaster also ran the local telegraph service. This meant that the postmaster, in addition to being the telegrapher, was also a sort of informal meteorologist as the telegraph, for the first time in the Caribbean, was being used to give advanced warnings of storms developing off shore. It was a duty that all the previous postmasters had taken very seriously. But none had thrown themselves into it with anything approaching the passion that Matias brought.

Matias and his wife lived above the post office in a house that, according to tradition, was paid and kept up by the municipality for the use of the postmaster and his family. It was a large house, two stories, with a wide balcony that wrapped around all four sides. But as Matias and his wife had never had children, vast areas of the house remained dark and unused. It was in one such sealed room that Matias established a small office. When he wasn't below in the post office reading other people's mail or receiving telegraphs about the latest events around the world, Matias was in his little office trying to predict the weather. He had all matter of instruments, barometers, thermometers. Probably, it wasn't too different from the type of things amateurs keep the world over. But Matias's secrecy about his room, even from his wife, soon led to talk in the town that Matias was an alchemist dealing in nefarious activities. It was the first chatter about Matias's supposed eccentricity. And just because it prefigured the extraordinary act he was about to embark on, it doesn't mean that it was necessarily a fair assessment. At that moment, I believe that Matias had truly developed a scientific interest in the weather. After all, not too many years had passed since a hurricane had devastated Varadero, cutting the narrow peninsula in half until both oceans met over the sand. Matias, I think, was trying to save Santiago from the next cataclysm.

He ordered all manner of new equipment from New York and tore at the packages when they arrived weeks later. Soon he built an observation deck on the roof and in clear weather began sending up weather balloons. At first, the balloons didn't carry anything—Matias merely used them to calculate wind speeds and air pressure. But as technology improved and radio transmitters began to gain wider currency, Matias arranged for bigger and bigger balloons that could carry more and more equipment. Soon he was launching balloons as big as oil drums carrying thermometers, barometers, humidity detectors all wired to a radio that could send the information back to Matias in his little room.

Every Friday, he posted the results on the front door of the post office as well as a small assessment of what the coming week's weather was likely to be. He was right more often than he was wrong and except for a few lapses when, for example, he announced that yesterday "rain had been very heavy" (something the townspeople could know well enough without consulting any instruments other than their memories), the people grew to respect his forecasts.

Cuba had prospered in those years and along with it, Santiago, and along with Santiago, Matias. The memory of hunger was fading. Children grew healthy. And Matias entered middle age in the prime of health. Even the hurricanes that had assaulted Cuba the previous decade seemed to ease and everyone everywhere seemed relaxed and content as if the more malevolent workings of the world had finally passed them by.

Matias continued to go into his office every afternoon and every Friday he emerged with the forecast for the following week. And of course he also continued to send up his balloons, each more elaborate than the last. The weather was not always perfect, but it was predictable. Soon everyone knew the rains would come in August and the heaviest thunder would be reserved for the late afternoon, when the sun began to dip low in the sky. By October, the skies would clear and the blue days return. Winters, whether Matias said so or not, were generally dry and pleasant.

Some nights, couples out for a walk noticed a dark figure above the post office—Matias with his hands on the railing looking up into the sky. But otherwise, few people paid much attention to Matias or his forecasts, anymore. They met him once a week, sometimes touched their fingers lightly to his when he handed them their mail and that was that. It seemed there was nothing left to fear.

There are eddies that develop in time, places where histories converge, and individuals caught inside the current find themselves suddenly unable to act for themselves. Perhaps this is what happened to Matias. Maybe everything that followed was as inevitable as history. I have to say things like this because there is really no other explanation for what came to pass. Outside of a family connection, there was nothing in Matias's character to suggest madness. The reports that came out later pointed out that there was no history of despondency. And nothing in the days preceding the event gave anyone any reason to believe that Matias had suffered a sudden depression. The weather, moreover, had been pleasantly uneventful, with, as Matias himself had noted, an abundance of bright days somewhat unusual for springtime.

And yet, the truth is this: One morning Matias was handing a stack of letters to Consuelo Perez and the next he was floating high above Santiago, his office chair dangling beneath four giant weather balloons with him in it.

Santiago had been the first city in Cuba to be linked by telegraph to the rest of the Caribbean. Santiago had been the first city to pioneer the use of observation balloons during war time. The telegraph had connected Cuba to the world, but in the end, the country learned it could not stand alone. Its prosperity and health were forever tethered to history and geography. Did Matias sense this? In those last years he had developed a habit of linking ideas one to the next until he'd convinced himself that there was an inherent logic running through the universe, governing even the impossible. When his own mind finally became untethered, where did it fly to?

His wife was the first to notice Matias had gone. She ran up to the observation deck and when she saw him just clearing the tops of the palms she began to shout at him, You insolent madman, you flying fool! Her shouting brought out a handful of people whose shouting brought out still more people. And soon the whole town was pointing at the sky where Matias floated, sometimes rising suddenly and sometimes hanging in the air, swaying from side to side just over the tree line, every second becoming a little bit smaller in the distance. A few of the men started off after him and when they were directly under his path began shouting instructions at him, in the venerable Cuban tradition: Cut one of the balloons! Jump now, the fronds will break your fall! When you make it over the swamp let the helium out very slowly! They continued to run and shout even after it became clear that Matias was not coming back. One of the men said that just when he was becoming so small that one could hardly make out his person, Matias glanced down at the others and there was a wide, white smile on his face. He was like a saint or a martyr, the man said. And for days, the man could talk of nothing else but Matias's calm happy gaze as he floated away from Santiago forever.

Matias seemed to know right where he was going. All those years of tracing wind patterns had given him a pilot's confidence. It was April, when the winds blow east to west. Before an hour was out he was a tiny speck out over the sea and then he was impossible to make out in the haze. After a while most of the people stopped searching the sky for Matias and began walking back to their homes. A few gathered in silence outside the post office. Matilde locked herself in the house and didn't emerge until the governor arrived two weeks later to take a report. Some days later, the police came for his papers. They carted off hundreds and hundreds of notebooks filled with strange drawings and algebraic calculations. But among the more curious of his possessions was a stuffed owl and a rare Cuban tern preserved in a bottle of formaldehyde.

Today, people in Cuba still say of an elusive fellow, "He vanished like Matias Padron." I think of Matias now and then. I am also a traveler. And nowadays after I have taken off my shoes and put them back on, after I have retrieved my naked laptop from the conveyor and had my purse rifled through, after I have emerged safely on the other side of the security cabal, I like to take a seat up close to the windows and watch the planes come and go. How generous of airport architects to design such large windows. And how good of the staff to keep them so clean and shiny. Coming upon these portals is like stumbling onto a new and intricate explanation of the possible.

I sit in one of the soft functional chairs and watch the planes land and I watch them lift off from the earth. And each time it seems like a miracle. There are so many planes flying in so many different directions that it is difficult to follow a single one. Too often, the flight path takes them beyond my line of vision. But now and then a plane will take off just so and fly straight out in view of all the airport, fly off to that point that everyone calls infinity but is really just the limits of our perception.

I'll follow the plane until it is nothing and know that soon I will be on one just like it. And I wonder, do we still know what it's like to dream about the other side of the mountain? At what point does one cross the crest of forgetting? And this is when I think of Matias, who breached the space of the known for nothing more than a glimpse of the white-blind city on the other side.

Austin, Fall 2004

Part III

The Philosophers

III THE PHILOSOPHERS

JORGE J. E. GRACIA

The contrast between the artists and writers whose interviews are included in this volume, on the one hand, and the philosophers, on the other, is quite sharp. The work of the writers in particular is deeply informed by Cuba and the experience of exile, diaspora, and memory. The stories the writers narrate, often autobiographical, reveal a sense of loss and a desire for recovery and wholeness even when not explicitly inspired by the Cuban experience. This is echoed in the work of some artists as well. The sense of separation from one's culture and nation, the idealization of the land, the sorrow associated with loneliness and alienation, and a nostalgic longing for a lost paradise are commonplaces in the work of the writers and artists. But this is not so with the philosophers. None of the work of the philosophers included here—Oscar Martí, Ofelia Schutte, Ernesto Sosa, and Jorge Gracia (the writer of this introduction)—displays any of these characteristics. We seem to be oblivious to the concerns present in most of the work of the writers and artists. Why?

Is it because two of us (Martí and Sosa) came to the United States before the Castro Revolution and cannot be considered exiles in the strict sense of the term? Is it because all of us have conducted our professional careers outside Miami? Is it because philosophy seeks to be universal and therefore immune to the particularity of memory and nostalgia? Or is it because our special subfields within philosophy do not lend themselves to the concerns writers and artists voice?

Only one of us, Schutte, is at all interested in Cuba in her work, and her interest in José Martí is rather devoid of the kind of reverence and emotional involvement that characterizes the work of some Cubans who have written about him. The work of Sosa lacks any reference to Cuba or issues of exile, diaspora, and memory. Martí's main work is on Latin-American philosophy, and particularly on Mexican philosophy, rather than on Cuban or Cuban-American thought. And although some of my work involves social identity, ethnicity, and nationality, none of it has had, to this day, anything directly to do with Cuba or the experience of exile, diaspora, and memory.

The philosophers seem to live in a different world from that of Cuban-American artists and writers. If they suffer from diasporic maladies and engage in bouts of nostalgia, this is not reflected in what they do professionally. One possible explanation for this phenomenon is the professional context in which they work, which is very different from the philosophical environment in Cuba. Technical philosophy, the sort of philosophy one associates with Aristotle, Kant, or Wittgenstein, has never flourished in Cuba, but this is precisely the kind that is practiced and rewarded by the philosophical establishment in this country. The history of Cuban philosophy understood in this sense is very limited. Perhaps the only author who could qualify as a philosopher of this sort is Enrique José Varona (1849–1933). But his thought, influenced by positivism, is not original, and Varona quickly gave up the attempt at developing it further in this vein, becoming what is more popular in the island, an essayist, *un pensador*.

Philosophers who live in the United States and have Cuban roots fall into two groups. The first includes what might be called "exiled Cuban philosophers." These philosophers were trained in Cuba and moved to the United States after 1959, but it would be difficult to classify them as Cuban-American philosophers except insofar as they may hold American citizenship. The case with the second group is different; it might be possible to claim that they are truly Cuban-American philosophers. They fall into three subgroups: children of Cubans who emigrated to the United States before 1959 and were trained as philosophers here; Cubans who left the island after 1959 but were young enough to be trained as philosophers in the United States; and children of Cuban exiles who grew up in the United States and have become philosophers. Of the ones interviewed here, Martí and Sosa fall in the first category, and Schutte and I on the second. All four of us live outside Miami, but Schutte lives in Florida.

The members of the exiled group found themselves in a different culture and isolated from its mainstream. Language is very important in philosophy, and members of this group had no easy way of developing the linguistic skills in English necessary for them to join the American philosophical community. In addition, their preference for writing essays rather than technical articles or treatises, made it impossible for them to find university or college positions except in Spanish or modern languages departments, which further isolated them from the American community of philosophers. Some of them continued to write essays in Spanish, but no one outside a very small circle of Cuban Americans has paid any attention to them, either in this country or outside it.

The lack of a tradition and even interest in technical philosophy among Cuban philosophers in general is reflected in the relative dearth of Cuban Americans who have chosen philosophy as a career in the United States. Except for a handful, no Cuban Americans have succeeded in securing jobs in PhD-granting philosophy programs in this country. Moreover, very few of them have shown any interest in issues related to identity and diaspora. Indeed, if we apply the criterion that some scholars use in literature, according to which one cannot qualify as Cuban American unless the work is informed by the Cuban experience, then there are no Cuban-American philosophers to speak of. But this is a too narrow understanding of what it means to be a Cuban-American philosopher, although it could perhaps be applied when speaking about a possible Cuban-American philosophy.

Indeed, it is quite obvious that all the philosophers chosen to be interviewed for this volume have in some ways been influenced in their professional lives by the fact that they are Cuban Americans, although not in the same ways or to the same extent. For some the influence has extended to preoccupations raised by issues of personal and group identity, for others it has translated into an interest in certain types of philosophy and philosophers, and still for others it has been a concern for the philosophical development of what the philosophers consider to be their ethnic kin, even if this is understood in different ways and broadly.

At the personal level, Ofelia Schutte is perhaps the one philosopher in the group whose work reveals more clearly a concern for issues related to her personal identity. She has had to struggle intellectually with the fact that she is a woman, a Cuban, a Hispanic, a Latino, an American, and a philosopher. All these "identities" create tensions, and as she argues in her work, need to be "negotiated": the relation and relative places of these identities in her experience need to be worked out.

How does she feel about, and how does she deal with, the pressures that these identifies bring to bear in her life and experience? As a philosopher she is pressured by the universalist claims of the discipline; as a woman she has to deal with the subtle discrimination that has replaced the former, explicit discrimination against women in various paths of life; as a Hispanic she is drawn by the Iberian heritage that ties her to Spain and its history; as a Latina, she needs to respond to the grassroots claims of other Latinos/as in this country; as an American she is bound by the laws and ideas of the United States Constitution; and as Cuban she feels the influence of her former life in the island, family ties, Cuban community, the Cuban culture, the political struggles of the Cuban people, and the frequently frustrated search for freedom for which Cubans have yearned throughout their history. This has led her to study Cuban thought and to visit Cuba repeatedly, establishing a dialogue with Cubans in Cuba so as to understand their point of view.

Rather than discarding some of these various identities, Schutte has tried to put them together coherently. She identifies what is important and characteristic in these for her to live an integrated life, and in doing so has elaborated a model for others to follow who are subjected to the same pressures.

Next to Ofelia, I am the philosopher of the group included here that most clearly has found inspiration in diasporic experience, but my work is intended to provide a metaphysical model of social identities in general. Cuban identity is present and surfaces in many ways in my life, but it has not been a professional focus for me. My work on identity began with an interest in Hispanic/Latino identities. I have not found in Cuban thought a source of philosophical inspiration, and have turned instead to the history of Hispanic thought. Even my interest in Latin-American philosophy was the result of a fluke, as explained in the interview.

I have never lived in Miami and have generally been insulated from the Cuban community there. I feel Cuban in some ways, but Cuba does not surface in my work. Still, the Cuban experience has not been lost, and the memories of the island, my departure, and all that it entailed have remained in the background. This is important for my work on social identities because it has led me to understand their strong personal dimensions. Social identities belong to groups of people, not to individuals, and it is in communities that they are found. For those of us who never lived in Cuban enclaves in this country, the community is one of memory.

Memory eventually led me back to Cuba in other ways. I had planned to become an architect in Cuba and also had a strong interest in art. These interests have not diminished over the years, but when I decided to take art seriously and build a collection, it was to Cuban-American art that I turned. I could justify this decision in many ways. For example, it was easier to buy Cuban-American art of top quality than mainstream art of top quality because it is less expensive. Moreover, Cuban-American art has experienced an incredible explosion similar in many ways to the well-known explosion in popular music. Still, a major factor for collecting this art is precisely that the art is Cuban: doing it takes me back to the foundations of my first ethnic and national identity, and with it I am giving life to memories that otherwise would lay dormant. Alberto Rey's moody painting of *El Morro* on the cover of this book brings back images of my departure, with all that it meant and still means. Collecting Cuban-American art has also helped me establish a relationship with the Cuban-American community that I never had, and helped me explore issues of exile, diaspora, identity, and memory. It has also opened avenues for the experience of these things not just in the Cuban context, but for all humans who have experienced alienation, displacement, and cultural shock.

Oscar Martí presents us with a different situation. He did not come to the United States as an exile in the early sixties. His family came to this country seeking opportunity, like so many other immigrants. But like me, his professional career took a turn related to identity based on a fortuitous event, the desire of one of his teachers to develop the study of Latin-American philosophy in this country. This teacher was a historian, and therefore must have become aware of the gap that the study of the history of philosophy in this country had with respect to Latin America.

Martí picked up the challenge, as he explains in the interview, and promptly became focused on Mexican philosophy. He could have gone back to his more general interests in biology, for example—nothing stopped him from doing so—but instead he joined the very small group of scholars interested in Latin-American thought in this country. Was this in part because he needed to work out the issues of identity that he experienced as a Cuban living in the United States? Not much of his work relates to the history of Cuban thought, but in Mexican philosophy he found a rich repository of philosophical speculation devoted to issues of identity. The great Mexican philosophers of the twentieth century, inspired by Spanish authors such as José Ortega y Gasset and José Gaos, had laid the bases for these discussions.

Ernesto Sosa's interview makes clear that he is the member of the philosophers included here who least of all has related his professional work to anything dealing with his background as Cuban, Latin American, Hispanic, or Latino. He works primarily in a technical field of philosophy, epistemology. Yet, Sosa has been a tireless promoter of Latin American philosophers, although he is not a promoter, or a student, of Latin American philosophy. Nor is he concerned with issues of social identity. His work deals with universal questions that he believes have universal value, but he has spent much of his professional life helping Latin American philosophers come to this country to receive what he regards as proper training and he has also traveled extensively in Latin America giving talks and promoting rigor and care in philosophical thinking.

Why has he done this? Sosa came to the United States at a young age and went through a standard education similar to that of other Americans. He worked with people who had no interest in Latin American philosophy or issues of social identity. The questions that Schutte and I have raised and explored do not appear in his philosophical horizon, and he has embraced completely the universalistic claims of the philosophical discipline. Yet, he has not forgotten the Cuban-American and Latin American communities, lending them practical support in the philosophical profession.

In closing, something must be said about the reason for the choice of philosophers included here. Three factors were particularly important. The first is the prominence that these philosophers have achieved in their areas of expertise. Although not all four have the same stature in the philosophical profession, the work of all four has been recognized in the fields of their expertise: Schutte in feminism, Latin American philosophy, and issues of cultural identity; Sosa in epistemology and metaphysics; Martí in Latin-American and Mexican philosophy; and in my case in history of philosophy, metaphysics, historiography, and social identity.

The second has to do with diversity; it is important to have voices that represent different perspectives and circumstances in the Cuban-American community. It was particularly important to include a female voice in the group and also to have representatives from the two main groups of Cuban Americans in the United States: immigrants and exiles. Schutte represents the female voice, she and I are the exiles, and Sosa and Martí are the immigrants.

Finally, it was desirable to have a range in the philosophical work and approach used: historians, systematic philosophers, representatives from both the analytic and Continental traditions, and philosophers who have somehow integrated issues of identity into their work and those who have not. For only by looking at a wide spectrum could the volume provide a representative panorama of the ways in which Cuban-American philosophers have dealt with the challenges posed by their identity, diaspora, and memories.

CUBAN, HISPANIC, AND LATINA?

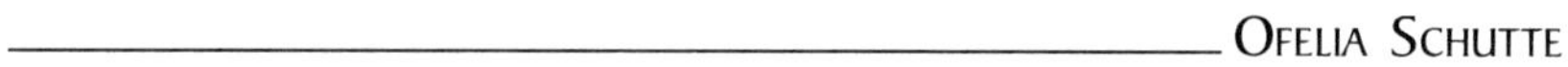

OFELIA SCHUTTE

Ofelia Schutte was born in 1946 and came to the United States in 1961. She graduated from Yale and has been a Bunting Fellow at Radcliffe. After having taught for many years at the University of Florida at Gainesville, she moved to the University of South Florida at Tampa, where she chaired Women's Studies and is currently Professor of Women's Studies and of Philosophy. Schutte has served as Chair of the American Philosophical Association Committee for Hispanics in Philosophy and is a leader among Hispanic women philosophers.

Schutte works in feminist theory, Continental philosophy, Latin-American philosophy, the philosophy of culture, and Cuban thought. She has recently undertaken a series of studies in the thought of José Martí that explore the foundations of his philosophical views. Her work on Nietzsche is the first that adopts a feminist perspective. Schutte is also the first North-American philosopher to attempt a comprehensive study of cultural identity in Latin America. She maintains close contacts with philosophers in Latin America and frequently visits Cuba and other Latin American countries.

Main works: Cultural Identity and Social Liberation in Latin American Thought *(1993) and* Beyond Nihilism: Nietzsche Without Masks *(1984). She is also author of numerous articles including: "Negotiating Latina Identities" (2000); "Cultural Alterity: Cross-Cultural Communication and Feminist Thought in North-South Dialogue" (1998); and "A Critique of Normative Heterosexuality: Identity, Embodiment, and Sexual Difference in Beauvoir and Irigaray" (1997).*

INTERVIEW

Conducted by Oscar Martí

[Martí] "Ofelia, let me begin by asking how you became interested, attracted to philosophy?"

[Schutte] "As soon as I took undergraduate courses in philosophy, it was an instant hit. However, it took a long time before it became a career choice. In those days, our recent arrival in the U.S. and the death of my father in Miami made personal circumstances quite difficult for me.

212

But eventually I went on to Miami University of Ohio for a master's degree in philosophy and to Yale (on a fellowship) for the PhD."

[Martí] "Who were your mentors at Yale?"

[Schutte] "My principal mentor was George Schrader, a Kant scholar. I owe a lot to him; he was very supportive. He especially encouraged me to develop a feminist perspective in philosophy, which, considering it was the 1970s, was fantastic."

[Martí] "Your dissertation was . . ."

[Schutte] ". . . on Nietzsche."

[Martí] "What attracted you to Nietzsche?"

[Schutte] "Lots of things. I had majored in English literature as an undergraduate and I had also taken a master's degree in English before I took the master's in philosophy, so I came to philosophy from an interest in literature and aesthetics. Nietzsche fits into this perfectly because of his literary work. He is such a pleasure to read as a writer. But philosophically, I was especially interested in the transvaluation of all values and the special approach to culture that Nietzsche takes, placing moral values in a cultural perspective. Even then, I was very interested in a cultural approach to philosophy, although I did not conceptualize it as such. My book on Nietzsche was not the dissertation; it was new work that I did after I started teaching. I began with Nietzsche's Apollonian-Dionysian distinction in *The Birth of Tragedy*; I was young at the time and I was very captivated by that."

[Martí] "Then, Latin American philosophy? How was that trajectory?"

[Schutte] "At Yale, Spanish did not qualify as a foreign language requirement in philosophy. It was assumed that no philosophy of significance was written in Spanish. On graduation in 1978 I accepted a job at the University of Florida in Gainesville, which has an outstanding program in Latin American Studies. In my second year, I was awarded a Lilly Postdoctoral Teaching Fellowship for which I obtained release time to develop and teach two new courses. That's when I developed my first undergraduate course in Latin American philosophy, which subsequently was made a permanent part of the curriculum. In 1981, Florida State University in Tallahassee hosted the Inter-American Congress of Philosophy. By this time I had already been teaching Latin American philosophy for a couple of years. At the Congress, I met Leopoldo Zea and Enrique Dussel for the first time. My North American colleagues kept asking me, what are the Latin American philosophers saying in the Spanish-speaking sessions? I found myself translating back and forth in a purely personal way. I vowed to myself that once my book on Nietzsche was completed, my next project would be on Latin American philosophy."

[Martí] "You were also in Mexico, at a Latin American Studies Association conference. Was that earlier?"

[Schutte] "That was a few months later, in 1982. Was that where we met?"

[Martí] "Yes, it was in Mexico, and we, sort of, rubbed shoulders in Tallahassee, but we were going in different directions. It was in Mexico that we started talking—it was a fascinating discussion. Now, you were actually teaching already."

[Schutte] "Right."

[Martí] "Then, you slowly but surely also moved toward gender issues."

[Schutte] "My book on Nietzsche was already feminist because of the type of reading I was doing in Nietzsche's social and political thought, and the approach I took to metaphysics, which questioned the mind/body dualism. When I was done with the book I was so happy—writing it was, by the way, a major effort. I didn't just write in the abstract; I traveled to Switzerland and Germany. I followed some of Nietzsche's steps. I actually stayed overnight at the Nietzsche Haus in Sils Maria, and I walked the trail where he claims to have had the vision of the eternal recurrence. It was in the Alps in this solitude, as Nietzsche describes it, that I was thinking so hard, trying to put myself in Nietzsche's shoes and trying to understand philosophy from his life experience that I told myself, 'This is too far removed from my concrete cultural situation: I'm a woman and I am Latin American and I'm Cuban, so I think that, once I'm done with this book, I want to write about women and about Latin America.' So it was right in the middle of doing the work on Nietzsche, right in the middle of writing *Beyond Nihilism*, that I decided the next time it was going to be closer to my own identity. After this, I got a Fulbright to go to Mexico and that started the next phase of my career."

[Martí] "You were in Mexico during the earthquake."

[Schutte] "Yes, it was traumatizing, and it influenced my philosophical outlook in yet another way. The society reacted to this tragedy, in a way completely differently from the way that say, people react or social institutions react in the United States or even in Cuba (from what I remembered in relation to hurricanes). I realized, then, the impact of culture on social being, as it were—the major differences that are evident in the reaction to natural phenomena given different cultural environments. So, again, this idea that culture is pervasive through everything influenced my work on Latin American philosophy. It became more oriented toward issues of cultural identity than I had even imagined at the beginning of my project. That's when I also had this incredible need to go back to visit Cuba because I had left Cuba at the age of fourteen in

1960 and I had not gone back. It hadn't been a burning issue for me as long as I was working on Nietzsche or was engaged in European philosophy. But when I started thinking through the issue of cultural identity in Latin America, I asked myself how could I even write about this without touching base with my own origins. Over a quarter century had passed, my life is finite, and I could wait no longer. That's when I began a kind of personal quest to go back to visit Cuba and to reestablish some cultural roots with the place of my origins."

[Martí] "How did it feel when you went back to Cuba?"

[Schutte] "Oh, incredible. It is so difficult to describe because before going back, especially after such a long time, people told me that I would break down crying the minute I set foot on Cuban soil at the airport. They all said that's what happened to them when they returned. But I wanted to be very cognitive about it. I thought, 'No, I'm going to come intellectually prepared: I am going to read about Cuban history,' just read some of the things that I had missed in my upbringing. So I read some of the texts on the Revolution. I studied some Marxists. I said, 'I am going to go intellectually prepared to face a place that's different from the one I left and try to at least understand intellectually a little bit of that historical development.' But neither of these two things happened: I did not break down crying when I set foot at the airport and all of my cognitive preparation went by the wayside as well. What happened was that as I was stepping off the plane and I was walking toward the airport terminal, the memory of the last steps I took going toward the airplane that led me out of Cuba became more and more vibrant. And I realized that these feelings had been repressed in my memory for over twenty-six years. I couldn't remember a thing of this until I was right there, at that moment. Then on the bus from the airport to Havana I recognized the road and the landscape, and I realized that somewhere in me I had kept all of these memories but that I wouldn't have known it unless I'd gone back."

[Martí] "That certainly influenced your philosophical outlook in deep ways."

[Schutte] "I think that it helps me as a writer. I have never written much about Cuba, but I think I'm at the point in my life when I'm allowed to do it. I've written about Latin America and from time to time I've written about José Martí. I have traveled to many congresses in Cuba and now I'm doing some individual research projects there. But I always thought, 'No, I'm too biased somehow. I'm too emotionally connected to this to be able to write something from the kind of philosophical distance that I think I need as a philosopher.' I think that now that I am getting older, and having had many experiences, I'm getting to the point where I will be able to do it."

[Martí] "Now, when you left Cuba, you came as a resident to the United States—you were not a refugee or an exile."

[Schutte] "That's right. Because we came so early on, I don't even think the program for political refugees had been instituted yet."

[Martí] "You came in 1960?"

[Schutte] "Yes, in April of that year. My dad was a doctor—and we were not involved in the previous political regime or anything. He was able to obtain U.S. residence papers and from the Cuban government a permit to reside abroad temporarily, so we left legally. We left with something like twenty-six bags—we took no money with us because you were not allowed to bring much money to the U.S. if you had U.S. residency papers. But we were allowed to bring some things. We brought the oddest collection of things, like our radio—things that you could easily buy here. I don't understand it, but, anyway, we brought them."

[Martí] "You didn't have to leave it, so you weren't forced or obliged to leave everything behind—you were able to bring some of your own personal belongings."

[Schutte] "Yes, we brought many personal belongings with us. Whatever was allowed. Not to say it was easy, by any means. My parents bore the burdens of translocation and economic survival."

[Martí] "Do you think that may have influenced your attitude toward Cuba when you returned?"

[Schutte] "Yes, the main influence is this: my dad sold the home where we were living to somebody else before we left Cuba and gave the money to his mother—the money he made out of the sale. So I did not feel that I had been stripped of my home by the state. At age fourteen I got caught up adapting to how to live in the United States. There was so much to learn."

[Martí] "Now let's go back to the vicissitudes that you've experienced—difficulties with your department, the discipline, questions of identity, particularly in the area of Latin American philosophy or feminism. How have you negotiated your own standing as a Latin American philosopher with your department or in a discipline that's relatively conservative like philosophy?"

[Schutte] "That's a really good question. In my own mind, I don't have the identity of a marginalized person. I believe that what I'm doing is really important and I don't see feminism as something that needs to be condemned to a margin. I don't see Spanish as something that needs to be placed at the margins of philosophical languages. And I am educated, I have had a really good education. Not everyone has the opportunity to go to an Ivy League university and get a PhD. So I think that I was very self-assured about my justification for doing philosophy by the time I entered the profession. Then I noticed as time went on that certain pressures were placed on the department in Gainesville to acquire more prestige, and people thought prestige meant doing only logic and analytic philosophy of a certain kind. I couldn't understand this—what, 'a Fulbright fellowship, isn't that prestige?' or the Bunting fellowship I got later on in my life to do feminist work at Radcliffe? Isn't that prestige? I thought this was a contradiction. It was a double message: on the one hand, they said, 'We want prestige'; on the other hand, they said, 'We don't want feminism. We don't want Latin American philosophy—or rather, it's not as if we don't want it but it should be located elsewhere. Teach it to non-majors.' So, I fought a long and hard battle to claim that this is just as integral to philosophy as anything else—not that I was believed! And I was an officer in many APA committees. I served on the International Cooperation Committee, on the Program Committee for the Eastern Division, on the Committee for Hispanics/Latinos. When the APA Committee on Hispanics was founded, I was one of the original members, and later I served as its chair. I was present at APA meetings where I could see this debate going on, people asking, 'What offers us prestige and what doesn't?' I participated in many efforts within the APA to make it more pluralistic, shall we say, or more multicultural? And so, I didn't think that my fields of specialization condemned me to the margin, but in the department where I was working in Gainesville this seemed to be the prevalent point of view of those in positions of authority. In 1999, I was offered and accepted the chair of Women Studies, at the University of South Florida in Tampa. For five years I enjoyed the freedom of teaching feminism in Women's Studies but I missed doing philosophy in the sense of its broader cultural scope. And I am very fortunate now at the University of South Florida in Tampa, where currently I am working again in a philosophy department, but in this case one that is happy to have me, and where I feel part of an inclusive philosophical community."

[Martí] "So, your essay on identity—also the focus of a book—has been informed by your academic experiences. The essay is quite profound. How do you see the stages that are occurring here, having developed in so many fascinating ways? We take pride in you: 'Gee, there's Ofelia again!' We're very, very proud of you. And do you see any directions or guide, or is this like the bend in the river, that you still don't know what's coming?"

[Schutte] "I have always surprised myself a little bit. This may be a Nietzschean side of me. I wrote *Beyond Nihilism* because I thought that there was a gap in the scholarship that I knew, with effort, I could fill. I was carving a path for myself and it turned out that I wrote what I think was the first feminist book on Nietzsche in the United States. The book was a little ahead of its time, because a few years later there was a whole generation of female Nietzsche scholars who are feminists. My second book, *Cultural Identity and Social Liberation in Latin American Thought*, was a little bit like this as well. I wrote this without a model either. In Latin America, some philosophers had built this tradition, but their works were not accessible in English translation. There was a rich tradition in the U.S. of interdisciplinary Latin American Studies, but not philosophy. Among senior philosophers, Jorge Gracia had done very important editorial work in this field. But I don't know of any Latin American or Latino philosopher working in a philosophy department at that time in the United States who had authored a book on the cultural tradition, cultural identity, and social/political philosophy in Latin America. So, again, there was no particular model. And I was gratified to see that a few years later there is an expanding group of Latina/o and Latin American philosophers in the United States. They are all writing their own works, they are developing the field, and this gives me much gratification. Currently I have another book project in mind—whether it materializes or not, we will see. But, again, it's in totally uncharted waters. It has to do with postcolonial thought, Latin American philosophy, and feminism and I am at the very beginning of putting it together."

[Martí] "So, in a sense, you are a pathfinder. This is a role that traditionally is said to belong to males and not to women, and yet you are a leading figure in gender issues and gender biases. How have those interfered with you career—gender biases?"

[Schutte] "There's a combination of internal and external factors—when one is raised, as I was, within a rather moderate if not conservative context—in what is expected of a young Cuban female. There are certain limitations that are imposed on you through your upbringing. And then there is the effort to overcome those limitations. But I can't psychoanalyze myself, so I have no clue about what happened. I'm just driven to know, I am driven by the quest for knowledge, and that is one of the things that attracted me to philosophy: the quest to know, the quest to ask questions, this passion to think things through and analyze and question them, taking a critical outlook if necessary. This attraction leads to unorthodoxy. But I have this interest in what is unorthodox because I think that knowledge can't progress unless you go beyond the limits of what is already there. It is the most commonsensical thing in the world to think this way. So, I had this internal drive, this passion to find things out and to question views philosophically, and I think this helped me tremendously. Some of the biases affecting women in philosophy have to do with stereotyped views of reason, with the gendering of reason as masculine (and emotion as feminine). But there are other biases women face daily in all aspects of our lives having to do with normative expectations regarding gender and sexuality. This is why I have also published some papers on the critique of normative heterosexuality.

[Martí] "Again, you're a very moderate, careful, introspective thinker, yet again you're what used to be called an activist, a philosophical activist, but that carries images of placards and marching . . ."

[Schutte] "I don't conceive of myself as an activist. What I'm referring to is taking the discussion one step further; basically, it is what I like to do. I don't like to repeat myself, and so I try to say new things. When I write a paper I don't like to repeat what I said in a previous one."

[Martí] "What about your relations with our Latin American colleagues? How do—Cubans or Mexicans, say—how have you been received as a woman, and as an American going to Latin America? Has there been any friction, any conflicts?"

[Schutte] "I feel that what interests people is my work, what I can contribute intellectually. That's how I connect with them, from my part. The reception has generally been very supportive and full of respect both from female and male colleagues. It has been one of my greatest sources of support—of moral support—because when I go to Latin America I see the way the people appreciate me, the way they appreciate my work. I also listen to them which, for me, is a learning experience. There is often an affinity between us because to some degree much of the work I do is a bridge for their work: the recognition that there are Latin American philosophers, that philosophical work gets done in Latin America. In one case I've collaborated rather closely in feminism with an Argentine colleague, María Luisa Femenías. We have had a very good collegial relationship and done some research together. It's been really great. I go to Argentina periodically. They invite me to read papers at their universities and we have social gatherings."

[Martí] Now, Cuba. Do you identify yourself as a Cuban in some sense other than simply circumstance? Is there something inside of you which is Cuban? Could you identify it?"

[Schutte] "That's so difficult to answer, but I think the answer depends on the context. I know I'm Cuban but it doesn't come out all the time. When I'm connected to something that has to do with Cuba—like a trip to Cuba or research in Cuba—in that case, I feel on the border between Cuban and Cuban American. I'm Cuban American, but a different species of Cuban American than the one most people know about in the United States. That's because I have very progressive political views. I've been living away from Miami most of my life and I have developed very independent views. But, yes, Cuba drives me in the sense that I care for its well-being. In this phase of my career, it is coming back with a force that it didn't have before. I have to ask myself, 'Why?' I feel I've achieved almost everything I wanted to achieve professionally. I feel rewarded in everything that I have achieved. And the one thing that I haven't written about is Cuba. This is why it's starting to have a certain weight on me that it didn't have before. Since the late 1980s I have been back to Cuba a number of times. I have read papers in Cuba, I have attended many professional meetings, and over the course of time I've been invited to present papers at various institutions. This has been very rewarding to me, in a personal sense. It means a lot to me. I think that's a very good thing and good for both sides, the exchange of ideas."

[Martí] ". . . the need to participate, to be able to influence the future somehow, to make things better. The need to, even though things could be bad, somehow or other make it better. Let's turn to another topic. We are now dealing with a bunch of young ones coming into philosophy—Latin American philosophy and we've prepared the way, what advice would you give these young people going into Latin American philosophy or into philosophy itself? What would you advise them to do?"

[Schutte] "In what sense?"

[Martí] "In their careers, in their facing philosophy. In both their personal and intellectual careers. How would you steer them?"

[Schutte] "It's essential to have a network of supportive colleagues, preferably both in your institution and outside, in the larger field of your profession. The Society for Iberian and Latin American Thought that you and I were a part of was a great source of support for me when I started doing Latin American philosophy. There I could find peers interested in the same topic."

[Martí] "You were president of the society."

[Schutte] "For a while, yes, and that was a huge source of help. I belong to many professional societies; on the cv, I have a long list of them. So I would say, just insert yourself in a group with whom you can discuss your work and where you can get helpful comments from other people in the field."

[Martí] "Nietzsche influenced you tremendously, but tell us what other, say, Latin Americans have influenced you the most?"

[Schutte] "Indirectly, I think, José Martí, not because I have written a book about him (I haven't), but because of the combination of the type of upbringing that I had in Cuba, where a certain ethos in affinity with many of his ideas was implanted in me from a very young age, and the concept of 'our America' that Martí proposed in his famous article by that title, and how that concept itself influenced the work of so many Latin American philosophers of my generation and of generations before mine. But I think the way that I experience Latin American philosophy is not so much through one great figure or one great philosopher, as through a combination of factors and a collection of different voices. My book itself reflects this because it's not focused on one single person; it's focused on social movements and intellectual formations and debates that relate to social movements. It tends to have a plurality of voices involved."

[Martí] "It's fascinating! Shall we end with that note?"

[Schutte] "Yes, thank you."

[Martí] "My pleasure."

June 11, 2005
Interviewed in the library of the Department of Philosophy at the University at Buffalo, filmed and edited by Jorge J. E. Gracia, and transcribed by Paul Symington.

THE SEARCH FOR IDENTITY OUTSIDE MIAMI

JORGE J. E. GRACIA

Jorge J. E. Gracia was born in 1942 and came to the United States in 1961. He holds the Samuel P. Capen Chair in Philosophy at the University at Buffalo, and is State University of New York Distinguished Professor. He has been president of several philosophical societies and has held grants and fellowships from the Canada Council, the National Endowment for the Humanities, and the New York Council for the Humanities.

Gracia was trained in medieval philosophy, but has published extensively on historiography, the interpretation of texts, and the history of Hispanic philosophy. Most of all, he has worked on metaphysics, particularly on individuality and on the identity of social groups (ethnic, racial, and national). He is also a collector of Cuban-American art.

Main Works: Surviving Race, Ethnicity, and Nationality: A Challenge for the Twenty-First Century *(2005),* Old Wine in New Skins: The Role of Tradition in Communication, Knowledge, and Group Identity *(2003),* How Can We Know What God Means? The Interpretation of Revelation *(2001),* Hispanic/Latino Identity: A Philosophical Perspective *(2000),* Metaphysics and its Task: The Search for the Categorial Foundation of Knowledge *(1999),* Texts: Ontological Status, Identity, Author, Audience *(1996),* A Theory of Textuality: The Logic and Epistemology *(1995),* Philosophy and Its History: Issues in Philosophical Historiography *(1992), and* Individuality: An Essay in the Foundations of Metaphysics *(1988, John Findlay Prize in Metaphysics). He has also published 250 articles and two dozen edited books.*

INTERVIEW

Conducted by Iván Jaksić

[Jaksić] "Jorge, let me begin by asking when, and under what circumstances, you came to the U.S.?"

[Gracia] "I came in 1961, I turned nineteen the day I arrived here. It was a result of the situation in Cuba, the Cuban revolution that started in January of 1959. Things had been moving toward the left, and after the

Bay of Pigs invasion, things changed drastically in Cuba. Before, there was always the possibility of openness, some more democratic ideas, some freedoms. But after the Bay of Pigs things deteriorated heavily. The regime took a turn to a more radical approach. The situation became impossible for people who disagreed, and at that time, I disagreed violently with the situation. So I decided to leave. I took the last boat—the last ferry boat—out of Cuba to West Palm Beach on July 17th."

[Jaksić] "The age of eighteen is interesting because you are old enough to have a sense of nationality, a sense of belonging, a sense of community, and at the same time it is an age in which you make drastic choices if you have to because you have convictions. I wonder, how did you handle that experience: on the one hand, being attached to a community and to a country, and on the other being so angry about it?"

[Gracia] "It was very traumatic as you can imagine. Of course, not as traumatic, I would say, as it was for someone who was, perhaps, forty-five and felt that he or she had to leave. But at eighteen, all of a sudden I felt that I couldn't continue in Cuba, yet, of course, the only place I knew was Cuba. My only language was Spanish, I had a very rudimentary knowledge of English. I had never been outside of Cuba. This was an enormous step outside of the place where I had lived all my life. I had just a few friends who had emigrated to the U.S. before this time, and some of them helped me when I got here. But it was extraordinarily traumatic. I agonized about it, but finally said, 'What is my future here?' There was no future, clearly there was none. I felt I had to leave. In a sense, I abandoned everything I had known. Of course, I came without any money at all; they allowed five dollars. I remember the moment in which that boat was leaving the Havana Bay. It was so extraordinary, it is a moment I can never forget because my family were on the pier, waving. . . . Everybody was there, and it was extremely moving. Late in the afternoon of the previous day we had been asked to go into the pertinent offices to see that everything was alright— to be cleared to leave the island—early the next morning, and it took all day to process us, even though there were not many of us. Around four o'clock we went into the boat and it started moving, very slowly, as ships do. All of a sudden, I realized that the world as I knew it was ending. I felt these things on my face and they were tears coming down! Yes, it was a very strong moment for me. Boats are particularly good at delaying departure, so it slowly moved out and I saw the fort of El Morro which is a symbol of Cuba and Havana. And slowly—and the sunset then was there—it was perfect—a perfect situation for sentimentality and nostalgia. Then slowly Cuba disappeared. Havana, you could observe the skyline from the perspective of the boat. Then it faded in the dusk, and then, of course, there was open sea, and the night, and I wondered, 'What's next?' "

[Jaksić] "So, when did you turn to philosophy? Was it in a college in the U.S. or at the graduate level? When did you realize that this was something that you really loved and liked?"

[Gracia] "When I came to the U.S. and went into college my knowledge of English was practically nonexistent and here I was thrown into a college environment trying to carry on—it was a tremendous shock. I realized right away that I needed to learn the language so I said, 'I'm going to isolate myself from all the Latinos or Hispanics that are in the college and I am going to associate only with Anglos until I learn English well.' And when I started taking courses, one of them was English literature and another was on the English language—composition and so forth. Imagine how I did on them, it was dreadful. But I became fascinated with the language. It was the first time that I had really been exposed to a different language, a different way of thinking about the world and this was hypnotizing to me. I was also fascinated by the literary aspect. We read Milton's *Paradise Lost*, imagine that, without knowing English! I guessed at its meaning, I suppose. But the richness of the language, the meter, the music, the rhythm, was just captivating to me. So what did I do? Well, what was the most difficult thing that you could have done at that time? First of all, I had declared a math major when I came in because I was a science type. Then, I took these courses. And then I said, 'Math is not that difficult, it is the same language all over the world!' So, what did I do? I changed my major from math to English. Can you believe it? One of the things that fascinated me about this exposure to the language was what makes a work of literature great. I wanted to know that. Unfortunately, the courses that I took in English literature did not stress that, they stressed the ideas. The teachers always talked about the ideas in the works. Never about what makes a poem so unique, aesthetically captivating, what makes a novel so fabulous. Then I took a course in philosophy and realized that, if you are going to talk about ideas, it is not in literature that you do it, but in philosophy. Although people in comparative literature today think that they're doing philosophy, but I didn't think that was right, so I moved to philosophy."

[Jaksić] "And at what point did you decide to do medieval philosophy?"

[Gracia] "Let me backtrack a bit. Wheaton College is a very religious, fundamentalist college—and of course, I was not a fundamentalist—I was Catholic—and on the other hand my Catholicism always has been a wavering type: I'm a roaming Catholic. At thirteen, was the first time that I decided religion just doesn't make any sense. I don't think that I've ever been an atheist but I certainly have been anti-Catholic, a non-Catholic, a this or that, but that doesn't mean that I have adhered to other religions; I have always found that if one's going to be religious, being

Catholic probably is what makes the most sense. But, I have certainly had periods in my life when I have not been Catholic and when I have been anti-Catholic and other periods when I have been very devoutly Catholic and where I have been a kind of an existential Catholic. I had an existential period in college, when I read *The Brothers Karamazov*, and Kierkegaard and so forth—oh, that was an extraordinary period. By the way, this is the sort of thing that my teacher was, and probably he enticed me into it. That pointed me toward the scholastics, particularly Thomas Aquinas. I have never been a disciple of Aquinas or an apologist for him or anything of the sort, but I became interested in him at Wheaton because, if you look at the history of Christian thought, there are very few authors who have the stature of Aquinas; and that rationality, that careful thinking, and so on. So there was a group of us at Wheaton—some of them Protestant and some Catholic—that actually took a particular liking to Thomas. But this is not really the reason why I became interested in medieval philosophy. The reason was that I thought the basic concepts of philosophy were framed in the Middle Ages—most of the concepts that we have, like essence, nature, quality, and relation. Where're these concepts from? My idea was that, yes, the Greeks had talked about these things but the bridge between the Greeks and us is the Middle Ages. The Middle Ages was the time when modern languages were formed, and where the first treatises and discussions of how these concepts relate to each other were made in the West. I was convinced that in order to do philosophy—and I've always wanted to do philosophy rather to be just merely a historian— I had to go back to the Middle Ages to find out the origin of the concepts that we use today. So when I went to the University of Chicago the idea was to study with the famous medievalist Richard McKeon. It turns out that he was not there, he was on leave and about to retire. The guy there at the time who did some medieval philosophy was not a famous person, but he told me that if I was really interested in medieval philosophy, I had to go to Toronto, the best place for it in North America at the time. So that's where I went."

[Jaksić] "So you did one or two years in Chicago, and then?"

[Gracia] "At Chicago, I did one year only. I got the MA and immediately left. But we have to put that in the context of the Vietnam War, because if I had stayed I would have had to go to Vietnam. Fortunately I had the legal option of not going by leaving the country. So two things worked out: first, I applied to Toronto, immediately upon coming to Chicago, because I realized there was no future there in medieval philosophy. I remember it was in November or October when I applied to the Pontifical Institute in Toronto, and I was notified that I had been accepted early in January. At that very time came the notification from the draft board saying that I had to go into the Army. I asked for a delay until I finished my MA and then, when I finished, I said, 'I'd rather not serve, I want to leave the country.' This was perfectly acceptable because I was not a citizen, I was merely a resident."

[Jaksić] "One other major issue that occurs to me is that by this time you are functioning in an Anglo world. And there are issues of language—it's more than language, it's identity. How did that happen? Did you notice some sort of lack?"

[Gracia] "Some people are very Cuban or Puerto Rican or Mexican, and they always stay there. In my case, I became conscious of a strong contrast between my being Cuban and being Anglo in college. But then, almost immediately, I became more pan-American or Latin American. I remember writing letters to former friends who lived in Miami and talking about Latin America and Anglo-America. This was something that they did not want to talk about, that they dismissed, that they were not interested in. They thought I was weird or something of that sort. Maybe this was a result of the fact that they lived in a very closely knit community. The people in Miami, to this day, still live in Cuba—probably a mythical Cuba, but it is Cuba. But I have lived outside of that milieu. I had to confront another world. Now, you remember that I said 'Until I learn English, I want to separate myself from anything that has to do with Spanish or Latin America and so forth.' And I did. But a year after that I already had sufficient confidence that I had mastered the language and that I knew how things worked—that I fitted in so many ways—that I went back. So we had—in college—a very nice group of friends that got together and did things together. I had some friends that were purely Anglo and did not mix with any of the Latin Americans, and then I had a group of friends who were Latin Americans and did not mix with any of the Anglos, and then I had a group of Latin Americans and Anglos that got together and did things together. So that's how issues of identity became very important at that time. Now, I did not have any philosophical interest in any of this at all. This was a personal matter, and then there was philosophy. Philosophy was universal and I was trying to learn about how the world is and how to talk about it cogently and present arguments, and about the history of philosophy, which of course became very important to me. I had not a great deal of interest in anything that had to do with Latin America or the Hispanic world."

[Jaksić] "In what form did your interest in Latin American philosophy develop, then? When I came to UB you already were established in the field as someone who knew Latin American philosophy, was actually writing about it . . ."

[Gracia] "The chairman of the department of philosophy here that hired me was Bill Parry. He was a well-known logician who had studied with some of the great logicians at Harvard. And he was also a Marxist and had suffered greatly in the fifties; his tenure was taken away in this University because of his Marxism. Can you imagine such a thing? Now, a Marxist and a Cuban. The Marxist hired the Cuban, who presumably was supposed to be a right-wing nut. So a left-wing nut, a communist—actually he'd been a member of the Communist Party—and a right-wing nut from Cuba, and we're supposed to get together, and we did. But he was not a left-wing nut, he was a reasonable, eminently rational, tremendously understanding person. And, I've always tried to be that way too. My anti-Castro bile had passed, so now I could look at this in a rational way. I had and still have objections, but they are not framed in a kind of personal, irrational fashion. So, I was hired as a medievalist in Buffalo, that was my field—but Bill said in a conversation we had, 'You're Cuban. I'm sure that there's Cuban philosophy, there is Latin American philosophy certainly. Why don't you look into it and see whether we can offer a course on Latin American philosophy?' So I wrote to Risieri Frondizi, and one of my issues concerned how to get any sources. There was nothing, nothing available. That old anthology by Sánchez Reulet was the only thing, and not available in English any longer. So, how to teach a course on Latin American philosophy under these conditions? It was heroic, like most of what has to do with Latin American philosophy. So, Frondizi and I started talking."

[Jaksić] "He was at Carbondale at the time?"

[Gracia] "Yes, and we became great friends. He was a marvelous human being. His personal history is extraordinary. He was a very important man, he came from a very prominent family in Argentina—people who were self-made in many ways. He had been president of the University of Buenos Aires. One of his brothers had been president of Argentina, and another was a prominent Marxist intellectual. The extraordinary thing is that Risieri never treated me like an underling or an upstart—which I was. I didn't know anything, my field was miles away from his field. He had been trained under Romero. And here I was, a medievalist—oh my God, this sounds like the odd couple. But, a couple we were, and we were not that odd, because we worked together extraordinarily well and we were very well matched, it was a marriage made in heaven."

[Jaksić] "And so you decided to do the collection on man and values, then."

[Gracia] "Yes, but we had tremendous trouble trying to publish it in English. It was published in Spanish, and there is even a second edition of it. But in English no publisher would touch it. The only one that took the risk was Paul Kurtz with Prometheus. Kurtz was a faculty member here, and he has always been a maverick, he's always been a sort of antiestablishment type. And so, I proposed it to him and he said, 'Yes, I'll do it.' "

[Jaksić] "Was the experience with the anthology discouraging in anyway?"

[Gracia] "Oh, it was horrible. I felt completely discouraged. I read all of these Latin American philosophers and I saw that, yes, they are talking about things that have a direct relationship to my own intellectual tradition—the Cuban tradition. There are common problems. They may have solved them in different ways, but the situation is somewhat similar."

[Jaksić] "I'd like to explore that sort of sense of discouragement and how it was transformed eventually in the sense that if you're removed from your community, your country, you make a choice to pursue a field seriously—in this case philosophy—and there is an engagement with it and then at some point you encounter the professional side of it and you see that side not recognized, something that is very close to your own past and identity. How did you negotiate that?"

[Gracia] "I was lucky to this extent: I had a field that was recognized. In a sense, my bread and butter, my stature, my recognition was not in play because I started publishing in medieval philosophy and what I published was regarded as good. When I published the first book that was not a translation or commentary, but a study—this was the *Introduction to the Problem of Individuation in the Early Middle Ages*—it established my reputation. By the way, I had some trouble publishing it also, because it's so different from anything that had been published before. Once that book came out, however, my reputation was very well established and the number of reviews was extraordinary: there were more than forty reviews of this book, all over the world. So, I received substantial recognition. Even before that, I was promoted to full professor here—everybody thought that what I was doing was great, I had this translation of Suárez with a commentary, and this work was respected and thought of highly in this university and in the profession at large. Of course, medieval philosophy is not the philosophy of mind—there is a bias against it. But medieval philosophy had already established itself somewhat because there was a group of analytic philosophers who had taken an interest in it. I was not part of this group, but the fact that a space had been opened in mainstream philosophy made it possible for people like me to work in it. Also because I was not just a text person, although I had done editions of Latin and other languages and had done very traditional historical studies—some of them even concerned with how manuscripts were dependent on each other and with chronologies and the like that historians love to do. But I was primarily interested in the conceptual analysis of historical figures. This opened doors for me and established my reputation. So what happens next? I have this other weird thing that I do—something that no one regards as important or interesting—which is Latin American philosophy. Alright, it is a quirky thing that Gracia does, maybe he has some mental—as one philosopher put it—some psychological problem, and we have to put up with it, because he does this other work that is very good. So we'll put up with this other, quirky thing. This is how my work on Latin American philosophy was regarded until very recently. What has changed is the demographic situation in the U.S. Another factor that has helped to open doors for this area of interest is the interest in black philosophy and issues that have to do with race. This groundbreaking enterprise has opened some space also for Latin Americans and Latin American philosophy."

[Jaksić] "Did you decide that this was going to be a field that you'd pursue, and the strategies to use?' How did you begin to conceptualize your new commitment?"

[Gracia] "I don't think this happened until relatively recently. I did have a commitment to it, but the commitment was to continue to maintain a presence of this field in philosophy in the U.S. This was very important to me because I was convinced that there was merit there, and of course, there was also a personal—one wants to say sentimental—investment in it. This is part of who I am. And you know what, Ivan, it is difficult for me to understand people who say, 'Oh no, I'm Mexican, I'm this or I'm that and I don't have anything to do with Romero or Sarmiento or someone coming from another part of Latin America. It is difficult because I read Rodó, for example, and I find so much that appeals to me in terms of who I am—my past, my history—just as I do with many things in the U.S. as well. So, there is a commitment, but the commitment has never been to make this my main field of study, because, first of all, I am a medievalist. I have a reputation in that field, and I have kept it up, not only because this is a bread and butter issue, but also because the Middle Ages are fascinating to me. Now, I can sit here with you and tell you several things that, if I had forty years ahead of me, I would do. And I'm dying to do them and saying, 'Oh well, my time is running out. I have to be very careful with what I do from now on.' But if I had time, it would be such a wonderful project to do this or that. For example, to study the development of category theory throughout the Middle Ages. This is something that has not been done. It would be fabulous. But it's not for me to do. But this main area itself evolved: the issue of historiography itself became important, because I had been doing history all this time. It happened because there was this faculty member here, Peter Hare, who organized a conference on historiography and he asked me for a paper. And I said to myself, 'I've been doing history all my life—of one kind or another, Latin American, medieval—so how is it that this should be done?' So I wrote an article and then of course I was totally dissatisfied with it, and proceeded to write a very thick book—*Philosophy and Its History*—which is the only systematic work in English on that topic. So I get asked all the time to contribute articles or to do this or that in the area of historiography—philosophical historiography. I have kept this up. Now there was a chapter in the book about texts and their interpretation which I found completely inadequate. So I went on to write two other books on the issues of texts and textuality. And since metaphysics has always been a concern of mine, then I thought I had to say something about it, so that's the book about metaphysics. This takes me to about 1996, somewhere around there. While I was writing the book on metaphysics, a change occurred in the climate of opinion in the U.S. as a result of the demographics: the increase of Latinos, Hispanics, was extraordinary. Things began to appear in philosophy about them. So I felt that the time was ripe for a major effort in this direction. This is the origin of *Hispanic/Latino Identity*. This book has opened new fields for me, including an interest in race and ethnicity, some new dimensions about Latin American philosophy, and the issue of Cuban Americans and how they negotiate their identities here. You asked me, 'Was there a point at which you decided to commit yourself more than you had, to have Latin American philosophy as more than a sideline?' I think I reached that point in the late nineties, although it is not so much Latin American philosophy as the issues that have to do with Latin American and Hispanic identity, ethnicity, and race."

[Jaksić] "At the same time your reputation in the field is more as a metaphysician, as Delfino's recently edited volume devoted to you indicates. How has your engagement with metaphysics been enriched or changed by your engagement with other aspects of philosophy? How has it influenced your work in metaphysics and medieval . . . ?"

[Gracia] "In medieval, it has enhanced my interest in authors that are part of this pre-Hispanic world, as I would call it. The interest in Suárez, the interest in the sixteenth century, has become greater in many ways. Although I should say that my work in the history of philosophy follows a topical or problems approach. My philosophical and topical concerns are always metaphysical, metaphysics really informs all of my work. I remember Lorenzo Peña telling me once, 'Jorge, the only thing that you do is metaphysics! You do metaphysics everywhere!' And I responded, 'What else is there to do?' This is a fascination. And now, what's happened is that I have been doing it in the area of ethnicity and race."

[Jaksić] "But what are the motivations and goals that you have? Are you contending against a metaphysical tradition or a set of authors?"

[Gracia] "I imagine that, as a philosopher, self-reflection is essential, and it would be weird, or strange, if I had not thought about this very question. You remember that I had mentioned that I was studying to be an architect. I think that has never left me in this sense: What is it that an architect does? An architect surveys the terrain and then designs a structure with foundations. And the structure is supposed to have a function; it encases a certain space to be used, so that people can move, work, and live in it. And he does it, also, in an appealing fashion; there is a strong artistic component in an architect that cannot be underestimated. So, what is it that I'm trying to do in philosophy? It is like that, in metaphysics in particular. All philosophy begins with experience—here and now. I look at my terrain, and my terrain is what? My experience: what I have perceived, what I have seen, what I have felt. There are parts of that experience that are, perhaps, incomplete. Let me put it in terms of a metaphor: the terrain, to serve its purpose, needs something more than what is there—maybe it is a swamp that needs to be drained. Or, maybe, I have certain needs that the terrain does not offer me. So what do I do? I try to build a structure and I begin by building up these foundations, this structure; and, that's the metaphysics of it. And slowly walls are added, and there are windows and spaces. And, what is it that I do? I dwell in those spaces, use them, organize this landscape where I am. My experience becomes the basis of my work, my metaphysical work, and the work is geared toward creating a structure that will serve me to live and function in—to put it all together. And there is an aesthetic sense that I would call almost narcissistic because it has to do, fundamentally, with my needs—to make sense of the landscape of my experience. And, not only to make sense of it, but to put me in a situation, namely a building, in which I can function comfortably."

[Jaksić] "When one thinks about architecture, one thinks about harmony. Is that a search or a desire in an intellectual field?"

[Gracia] "Yes, to put it all together in a way that there are no clashes. This is a fundamental requirement. To be comfortable with one's experience, with one's history, most of all to be comfortable with yourself, who you are. Many people are unhappy and one source of their unhappiness is their dissatisfaction with themselves. They haven't come to terms with who they are. The older I get the more important this is for me—that I think I have. I'm quite comfortable with who I am, with what I do, with my goals—I have put it all together in a sense. What I've done has cohesion, has threads tied together and they are all integrated into my life, my needs, my views, my values. This sounds very selfish, perhaps, but ultimately—yes, there are other people, and the other people are there as part of myself in some way, as in relationship to me—but everything is in a sense centered around this identity, who I am and what I have done. I often say, well, actually I am quite comfortable; if I were going to die tomorrow, or even in an hour, or in five minutes, or whatever..."

[Jaksić] "...not before the end of the interview!"

[Gracia] "Alright, I won't do it before then! I'll have to stop that heart attack when it's coming! But, you know, I don't feel that I have regrets. I'm not going to say something that some people say: 'I would never change anything!' Oh, for God's sake! I would change endless numbers of things, naturally, I would! And who knows what would happen.... The point is: How is it all tied together? How is that experience of the world and what I have been able to build—the house in which I live intellectually—how is that functioning? Is it functioning well for me, and for those around me? There are many theories about the nature of philosophy and we've talked about this often—the Socratic idea that you really are not sure of anything. I know that some people hearing me say this are going to be terribly scandalized, because 'we know certain things for certain, obviously.' Well, do we? The job of philosophy is always to undermine those certainties and make you think, and then try to put something together again. But that house that we were talking about is never complete, there is always remodeling to be done. There is always a window that needs to be opened, one that has to be closed; there is a wall that has to be moved, a particular couch that you want here, but then you want it there. It is a constant flow. My mother was one of those people who hated old things. As a result, there was nothing old in my house. Nothing. No piece of furniture that was antique, nothing, nothing, nothing. She was always on the hunt for the latest in furniture, fashion. So, I was used to having a house in which every two years all of the furniture would change. I am not sure that this is quite the way I feel in philosophy, because it's not that everything changes, but there's always tinkering. And sometimes, there has to be substantial change."

[Jaksić] "I have a question about yourself as a Cuban and a member of the Cuban-American community. Its been tough, you know, the public perception of Cubans, the Cuban movement. You are part of the community, but you do things so contrary to the stereotype of Cubans. So my question to you is, How do you wish this to change, or what would you like to do that would in some ways serve the memory of more complexity or register the fact that this is not exclusively a political experience alone, but is a human experience—what are your wishes and in which direction would they go?"

[Gracia] "My wish is precisely to bring to the American people and the world a sense that there is a Cuban experience outside politics. That the Cubans here in the U.S. have had to face other issues that are as important or more important than the political ones. And that they had to deal with them. This interview is part of an overall project entitled, 'Negotiating Identities in Art, Literature, and Philosophy,' and my whole idea about it was precisely that: to try to open a space for a discussion of the Cuban experience apart from the political dialectic that is completely destructive, because once you get into it, there is no way out. Opening this, seeing how, for example, some Cubans—some artists, say—have integrated into their work some of their concerns, some of their memories, some of their ambivalence between the Cuban identity and the American identity. How do they fit with other Latin Americans? And all of this apart from the political situation and rhetoric. The same thing with me, for example, what we've talked about in this interview. How is it that I, as a philosopher, relate to issues that have to do with being Latin American, Hispanic, Cuban, part of North America, and keeping the political situation from interfering? The political situation can be brought in, but it has to be brought into the context of this larger picture. The thing that really hurts is that politics is the only thing that's brought in and everything else is either forgotten or broached in the context of politics. The experience of Cuban Americans has a universal dimension of all peoples who are for one reason or another, alienated from their native lands, away from their nations, away from their cultures. How do they cope? How do they respond? Do they assimilate? Do they gather together? All of these questions are extraordinarily important. How do they negotiate these things? Apart from the causes that brought them out. And, if the causes were political, or the causes were other than political, such as, for example, economic, does that affect their experience and what they do in the new place where they live? These are very rich, very interesting, very extraordinary, issues. One thing that is certainly forgotten is that the Cubans that have come to the U.S. have come in waves. They have been part of different classes, with varying degrees of professional training and education. This has created a Cuban community that is perhaps different from other communities of immigrants who are primarily, let's say, economically deprived and come to this country to work and earn a living, and therefore, have little education. All these questions and issues seem to me fascinating, interesting, and worthy of consideration when people think about Cubans."

[Jaksić] "Well, that about answers my questions. Thank you."

June 23, 2005
Interviewed in Jorge Gracia's office at the State University at Buffalo, filmed and transcribed by Paul Symington, and edited by Iván Jaksić.

CUBAN AMERICAN OR LATIN AMERICAN?

———————————————————————— OSCAR MARTÍ

Oscar Martí was born in 1942 and came to the United States in 1956. He has taught at The City College of New York, San Diego State University, University of California at Los Angeles, the Universidad Nacional Autónoma de México, and Goddard College. He currently teaches in the Department of Chicana/o Studies and is the outgoing director of the Center for Ethics and Values at California State University at Northridge. He has also been Director of Publications at the Chicano Studies Research Center, and associate director of the French Revolution Bicentennial Program, both at the University of California at Los Angeles. He was a postdoctoral fellow at the UCLA Institute for American Cultures, and a Fulbright Scholar to Mexico.

His general research interests are on Latin American philosophy, logic, and medical ethics. But his recognized area of expertise is Mexican philosophy and Latin American positivism.

Main works: editorship of the Gabino Barreda Commemorative Issue, Aztlán: International Journal of Chicano Studies Research *(1983); a collection of essays on the influence of Gabino Barreda and Comtian positivism on nineteenth-century Mexico. He also co-edited* Las Revoluciones en el Mundo Ibérico, 1766–1834 *(1989), which appeared in a revised edition as* Les Révolutions dans le monde ibérique, 1766–1834, 2 vols., *(1989–92). Articles include: "Is There a Latin American Philosophy?" (1983); "Auguste Comte and the Positivist Utopias" (1982); "Sarmiento y el positivismo" (1989); "Gigantes y cabezudos: La querella entre los historicistas y los analíticos" (1992); "El positivismo del siglo XIX" (1998); "José Martí and the Heroic Image" (1998); and "Aportes de cubanos fuera de Cuba a la filosofía actual" (1999).*

INTERVIEW

Conducted by Jorge J. E. Gracia

[Gracia] "Oscar, how did you get into philosophy, for philosophy is not one of those fields that a Cuban would favor! After all, there's the matter of money!"

[Martí] "It's a very long story. For one thing, I did like philosophy since I was a kid. When I was about ten or eleven I found this book on

234

Plato. It had dialogues—and I started reading one of the early dialogues and thought, 'Hey, how interesting!' In 1955, I entered the 'Instituto' [secondary school], but then they closed it and there were student revolts. So, my father said, 'This is no good,' so we came to the United States. It was rough because I was very young: thirteen, fourteen years old and I didn't speak English."

[Gracia] "Where was it that you settled?"

[Martí] "New York City. We were on our own and my mother had to work—this is the fifties. She landed a job as a wig maker at a company that made wigs and moustaches and beards for the theater. I was a young man, you know, fourteen, fifteen, sixteen. My mother talked to the owner of the wig house and he offered me a job as a delivery boy, but she wanted to keep an eye on me so I ended up with a job as a wig maker. I was going to school and working as a wig maker; and I specialized in Santa Claus beards. That was a big thing. Then I started working on the theater. When I got to college, I was sixteen, and the horror of a sixteen year old surrounded by all these gorgeous girls, and still speaking with a high voice. . . . I couldn't integrate. I grew a beard. I started working in biochemistry; my actual bachelor's degree is in biochemistry and in the sciences. Then I got a scholarship to medical school—Albert Einstein medical school—it was a four-year scholarship, I got into first year medical school and I was given a cadaver to dissect, and I fainted. I discovered that I just didn't have what it takes to be a doctor. I felt ethical and stomach difficulties. So I went into clinical psychology instead. Then I was walking down the hall one day and I heard someone giving a lecture. I stood by the door and I sneaked in and sat down. After he finished, I went down and introduced myself and the rest is history. I went in to talk with the Chair, who at that time was Philip Weiner, and I started graduate work in philosophy. I was working on a thesis on Descartes for the MA and Weiner said, 'You might as well do it for the doctorate.' So, they advanced me to the doctorate without a master's. My proposed dissertation was on Descartes and Freud."

[Gracia] "Naturally! You were interested in psychoanalysis."

[Martí] "It was around the time that they had one of the Inter-American Congresses of Philosophy. Weiner calls me up and says, 'Oscar, you speak Spanish, right? Do you know anything about Latin American philosophy?' I said, 'No, I've never heard of it.' So he says, 'Well, there's all kinds of opportunities there; I want you to make it exist. You have four weeks to do it. I would like a proposal, a doctoral proposal on my desk in four weeks."

[Gracia] "Is this your entry into Latin American philosophy!"

[Martí] "Yeah, completely by surprise. I went down to the Forty-second Street library and there was Augusto Salazar Bondy's 'Is There a Latin American Philosophy?' I had the pressure of having to prepare a program, so I did. My idea was Positivism.'

[Gracia] "This was a very logical place to go because of your background."

[Martí] "Correct. I discovered a man called José Ingenieros, who was a doctor, a philosopher, an activist . . ."

[Gracia] ". . . and interested in psychology!"

[Martí] "Yes, he had actually done some work in the field. I had come across his name in a couple of footnotes and I had never connected them. The other person that I studied was Vaz Ferreira who appealed to my interest in logic. I started working on these two individuals and decided that chapter one or chapter two was going to be on Positivism, or the development of the reaction against Positivism in Argentina and Uruguay. Weiner retired, but I was lucky enough to get passed on to Peter Caws—very, very open, very tolerant, and very sharp mentor. He left me alone when I had to be left alone and pressured me when I had to be pressed. But I discovered that Latin American philosophy became more and more all-absorbing. So I dedicated myself to work primarily in it. This is 1976, 1975. At the time the University began to have financial problems related to the New York State crisis, so I started looking for a job. I ended up in San Diego State with a one-year position. But there was a fellowship to specialize on Mexican philosophy. Part of my original ambitious plan was to first look at Argentina, Uruguay, then Venezuela, and Colombia, and then Mexico. But, I said, 'Okay, fine. I'll begin with Mexico.' That turned out to be a major decision. It was very, very fortunate. I was given a one year, well paid fellowship of the Institute of the Americas. UCLA always had money. After the fellowship, they asked me if I wanted to stay a second year, and at the end of the second year they asked me if I wanted to go into administration. During my tenure as fellow I organized several conferences and I was doing work on a journal, and the papers from one of the conferences were going to be published in the journal, *Astlán*. So they asked me if I wanted to be the editor for *Astlán*."

[Gracia] "You had also worked with Weiner editing the *Journal of the History of Ideas*. So you had all this experience."

[Martí] "Yes, but like the guy at the Xerox machine, I was a graduate student and I had to do some editing. I mean, they exploit the labor. Afterwards, the university awarded me money to go to Mexico to establish an American Studies program at Guadalajara. That was the year of the Inter-American Congress held there, 1985? When I came back to UCLA, Bob Manicas, who was the director of the French Revolution program invited me to be his assistant director in charge of Latin America. So, the university gave me a sabbatical and I got a Fulbright to work in Mexico. We spent two years in Mexico City. By then I was beginning to be recognized as a major potential Mexicanist. So, when I got to Mexico they allowed me to teach in the chair of Mexican philosophy. I brought in analytical tools to study the history of philosophy. When I finished there, I got into the French Revolution project, and that was an entirely different world, dealing primarily with the French. Suddenly I began to get invitations to historical congresses in Europe—the Europeans know me as an historian! 'Oh, Oscar the historian who does philosophy.' I felt like David Hume, who was known for many years as that great historian of English history who did some minor work in philosophy. It is only until Russell discovered him in the twentieth century that people began to think of him as a major philosopher who did some history work. Now I'm waiting for someone to discover my work."

[Gracia] "There you go, you might still get discovered!"

[Martí] "Actually, no, my view of philosophy is not all that—I don't have a system of philosophy at one time. Philosophy for me is a trip, and on a trip you carry some baggage—bags, baggage is a bad term—so what I do is I have some philosophical techniques, some analytical techniques that allow me to travel from point to point with what I'm dealing with in my career. First—well, not as a wig maker—but certainly in clinical psychology, and then in history. Philosophy allows me to deal with the arguments from a broader, more analytical perspective. After the French Revolution I retired from UCLA. Eventually I organized a Center for Ethics and Values. The center has been very profitable and the dean has been very supportive. But Chicano Studies needed a specialist in critical reasoning, a logician to upgrade the courses on critical reasoning. So I moved to Chicano Studies and that's where I am right now."

[Gracia] "Obviously, there is the interesting way in which you got into the field of Mexican philosophy, Latin American philosophy, which seems to be a very prominent part of your career. This seems to have been a result of both circumstances and an interest. That is, there was an external cause, you were asked to do certain things and so on, and then you got into it and very much liked it. But the question is, was there ever any kind of personal motivation because you're Cuban American or because you are Hispanic or Latino or whatever you want to call it? Was there ever something—well, you have done work in psychology and psychoanalysis—is there something that you think was at work there or was it simply that the philosophical works from Latin America interested you? Once you got into them you found them philosophically interesting and rewarding?"

[Martí] "That is a very interesting question for a variety of reasons. First, there is a curiosity that you have. I was interested in the mind, body, individuals, and medicine. I find that those questions in a way tackle a number of even broader more interesting questions in philosophy. So when I went into philosophy, it was because the questions philosophers were asking were the questions that I was asking all the time, I just didn't know about them. When I got into Latin American philosophy, what I discovered, which shocked the daylights out of me, was that Latin American philosophers were asking the same type of questions, only their relations and their examples and their concerns were about Latin America, about Mexico, about Mexican politics, about literature, and about politics. Being reflective, I looked at it and said, 'When I ask these questions, I'm also thinking about American realities.' There's a war in Vietnam, I'm constantly thinking about American realities. So in a way they're not really different from us, its just that their interest in topics and concerns are centered on a different set of problems. I found similarities. However, one thing that I did find that was very interesting is that in the sciences you're a scientist, you work in your lab, you got your patients, and they leave you alone. Now many scientists—clinicians whom I was working with—were from Pakistan, from Uruguay, but it never occurred to us to ask about ethnicity. But when I got to the humanities, suddenly ethnicity became a question. Well, I was going to do work in Freud, remember, and instead I ended up doing work on Latin America. I was at a party talking to somebody and I said, 'My original thing was Freud, but now I'm doing work on Latin America.' So, this man said, 'Well, of course— Latin America—you'd understand it more!' And I looked at him and said, 'Why?' 'Well, Freud, you know, German, you know.' I said, 'I find myself very akin with Freud.' I speak German, I've read his material all in German, I probably know more about Freud than he did himself. But, no, no, no, you're Latin American. I'm being pigeonholed. I got to assert my identity now. The identity notion started occurring in the humanities. A couple of people in the department did not want me to do work in philosophy of science because I was Cuban. 'Oh, let him do his Latin American stuff.' This was a problematic person, he's still a problematic person, but there were other people who also pigeonholed, pushed me— whether you were a threat to them or whether an annoyance or whatever, it was there, and I became quite conscious of it. Now, there were many things I could have done, but I did the one thing that no one expected: I went into Chicano Studies. I said, okay, you want to pigeonhole me, I'll pigeonhole myself and I'll be in your face pigeonholed. Chicano Studies is very active, and very in your face. So, I chose that and I chose to do philosophy, not from the philosophy department, but from the Chicano Studies department. People ask me, 'You're in Chicano studies?' and I answer, 'Oh, it is still philosophy. Yeah, we are in fact probably a better philosophy department, probably better philosophers, than some in the philosophy department.' "

[Gracia] "It is interesting that, in a sense, the people that were your colleagues, or this particular man that you were talking about, were perfectly happy to have you doing Latin American philosophy. I perceive that's like saying, 'If he's doing that, he's sort of a marginal person, and therefore, there won't be any interference with the real business of the department which is, you know, doing philosophy.' So, it was a way of pushing you aside. But you embraced your marginalization in a sense because you went into it—Chicano Sudies. And this is . . ."

[Martí] ". . . very Cuban. This is very Cuban"

[Gracia] "How do you see your Cuban thing, your Cuban identity. Does it show? The fact that you joke and you're always looking at the funny side of things, and that wit, is that Cuban?"

[Martí] "Yeah, although my wife doesn't see me as a Cuban. She says I am so international. We've been all over the place and in many situations—the Middle East—and I've managed to integrate myself well. But again, that's very Cuban! Cubans don't have a problem with identity. The problem is that others have problems with our identity. This is something my daughter realized when she went to Berkeley. When she got to college they wanted to know what she was. And she said, 'What's your problem?' 'Well, are you American? Are you Cuban?' She answered, 'No, I am all, and I am none. I am myself. What is your problem? Why should I be labeled?' Because, I told her 'You don't have to be labeled.' You wear the labels that you choose. Now, it so happens that I liked the label 'Cuban.' For all our difficulties, and for all our problems, and for all the tremendous burdens that we as Cubans have, we're still very nice people. We have had our bad moments, but of all the people in the world, yeah, I'd rather be Cuban. Now, being Cuban here has been a very interesting thing, especially when I first came to the United States. Being a Cuban was alright then, 'Oh, he's Cuban, can you say something in Spanish?' "

[Gracia] "This was in the nineteen fifties."

[Martí] "Yes, before the Revolution. You say something in Spanish and everybody laughs. We were left alone, no problem. When Castro came to power things changed. A Cuban became an enemy. You were an enemy combatant, an alien. You're like Alqueida, suspicious. Cubans after nineteen fifty-nine, sixty, who lived here, were looked upon very suspiciously. People looked at them and said, 'What are you? Are you for Castro or against Castro?' And they tried to pigeonhole you. I saw bad and good parts—this was before the major migration. When Cubans started migrating there was another shift. Cubans needed help. In the seventies—Cubans own Miami—started to become part of the nation. So there was another shift. I never shifted, I am myself and I've done the things I've done because this is what I wanted, based on careful, rational thinking; careful discussion with my wife—we have been married thirty-some-odd years, thirty-six, thirty-seven years. Ethnicity has and has not played an important part in my life. Ethnicity in the sense in which at home we are a very warm family, a very Cuban family. Someone asked my son, 'What are you?' And he said, 'I'm Cuban.' So ethnicity has and has not played an important part in my life. It did in the sense in which I chose to be Cuban. And it didn't in the sense in which when I had to make any decisions I didn't feel that I couldn't do something because I was Cuban. My wife said that, in a way, she married the other. And I said, '*I* married the other.' But Americans don't like to look at themselves as the other. They are the center of the world. And, why should they be? When I was a kid, I remember a map of Cuba—a map of the world—and Cuba was right in the center of the map."

[Gracia] "And it was big!"

[Martí] "It was huge! And it had the lines to New York, to France, all of it. And it had a little tugboat. I never stopped realizing how central Cuba was. It is not ego—it is ego and it isn't ego—it is a strong sense of identity that I find most Cubans have. Now, when you're working with Chicanos, it is a slightly different situation. We came from a social stratum with a certain education, a certain self-identification. When I worked with Chicanos, many farmers. The parents had no education, they were really mistreated, they worked in the fields, and they had to be smuggled into this country. So they don't have that strong sense of identity and they are very fragile. So the question of their identity is very different from that of my identity."

[Gracia] "Do you think that it might have to do with the fact that Cubans come from an island and there is a certain independence, separation, and self-sufficiency?"

[Martí] "Yeah, it's like the Greeks. They live on an island, sort of, and they have a very strong sense of history even though it is a very different history, although it is not always very real. Well, we Cubans have also a very strong sense of history and it is also not very real. . . . It's a big construct. But yeah, I remember as a kid going all over Cuba, going to Santiago, Matanzas—all those things. Every once in a while I find myself singing some old songs. . . . It is a part of myself, but it is also part of being on an island where people literally share with each other, which is not bad. This is one of the reasons why we left, because you couldn't have privacy—you couldn't get away from the family. And when we came to the United States it turns out that the whole family started coming over."

[Gracia] "So you can't get away from the family period!"

[Martí] "Every once in a while I find myself mentally walking through those years. Every once in a while I find myself remembering a street, and I would like to walk that street. And people ask me, 'Why don't you go back?' And that's an important question."

[Gracia] "You haven't actually gone back to Cuba?"

[Martí] "I refuse to go back for very personal reasons. My memories of Cuba as a kid were very happy. There were problems, my brother got run over by a bus once and he was very ill, almost lost a leg. But Cuban doctors saved his leg—and so it wasn't that easy. But I had a very happy childhood. My parents were extraordinarily good people. They had had problems with their parents, so they didn't want to have the same problems with us—they bent over backwards to be good parents. So my memories of Cuba are always of laughing and having fun. Now, my grandmother was born in, I think it was in, Key West or Tampa. Her father had been one of those traders of tobacco. . . . Apparently he traveled back and forth between Cuba and the United States. My grandmother's house was in Tampa. In nineteen eighty, during the Inter-American Congress in Tallahassee, we went over there, I wanted to show my wife Tampa. We drove by and there was a shopping center in the area. There had been a tree there that had an automobile tire and we used to swing on it. For about a week I was quite depressed. What ever happened to all this? I figure that if I go back to Cuba, the same will happen. I want to keep certain memories pristine. That's one reason why I haven't gone back to Cuba. God knows I've been invited: Guadarrama has asked me, but I've told him, it's not a political reason, its just I want to hold some things dear to me."

[Gracia] "Now tell me whether your Cuban connection, as it were, has ever informed some project or some scholarly publication or your philosophical work? It's part of your history, your personality, but your work is fundamentally on Mexican philosophy, although you've done some work on Martí also; has this been because of the Cuban connection or because of something else?"

[Martí] "Both. First, the piece on Cuban philosophy published by Raúl Fornet Betancourt in Germany was because I'm Cuban. That was important because these are my colleagues. Some of them I don't know, some of them I do, some of them I know but I haven't seen in years. It was important as an homage to them, to try to put on paper as much as I could about how extraordinary they are as a group. I recognize that as a Cuban I take pride in the fact that I'm in the company of extraordinary philosophers. I said at the end of the article that these people are relatively young. If they—this was, what, five, eight, years ago—they've done so much up to this point, you can imagine what they can do in the future. You know Ernesto, yourself, Ofelia, and a number of other smaller figures; they have made quite a contribution to philosophy. So that article was written precisely because these are my colleagues and I wanted to pay homage to them. The Martí article is a different thing. Martí was drilled into us as kids—sometimes I felt that it was propaganda. But I tried to figure out whether it was really propaganda. What is the value of Martí? So I did a piece on how Martí's image has changed through the years.

This image has changed from a young activist to a political organizer, then to a martyr, and eventually to a minor figure, and then again to become the hero and the apostle of the thirties to the fifties. I also found that there was something at the core of those images, there's an essence, and I found that to be the writer, his power as a writer. I had to get this out of me—I had to do it as a Cuban, as an admirer of Martí. My wife thinks that it's one of the best things that I've written outside of philosophy. I don't, because I never was able to put everything I wanted down—I had an editor who didn't know what the heck he was doing. But as a Cuban I had to do that. Also, every once in a while I give a lecture to students, and so on, and I explain to them what my ethnicity means and so on, and I do it as a Cuban also. I tell them, 'Look, I'm a Cuban, you're Chicano, you're Salvadoran, you're Venezuelan, and this is how I've dealt with my identity, this is how you can deal with it—I'm giving you certain tools, certain strategies, for dealing with your identity in this environment. Most of them find it not useful, but at least soothing."

[Gracia] "You obviously are well known as a historian and as a historian you recover the past, you recover Mexican philosophy, Mexican thinking, some things of Martí, and in other places as well, the Enlightenment and so forth. Is this something that you need, that somehow you want to do for yourself? Or is it something that you feel needs to be done for posterity, for others? How do you negotiate these two urges?"

[Martí] "Are there two urges or just one? It's a teaching thing."

[Gracia] "But the historian can do—although history is very difficult to recover, except for basic facts, intellectual history is very difficult as you know—approximations which are pretty good in some cases. But answering philosophical questions . . . is there any answer to any philosophical question? Is there or is there not? Tell your opinion, what is it?"

[Martí] "Philosophy is like a big garbage heap. You have huge amounts of stuff that's there. Somebody comes in rummaging, grabs something, 'Oh, look at that! Physics!' and walks off. Somebody else walks up, 'Oh, look at that! Ethics!' and goes off. And then, the latest rummaging has been, what, artificial intelligence. Before that it was economics, linguistics, and before that it was psychology . . . I was there when the linguistics department separated from psychology—from philosophy. I was there when artificial intelligence was a philosophical problem which is now a computer problem."

[Gracia] "Do we have anything left?"

[Martí] "Oh, plenty! You know we have plenty of stuff there, the garbage heap seems to be just as high . . . For me, philosophy is a voyage: it is not getting to the point, it is the actual trip itself that's fun."

[Gracia] "So you're a Faustian, with respect to philosophy at least."

[Martí] "Yes and no. I don't doubt that there are solutions, I think that there are provisional solutions. It would be bad for me as a logician to say that there is no such thing as a philosophical solution. Some of the solutions become very boring, and then we sort of leave them. Philosophy is strewn with solutions that were given to stuff that we don't talk about anymore. There are other questions that seem to be recurring—I wouldn't call them eternal. I don't think that there are any universal questions, only what we make of them and how we feel about them. There are some universal questions, but they have little to do with philosophy: the question of death and as I said, the question of facing the unavoidable, the ability to deal with your own situation. Sometimes, to some people, the question of God. Those are problems that need not be philosophical, and oftentimes they are not philosophical. It is when the philosopher tries to make sense of them that they become philosophical."

[Gracia] "Do you see any difference between your role as a philosopher and your role as a Cuban philosopher or a Latino, or Hispanic philosopher? Is there something in your goals or in the way you do philosophy or anything related to this enterprise that would introduce a bridge or a gap between these two things?"

[Martí] "In my logic class—logic is about as unethnic as you can get—I use a lot of ethnic examples, partly because students seem to relate to what looks like an abstract concept in very concrete ways. Sometimes you approach a problem from a specifically ethnic position and you want to deal with, say, questions of rights, of duties, of the state, for instance. So you have to approach it from a very concrete position. In that case, I am very ethnic. I talk to my students about stuff that happened to me as a kid, and how I related certain questions of cause and effect and so on, very concretely. Once you use the concrete you can move to the abstract; and there is a common language with a common point of reference. Does it build a bridge? Sometimes it does. Particularly when you're talking with others, with colleagues. You try to explain to people the Cuban situation and people tend to politicize it. They really don't understand Cuba here in the United States. This happened some years ago—a man was talking to two Cubans, one from Cuba and the other from the United States, and he said something disrespectful about Castro and about Cuba in general. Both the Castro Cuban and the Miami Cuban turned on him savagely and they left the room arm-in-arm. The guy was quite surprised—he thought they were enemies! Well, yes, and no. It is not black and white. The Cuban situation is so complex, it is so intricate; when you have brother against brother, when you have family against family."

[Gracia] "One last question. Do you find that the philosophy that is done by Cubans, or has been done by Cubans let's say, historically, up to the present, has something distinctive about it or not?"

[Martí] "To find something distinctive in it you need a larger period of time. What you might call British empiricism includes an Englishman, Locke, an Irishman, Berkeley, and a Scottsman, Hume; very different cultures—I point out to my students that Hume was a sort of British Chicano. He was really alienated from the mainstream though now we look at him as being in the center—he was, in fact, some dumb Scottsman coming over to teach us philosophy. We need more time for that. There are some commonalities but they are not necessarily philosophical. This is an area of conflict and we all share some problems and we all share some differences. We do share, probably, a certain approach to philosophizing. I was talking to Ernesto Sosa some time ago and I was listening to him and I said, 'You don't know how Cuban you are!' We are very much alike in the sense that we think and joke and so on, and our approaches, even though we do philosophy differently, there are certain commonalities. And the same with Ofelia, although with Ofelia there is an important difference in gender."

[Gracia] "But what about the past? What about Varela, Varona, Martí? Is there something that ties us to them?"

[Martí] "They are part of a larger tradition, but there has to be a critical mass, and there is no critical mass. I don't see anything uniquely distinctive there. There is not something that is Cuban philosophy. You might find some common ground in political philosophy that is distinctly Cuban. I don't know."

[Gracia] "Ofelia says something about the search for freedom and the interest in this idea. But I share with you a certain skepticism."

[Martí] "We are too close to determine it."

[Gracia] "And then the critical mass business. There hasn't been enough philosophy."

[Martí] "That is a superb insight and very important. You have to have a sufficiently large group of individuals. Maybe in ten years, twenty years—maybe there is someone a hundred years from now who can see our work and say, 'Hey, look at that, they didn't realize that there were trends.' Someone has gotta write a dissertation; their doctorate and tenure hang on it, he's going to discover something that we've done—we don't know what it is but . . ."

[Gracia] ". . . it will be there. And with this we end. Thank you."

June 9, 2005
Interviewed in the Library at the Department of Philosophy of the University at Buffalo, filmed and edited by Gracia, and transcribed by Paul Symington.

UNIVERSALISM OR PARTICULARISM?

———————————————————————————— ERNESTO SOSA

Ernesto Sosa was born in 1940 and emigrated to the United States in 1954. He was recently elected president of the Eastern Division of the American Philosophical Association, is Romeo Elton Professor of Natural Theology and Professor of Philosophy at Brown University and Distinguished Visiting Professor every spring at Rutgers University, and was elected in 2001 to the American Academy of Arts and Sciences. He has been editor, since 1983, of Philosophy and Phenomenological Research, *and of* Noûs *since 1999, and was General Editor, from 1992 to 2003, of the Cambridge Studies in Philosophy. He has received grants or fellowships from the Canada Council, the American Council of Learned Societies, the National Science Foundation, the Exxon Educational Foundation, and the National Endowment for the Humanities.*

Sosa is one of the leading epistemologists today, but he has also made important contributions in metaphysics and the philosophy of mind. In particular, he is known for his attempt to reconcile "coherentist" and "foundationalist" epistemological concerns.

Main works: Knowledge in Perspective: Selected Essays in Epistemology *(1991);* Epistemic Justification: Internalism vs. Externalism, Foundations vs. Virtues *(2003);* On Virtue Epistemology: Apt Belief and Reflective Knowledge *(2007); and* Virtuous Circles: Apt Belief and Reflective Knowledge *(2007); and many articles in journals (many reprinted in collections, and two selected for* The Philosopher's Annual, *each as "among the best ten articles" in its year of publication).*

INTERVIEW

Conducted by Jorge J. E. Gracia

[Gracia] "Let's begin by asking when you left Cuba.

[Sosa] "I left Cuba permanently, with my family, in early 1954, at the age of fourteen."

[Gracia] "Would you like to say something about the circumstances in which, and the reasons why, you left Cuba?"

[Sosa]: "A precipitating cause of our departure was my sister's very serious asthma, and a doctor's recommendation that she be taken to a dry

245

climate. My father was a Presbyterian minister, so he was able to find a church in El Paso, Texas, an extremely dry place, and off we went. Once my sister was cured after adolescence, my family went to Miami. Of course, she might have been cured of her asthma not by El Paso but by her adolescence. However it may have happened, the fact is that she was cured and we dared once again to venture beyond our dry Southwestern setting to lush and humid South Florida."

[Gracia] "Where have you been after you left Cuba?"

[Sosa] "I have lived for months in Mexico, in Spain, and in England. I also lived in Canada—in London, Ontario—for a couple of years, while teaching at the University of Western Ontario. Those are the relatively long stays; I've also traveled extensively, in all continents, for conferences and lectures."

[Gracia] "When did you decide or discover that you were going to be a philosopher, and under what circumstances?"

[Sosa] "At the University of Miami I was studying mainly science courses, which though interesting I found unsatisfying, since I wanted to question things that must of course remain unquestioned if one is to do science within the confines of its required presuppositions. I did not imagine that there was a discipline in which radical questioning is prized, and was delighted to find it in the writings of Bertrand Russell."

[Gracia] "How did your family react to this possibility?"

[Sosa] "My family would have liked me to follow my father in the ministry, but were quite supportive of my career choice, for which I have always been very grateful."

[Gracia] "Where were you trained?"

[Sosa] "Once I found philosophy in the writings of Russell in my last college summer, having hardly encountered so much as the word philosophy before that, I became a philosophy major and my senior year consisted of little more that twelve philosophy courses. With no record in philosophy by the time applications had to go out, however, I did not apply until the second semester of the 1960-61 academic year, and was lucky to be accepted with some aid in what was then a lowly program, at the University of Pittsburgh. To my great good fortune, the Pitt department was just then beginning its transformation from a bottom-ranked to a top-ranked department, where it has remained throughout all these decades. I was thus blessed with superb fellow students and professors. Although I moved quickly through the program, my two years at Pitt were transformative."

[Gracia] "What were the main challenges you faced in becoming a professional philosopher?"

[Sosa] "I took to philosophy easily, and it quickly became a passion (two closely related facts). Only three years span the time when I first encountered the discipline in the writings of Russell, and the moment I because a full-time teacher of philosophy at the University of Western Ontario. Having completed the course work at Pitt in two years, I then wrote my dissertation during my first year of full-time teaching. Since I had been in this country only six years when I began the serious study of philosophy, and since I arrived at what was already a top-flight program, though small and intensive, it took a lot of passionate concentration and effort to get up to speed. It also involved a struggle to gain facility, not only with philosophy but also with the English language. That meant many hours a week, including nights and weekends, and this work ethic has stuck with me ever since."

[Gracia] "Did the fact that you were a Cuban American ever play any role in these difficulties?"

[Sosa] "Ten years span the time between my arrival in this country in Miami at the age of fourteen, with great linguistic and cultural lacunae, and my joining the faculty at Brown University (where I would remain for forty-two years). Those early years were difficult, since during much of that time I felt quite different and alien, and moved repeatedly from setting to quite different setting. These uprooting moves kept me in a constant state of unfamiliarity and even alienation. But I believe that they also forced me to draw on and perhaps develop inner resources, attaining a kind of sturdy self-reliance that has proved helpful in dealing with later adversity and with the requirements of the committed scholarly life of the mind, with its long daily stretches of concentrated solitude."

[Gracia] "How would you describe your work? What is unique about it? What do you consider to be your contribution to philosophy? How do you see your work in the context of philosophy at large?"

[Gracia] "I have published on almost every subdiscipline of philosophy (including not only epistemology and metaphysics, but also logic, philosophy of mind, theory of action, metaphilosophy, philosophy of language, and ethics). I have sometimes thought that it might have been better to specialize earlier and more intensively. That might have led to books, where I have instead published articles. I suppose it has been self-indulgent to just follow my interests of the moment, or of the year. On the other hand, one benefit of philosophy is to give a view, if only a glimpse, of how things hang together, as Sellars once put it. Even masters of close analysis, like Chisholm and Moore, take up an impressively broad spread of issues."

In any case, my main contributions have been to epistemology, where I originated an approach, known as virtue epistemology, that has grown in prominence over the last couple of decades. I think this is reflected in the contents of *Ernest Sosa and His Critics*, ed. by John Greco (Blackwell, 2004).

[Gracia] "Which philosophers have influenced you the most?"

[Sosa] "Plato, and hence Socrates, Aristotle, Descartes, Berkeley, Mill, Moore, Russell, Chisholm, and Sellars."

[Gracia] "Has anything in particular outside philosophy influenced your philosophical thinking, such as literature, art, certain experiences as a Cuban American? Do you feel or think of yourself as primarily Cuban, Cuban American, Latino, Hispanic, Latin American, American?

[Sosa] "No. I think of myself as all of the above. But really I think in such terms mostly within social settings—for example, as I travel around the world, or as I visit my relatives in Miami. My daily life is absorbed by just thinking hard about philosophical questions, or by work on philosophical projects, such as those that I undertake as journal editor, or as chair of the APA Board of Officers, or as director of Graduate Studies at Brown. In these settings I do not really think of my identity in those terms. If I can be said to think of myself in any such social way at all, it is not in terms of cultural or ethnic identity, but rather in terms of my social roles in the world of philosophy, as author, teacher, editor, administrator, et cetera."

[Gracia] "How do you negotiate your cubanness and your americanness, as a person and as a philosopher? You married another Cuban, and a very Cuban Cuban, how has that affected you? Do you go to Miami often? Have you kept in touch with the Cuban community in Miami and elsewhere, and if you have, how has that affected your career?"

[Sosa] "From the time I left Miami in 1961, I have been away from any Cuban community, and indeed away from Cubans generally except for my wife. However, we would make several long drives a year, for Christmas and summer vacations. These extended stays in Miami kept me in touch with my roots, which was emotionally quite sustaining and enriching. This also accounts for the fact that my sons too have retained a strong connection with their Cuban origins. Though of course their connection is less thick and strong than my wife's or my own, it has I think been quite enriching to their lives, and has also been an important part of our sense of family. Clearly they are fully assimilated and integrated Americans, and are not marrying Cubans or even Hispanics. But they retain much from their background, much that they also share with us."

[Gracia] "How do you feel about philosophy in Cuba today? Is there any? Is it worth exploring? How do you feel about Latin American philosophy? Do you see any value in exploring the history of Cuban or Latin American philosophy? Is there anything in your career that can be explained because you are a Cuban American?"

[Sosa] "What is mainly explained by my being a Cuban American is a long-standing and very intensive participation in the life of philosophy in the Hispanic and Iberian world, in the broadest sense. It is true that I have been very active on the international scene much more broadly, in all continents, in Britain and the Commonwealth, and even in Russia, and the Far East. But, for several decades now, I have made philosophical visits several times a year to Hispanic countries far and wide, and I have published extensively, and joined editorial boards of Spanish-language philosophy journals, and have refereed extensively for them. Unfortunately, this has not extended to Cuba itself. Although I have shown my interest in making connection with colleagues in Cuba, this has not happened, for whatever reasons. Maybe it is because I am seen as too alien in my philosophical interests. In any case, for whatever reason, to my regret I have not joined with fellow Cubans for philosophical exchange. The only exception is that, as Chair of the APA's Committee for International Cooperation, I arranged a visit to an APA meeting by several Cuban philosophers. But I have never visited Cuba as a philosopher. Consequently, I am not well informed about the state of philosophy in Cuba, and am not well-positioned to discuss it in any detail."

[Gracia] "What are you trying to do as a philosopher? What moves you? What is your aim? Is philosophy and your philosophical career integral to your identity, who you are as a person? Could you have been anything else but a philosopher, and if so what? You are now approaching seventy. Has this fact prompted any thoughts you would like to share with us?

[Sosa] "Philosophy has indeed been a huge part of my identity and of how I think of myself. This is partly because so much of what I do is in the world of philosophy, either as thinker, or scholar, or teacher, or speaker, or mentor, or editor, or administrator in the life of the profession. (That work ethic again!) Inevitably, then, philosophy in one way or another very largely fills my days. It is rewarding indeed to be part of a community and its institutions that way. It gives much structure and meaning to one's existence. My son David is also a philosopher, at Texas/Austin, and it has been wonderful to share so much with him.

I suppose I could have done okay in other roles, with other careers. But I very much doubt that I could have been as well suited for them as, to my great good fortune, I have turned out to be for my life in philosophy. In retrospect, I instinctively took a good course by just allowing myself to be absorbed by what I found naturally absorbing, while also retaining the human element, and joining in institutions and joint endeavors at every level. It is this combination of scholarly solitude and supportive community that has proved so deeply rewarding to me. I doubt that I am peculiar in that respect, and I would recommend the same to young colleagues starting out, though of course we all must find our own particular niche with its specific options and rewards.

And then there is the element of luck, in all its many varieties!

May 2006

Interviewed through the Internet, and edited by Jorge J. E. Gracia.

The Philosophers' Work

THE PHILOSOPHERS' WORK

—————————————————————————— OFELIA SCHUTTE

IDENTITIES IN TENSION

In her now classic work *Borderlands/La Frontera*, Gloria Anzaldúa provides an illustration of the multifaceted identity of a Chicana feminist. Anzaldúa reflects on growing up in south Texas, where the legacies of different cultures intersect. She mentions how easy it is to be torn apart by the variable and sometimes conflicting demands of a multicultural background composed of Indian, Mexican, and North American elements. "Like all people," she says, "we perceive the version of reality that our culture communicates. Like others having or living in more than one culture, we get multiple, even opposing messages." There is, above all, the pain of realizing that some of these elements have been oppressors of others: the Mexican has oppressed the Indian, and the North American has oppressed the other two. It is important for her to overcome the anger and the resentment that can build up when she sees the ways Chicanos are discriminated against. Anzaldúa realized one must be strong to fight and overcome the effects of discrimination on one's people and on one's self. In her own self, however, she has to bring together her complex identifications, and not let one or another of them exploit another. She has to create a healing relationship between the Indian, the Chicana, and the north American aspects of herself. I think that, apart from her psychological attitude of inclusiveness and respect for all the different elements that make up her self, she succeeds in creating this balance through the use of language, alternating between English and Spanish in much of her prose, from time to time using indigenous imagery to ground her thought. In other words, in her writing and choice of how to define the topics she writes about, she is able to bring together creatively the different elements of her self. "The possibilities are numerous," she writes, "once we decide to act and not to react." Yet she adds a warning in a mixed tongue: *"Pero es difícil* differentiating between *lo heredado, lo adquirido, lo impuesto"* (Yet it is difficult to differentiate between what is inherited, what is acquired, and what is imposed).

Anzaldúa's example shows one creative way to approach the heterogeneity and mixture of elements in a person's multicultural background.

In fact, she describes her consciousness as one that speaks up for *"la nueva mestiza"* (the new *mestiza*), where the word *mestiza* already indicates the concept of mixture. In reference to her position as that of "la *nueva mestiza*" (emphasis added), a new cultural horizon is opened—one that allows us to move to a larger category than "Chicana/Tejana." The concept of *"mestiza"* is transferable to the category "latina," which, like *"mestiza,"* encompasses far more than a reference to Chicana feminists. Since the 1980s "Latina" has been used increasingly to describe women of Hispanic-American backgrounds residing in the United States. It allows Hispanic-American women the use of a common designator, surpassing the more specific designators of "Chicana," *"puertoriqueña,"* *"cubana-americana,"* . . .

From "Negotiating Latina Identities," in Jorge J. E. Gracia and Pablo De Greiff, eds., Hispanic/Latinos in the United States: Ethnicity, Race, and Rights, *p. 68 (New York: Routledge, 2000).*

ETHNIC IDENTITY

Certain groups of people are best conceived as extended historical families whose members have no identifiable properties, or set of properties, that are shared by all their members throughout the existence of the groups. This accounts for the lack of agreement concerning any particular conditions, or even kinds of conditions, that are necessary and sufficient for Hispanic identity in general, or any Hispanic identity in particular. Even the most superficial consideration of available research points to difficulties in the identification of any such conditions. . . .we must abandon the project of trying to develop conceptions of identities of this sort in terms of discernible common features.

. . . [I]n order to have any of these identities, it is not necessary that one share a property or set of properties with others who also have that identity. . . . It is not even necessary that the members of the group name themselves in any particular way or have a conscious sense of belonging to the group. Some of them may in fact consider themselves so and even have a consciousness, or sense, of themselves as a group, but it is not necessary that all of them do. Are all Latin Americans conscious of a Hispanic, or even a Latin American identity? Do all Mexicans have a sense of their Mexicanity? How about the *campesino* lost in the ravines of the Copper Canyon? How about the descendants of the Maya living in isolation somewhere in Yucatan? And this extends to knowledge of the group's history. Belonging to a group does not entail knowing anything about the history of the group, and even less having an accurate knowledge of that history.

Latin Americans . . . or Cubans . . . are tied by the same kind of thing that ties the members of a family. There may not be any common features to all of them, but nonetheless they share an identity because they are related in ways similar to those in which members of a family are and this identity is a source of feelings and actions. The metaphor of family is helpful in this case, for one does not need even to be related by descent to other members of a family to be a member of the family. Indeed, perhaps the most important foundation of a family, namely marriage, takes place between persons who are not related by descent, but by contract. . . .The family metaphor also entails that any requirements of coherence or of homogeneity among members of the group do not apply. Families are not coherent wholes composed of homogeneous elements; they include members that differ substantially from each other and often clash. . . .

An identity is merely a historical marker. It tells me that I am here and I am now a part of a group within which I fit in many ways. It does not tell me that I am like everyone else in the group and different from everyone else who does not belong to the group, or that I have been and will continue to be what I am. Rather it tells me that I am part of the group because I share various relations and properties they generate in context with some of its members and that these relations set us apart from other groups. I am not part of those other groups because either I have no relations with their members or because the relations I share with them do not justify membership and thus identity, or even because I do not share with them certain properties that in context identify the groups that have them. Clearly I am not Jewish—I share no history with the Jews and there are no properties resulting from that history that I also have. And the citizenship relation I share with other Americans does not warrant Hispanic identity, because citizenship is not an ethnic marker for Hispanics.

From "Identities," in Jorge J. E. Gracia's Latinos in America: Philosophy and Social Identity *(Oxford: Blackwell, forthcoming).*

BREAKING WITH THE PAST

It has been argued here that the lack of histories of philosophy—and by extension, the lack of a clearly identifiable philosophical movement in Latin America—is due to an antipathy toward the past, an antipathy that others have seen as the cause of self-hatred, inferiority complexes, or lack of identity. Evidence is drawn from historical accounts, from the philosophical texts, and from the practice of philosophy itself. They range from the concrete to the abstract. Let me now raise some objections. Explaining an aversion to the past in terms of the just-outlined conditions for doing philosophy could lead to a charge of triviality: If this is the lot of philosophers, then any form of critical thinking so typical of the profession would lead, by definition, to a demeaning of the value of the past.

If acceptance of the past were a parrotlike repetition or imitation, then, trivially, everyone is breaking with the past. But there are alternative acceptances of the past. For one thing, a person could espouse a traditional model of philosophizing, to the exclusion of other models, and employ it to examine emerging problems. Modes of philosophizing are, normally, flexible enough to survive criticism and flexible enough to allow patches to doctrinal difficulties, as Díaz de Gamarra or Alzate found out from the scholastics. Another option is simply to ignore history. Nothing wrong with this—there were many philosophers who, instead of worrying about history, concentrated on philosophic problems. To this group belong those very few philosophers who offered solutions to the traditional logical, metaphysical, epistemological, or ethical problems—the kind of stuff I was expecting—Vera Cruz, Díaz de Gamarra, Lafinur, Ocampo, and later, Vaz Ferreira and almost Ingenieros. They might even use historical materials, but always reinterpreted in contemporary terms, distilled from local color and accidental flavor. But their disdain of the concrete, of history, of time and place, made them unlikely authors of historical accounts. So much for the charge of triviality.

Nonphilosophical factors have been blamed for the rejection of a Hispanic past. Many think that practical and concrete reasons—if not crass pecuniary gain—lurked behind the high rhetoric that cried for intellectual autonomy during the Ilustración, and for political autonomy during the Independencia. Equal arguments can be made against those who wanted to keep political ties to Spain. They might have made their personal gain more palatable by invoking the high road represented by tradition. It can be objected that we are dealing here with material conditions rather than conclusions drawn from accepted philosophical premises or the entailment of the meanings of concepts. Actually, the dichotomy between ideals compelling action, or of action seeking a justification in ideals seems like a pseudoproblem. But to decide which alternative is correct, would prove an arduous task, in particular since it's hard to imagine—other than personal preference—the kind of reasons or evidence that would decide one way or another.

An inquiry into the absence of a history of philosophy in Latin America has some remarkable implications. For one thing, its absence can be explained by a series of accidental factors, as opposed to intrinsic properties of philosophy in the region. A dominant factor is the distrust of the intellectual past, our original hypothesis. After all, if you consider the past something to break away from, you are not going to spend too much time dwelling on its features. Yet other temporal factors have emerged. During the seventeenth century, squabbles among scholastics and a devaluation of what criollos do by proximate and distant critics are not a stimulus to the writing of histories of philosophy. And in the nineteenth century, with the revolutions that led to a political and social break with the metropolis and the instauration of new republics, with their own identities, beliefs, conceptions of the future, the good life, the best polity, the past that narrated, explained, or even justified in rational terms, the ills they had just revolted against, is not a past they would want to examine philosophically.

It isn't that in Latin America there was a lack of philosophy, or a defective philosophy that merited no history. What we have is, instead, a refusal to look at its history out of a desire to thoroughly break with it. The moral of the story is somewhat disquieting for it undermines some ingrained habits. Whereas one way to approach a field is to look for its history, its existence determined in chronological terms, it seems that some fields, like Latin American philosophy, in their desire to be future, have endeavored to be not ahistorical but nonhistorical. This is a curious twist of Hegel's dictum that "Latin America is the land of the future."

From "Breaking with the Past: Philosophy and Its History in Latin America," in The Role of History in Latin American Philosophy, *edited by Arleen Salles and Elizabeth Millán-Zaibert (Albany, NY: SUNY Press, 2005).*

PHILOSOPHY, THE HISTORY OF PHILOSOPHY, AND SCIENCE

Both Roderick Chisholm and Wilfrid Sellars combined their focus on contemporary issues with a serious interest in the insight that could be gained into these issues through study of their history. Sellars also thought that when we join in study of a philosophical canon we gain something as a community, namely, a common framework within which to join together in discussion, a common vocabulary and set of issues. Of course, it is not just a matter of agreeing arbitrarily on some readings so as to form a community, in the way of a book reading club. There is rather an ongoing mutual adjustment. First might come some initial interest in certain sets of issues, and further definition of these issues, and of the concepts they presuppose. Such interest, if pursued, may then lead to additional, related concepts, which in turn may enable appreciation of further related issues, and the cycle thus continues. This all may then lead in turn to study of other historical contributors to the conversation with helpful things to say about issues already gripping, who may in turn introduce yet further issues and concepts. And so on and so forth.

On almost any major question of philosophy there are alternative pictures that can be developed in different ways, with different emphases, and to differing levels of specificity and detail. Despite the differences that one would expect across cultural and historical divides, there is a truly impressive commonality of basic issues and alternative ways to deal with them. In developing as a philosopher one deepens one's insight into the alternatives and their costs and benefits, and one broadens one's understanding of how a position on one issue may bear on other issues. Because large philosophical views are combinations of more restricted pictures, and because such panoramas are rarely refuted beyond redemption, it is always possible to learn from our most brilliant predecessors, if only about how things might look along a road not taken. And this might occasionally even lead us to retrace our steps and explore seriously an avenue previously overlooked.

Equally rational, well-informed philosophers work their way to their respective positions with less agreement than one finds in other disciplines. Philosophy tailors its benefits to the individual thinker, and on many issues there is no one cut that will suit everyone equally. Why is this so? That is itself a philosophical question, and will of course receive a variety of still defensible answers, from a variety of perspectives. At one extreme stand those who take all questions of philosophy to be fully objective, and factual, and the diversity of opinion to derive from the difficulty and complexity of the questions. At another extreme will be those radical skeptics or relativists who find a great many philosophical questions to be either pseudoquestions, or subjective matters of taste. On this issue I myself find it difficult to settle on a stable and definitive stance. What is more, this attitude seems to me appropriate not only with regard to the general issue of the kind of objectivity that might be available generally in philosophy, but also with regard to more specific ranges of philosophical questions. In any case, one thing I do find obvious: philosophy is very, very hard, very complex, and multiply ramified. Our disagreements may derive simply from that, or they may also derive at least in part, at least on some questions, from the fact that different views seem defensible, though not coherently combinable, and one can hope at best to develop a coherent, defensible picture that has the broadest defensible scope. Of course one hopes that the apparent incompatibilities derive ultimately from varying interests and emphasis, and corresponding terminological diversity and ambiguity, and not so much from outright logical conflict. Progress is then to a large extent a matter of the deeper appreciation of such differences. I think recent epistemology presents an excellent case study.

From interview with Juan Comesaña, http://homepage.mac.com/ernestsosa/Menu2.html.

Bibliography

Alonso Gallo, Laura P. and Fabio Murrieta, eds. 2004. *Guayaba Sweet: Literatura cubana en Estados Unidos*. Cádiz: Aduana Vieja.

Alvarez, Pedro. 2000. *How Havana Stole from New York the Idea of Cuban Art*. Santa Monica, CA: Smart Art Press.

Alvarez Borland, Isabel. 1998. *Cuban-American Literature of Exile: From Person to Persona*. Charlottesville and London: University Press of Virginia.

———. 2004. "Las raíces al desnudo: narradores cubanos en los Estados Unidos," in *Guayaba Sweet: Literatura cubana en Estados Unidos*, Laura P. Alonso and Fabio Murieta, eds., 37–50. Cádiz: Editorial Aduana Vieja.

———. 2004. "Gustavo Pérez Firmat," in *Latino and Latina Writers*, Alan West and Cesar Salgado, eds., 717–36. New York: Charles Scribner's Sons.

———. 1994. "Displacements and Autobiography in Cuban-American Fiction," *World Literature Today* 68: 43–49.

Araújo, Nara. 2003. "Zonas de contacto: narrativa femenina de la diáspora y de la isla de Cuba," in *Guayaba Sweet: Literatura cubana en Estados Unidos*, Laura P. Alonso and Fabio Murieta, eds., 73–93. Cádiz: Editorial Aduana Vieja.

Ballester, J. P., M. Escalona, and I. la Nuez, eds. 1995. *Cuba: la isla possible*. Barcelona: Ediciones Destino.

Barquet, Jesús, and Rosario Sanmiguel, eds. 1995. *Más allá de la isla: 66 creadores cubanos*. Puentelibre: vol. 2, nos. 5–6. Chihuahua, Mexico: Puentelibre Editores.

Behar Ruth, ed. 1995. *Bridges to Cuba*. Ann Arbor: University of Michigan Press.

Begley, Louis. 2004. "On Being an Orphaned Writer," in *The Genius of Language*, Wendy Lesser, ed., 165–85. New York: Pantheon.

Belnap, Jeffrey, and Fernández, Raúl, eds. 1998. *José Martí's 'Our America': From National to Hemispheric Cultural Studies*. Durham: Duke University Press.

Berthot, Lillian. 1997. *La generación del Mariel*. Miami, FL: Cuban-American National Foundation.

Blanc, Giulio. 1993. *Cuban Artists of the Twentieth Century*. Fort Lauderdale, FL: Fort Lauderdale Museum of Art.

———. 1984. *The Miami Generation*. Exhibition Catalogue. Miami, FL: Cuban Museum of Arts and Culture.

———. 1990. *The Post-Miami Generation*. Exhibition Catalogue. Miami, FL: Cuban Museum of Arts and Culture.

Block, Holly. 2001. *Art Cuba: The New Generation*. New York: Abrams.

Boswell, Thomas. 1994. *The Cubanization and Hispanization of Miami*. Miami, FL: Cuban American National Council.

Boswell, Thomas D., and James R. Curtis. 1984. *The Cuban-American Experience: Culture, Images and Perspectives*. Totowa, NJ: Rowman & Allanheld.

Bosch, Lynette M. F. 2006. "Layers: Collecting Cuban-American Art," in *Layers: Collecting Cuban-American Art*. Exhibition Catalogue. Buffalo, NY: University at Buffalo Art Galleries.

———. 2004. *Cuban-American Art in Miami: Exile, Identity and the Neo-Baroque*. London: Lund Humphreys Press.

———. 1997. *Past Cuba-Identity and Identification in Cuban-American Art*. Exhibition Catalogue. Fairfield, CT.: Fairfield University and St. Lawrence University.

———. 1993. *Islands in the Stream: Seven Cuban-American Artists*. Exhibition Catalogue. SUNY, Cortland.

Burunat, Silvia, and Ofelia García, eds. 1988. *Veinte años de literatura cubano-americana*. Tempe, AR: Bilingual Press.

Camnitzer, Luis. 1994. *New Art of Cuba*. Austin, TX: University of New Mexico Press.

Casal, Lourdes. 1978. "Memories of a Black Cuban Childhood," in *Nuestro 2*, 4: 61–2.

Cockcroft, James D., and Jane Canning. 2000. *Latino Visions: Contemporary Chicano, Puerto Rican and Cuban-American Artists*. New York: Franklin Watts Press.

Cuba Siglo XX: modernidad y sincretismo. Exhibition Catalogue. 1996. Canary Islands: Centro Atlántico de Arte Moderno.

Damian, Carol. 1997. *Breaking Barriers: Selections from the Museum of Art's Permanent Contemporary Cuban Collection*. Exhibition Catalogue. Fort Lauderdale, FL: Fort Lauderdale Museum of Art.

Davidson, Cathy, and Linda Wagner-Martin, eds. 1995. "Cuban American Writing," in *The Oxford Companion to Women's Writing in the United States*, 228–30. New York: Oxford University Press.

Delfino, Robert, ed. 2006. *What Are We to Understand Gracia to Mean? Realist Challenges to Metaphysical Neutralism*. New York: Rodopi.

Delgado, Asunción Horno, et al., eds. 1989. *Breaking Boundaries: Latina Writing and Critical Readings*. Amherst: University of Massachusetts Press.

Espinosa, Carlos Domínguez. 2001. *El peregrino en comarca ajena*. Boulder, CO: Society of Spanish and Spanish American Studies.

Febles, Jorge, ed. 2001. *Narradores cubanos fuera de la isla*. Anales Literarios 3. Miami, FL: Universal.

Figueredo, Danilo. 1997. "Ser cubano/To Be Cuban," in *Multicultural Review* 6:18–28.

Fornet, Ambrosio. 2000. *Memorias recobradas*. Santa Clara, Cuba: Capiro.

Fornet-Betancourt, Raúl, ed. 1999. *Filosofía, Teología, Literatura: Aportes cubanos en los últimos 50 años*. (Concordia Monographien: Verlag Mainz). Translated into German as *Philosophie, Theologie, Literatur: Kubanische Beiträge aus den letzten 50 Jahren*. Alena Retoba, translator. Aachen: Wissenschaftsverlag Mainz.

Fuentes-Pérez, Ileana, et al. 1987. *Outside Cuba/Fuera de Cuba*. Exhibition Catalogue. New Brunswick, NJ: Rutgers University Press.

García, M. 1996. *Havana USA: Cuban Exiles and Cuban-Americans in South Florida*. Berkeley: University of California Press.

Gil, Lourdes. 1997. "Cuban Writing in the United States." *Encyclopedia of Latin American Literature*. Verity Smith ed., 242–44. London: FitzRoy Dearborn Publishers.

———. 1999/2000. "La apropiación de la lejanía," *Encuentro* 15: 61–70.

Giulio Blanc, et al. 1991. *Cuba/U.S.A.: The First Generation*. Exhibition Catalogue. Washington, DC: El Fondo del Sol.

Gómez-Sicre, José. 1987. *Art of Cuba in Exile*. Miami, FL: Editorial Munder.

González Mandri, Flora. 2006. *Guarding Cultural Memory: Afro-Cuban Women in Literature and the Arts*. Charlottesville: University of Virginia Press.

Gracia, Jorge J. E. 2003. "Ethnic Labels and Philosophy," in *Latin American Philosophy: Currents, Issues, Debates*, Eduardo Mendieta, ed., 57–67. Bloomington, IN: Indiana University Press.

———. 2007. *Latinos in America: Philosophy and Social Identity*. Oxford, MA: Blackwell.

———. 2000. *Hispanic/Latino Identity: A Philosophical Perspective*. Oxford, MA: Blackwell.

———. 1998. *Filosofía hispánica: Concepto, orígen y foco historiográfico*. Pamplona: Universidad de Navarra.

Gracia, Jorge J. E. and Millán-Zaibert, Elizabeth, eds. 2004. *Latin American Philosophy for the Twenty-first Century: The Human Condition, Values, and the Search for Identity*. Buffalo, NY: Prometheus Books.

Greco, John, ed. 2004. *Ernest Sosa and His Critics*. London: Basil Blackwell.

Guerra, Lillian. 2005. *The Myth of José Martí: Conflicting Nationalisms in Early Twentieth-Century Cuba*. Chapel Hill: University of North Carolina Press.

Hernández-Miyares, Julio, ed. 2002. *Cuba: exilio y cultura: Memoria del congreso del milenio*. Miami, FL: Universal.

Herrera, A. O'Reilly ed. 2001. *Remembering Cuba: Legacy of a Diaspora*. Austin: University of Texas Press.

Hospital, Carolina, ed. 1988. *Cuban-American Writers: Los Atrevidos*. Princeton, NJ: Linden Lane Press.

———, ed. 1996. *A Century of Cuban Writers in Florida*. Sarasota, FL: Pineapple Press.

Jaffee McCabe, Cynthia, and Daniel J. Boorstin.1976. *The Golden Door: Artist-Immigrants of America, 1876–1976*. Exhibition Catalogue. Washington, DC: Smithsomian Institution Press.

Kirk, John M. 1983. *José Martí: Mentor of the Cuban Nation*. Tampa: University of Florida Presses.

Levine, R. and M. Asís. 2000. *Cuban Miami*. New Brunswick, NJ: Rutgers University Press.

Llanes, J. 1982. *Cuban-Americans: Masters of Survival*. Cambridge, MA: Abt Books.

Loin de Cuba. Exhibition Catalogue. 1999. Aix-en-Provence, France: Musèe des Tapisseries.

Loomis, John A. 1999. *Revolution of Forms: Cuba's Forgotten Art Schools*. Princeton, NJ: Princeton Architectural Press.

López, Iraida. 2001. *La autobiografía hispana contemporánea en los Estados Unidos: a través del caleidoscopio*. Lewiston, NY: The Edwin Mellen Press.

Luis, William. 1997. *Dance Between Two Cultures*. Nashville, TN: Vanderbilt University Press.

Maratos, Daniel C. and D. Hill Marnesba, eds. 1986. *Escritores de la diáspora cubana; manual bibliográfico/ Cuban Exile Writers: A Bibliographical Handbook*. Metuchen, NJ: Scarecrow Press.

Martí, José. 2002. *José Martí: Selected Writings*. Ed. Esther Allen. New York: Penguin.

Martí, Oscar. 1999. "Aportes de cubanos fuera de Cuba a la filosofía actual," in Raúl Fornet-Betancourt, ed. *Filosofía, Teología, Literatura: Aportes cubanos en los últimos 50 años*. (Concordia Monographien: Verlag Mainz, 1999), 110–39. Translated into German by Oscar R. Martí as "Der Beitrag der Kubaner außerhalb Kubas zur Philosophie der Gegenwart," in R. Fornet-Betancourt, *Philosophie, Theologie, Literatur: Kubanische Beiträge aus den letzten 50 Jahren*. Alena Retoba, translator, 99–127. Aachen: Wissenschaftsverlag Mainz.

———. 1983. "Is There a Latin American Philosophy?" *Metaphilosophy* 1: 46–52.

Martínez, Juan A. 1994. *Cuban Art and National Identity: The Vanguardia Painters 1927–1950*. Gainesville, FL: University Press of Florida.

———. 2000. "Lo blanco-criollo as lo cubano in the Symbolization of a Cuban National Identity in Modernist Painting of the 1940s," in *Cuba, The Elusive Nation: Interpretations of National Identity*. ed. Damian J. Fernández and Madeline Cámara. Gainesville: University Press of Florida.

Martínez, Julio, ed. 1990. *Dictionary of Twentieth Century Cuban Literature*. Westport, CN: Greenwood Press.

Masud-Piloto, Felix Roberto. 1988. *With Open Arms: Cuban Migration to the US*. Totowa, NJ: Rowman & Littlefield.

Méndez Rodenas, Adriana. 2000. "Diáspora o identidad: Adónde va la cultura cubana?" *Revista Hispano Cubana* 8: 43–66.

Mendoza, Tony. 1999. *Cuba: Going Back*. Austin: University of Texas Press.

Mosquera, Gerardo. 1999. *Contemporary Art from Cuba*. New York: Arizona State University Art Museum: Delano Greenridge Editions.

Pérez Firmat, Gustavo. 1994. *Life on the Hyphen: The Cuban-American Way*. Austin: The University of Texas Press.

———. 2003. *Tongue Ties: Logoeroticism in Anglo Hispanic Literature*. New York: Palgrave Macmillan.

Philosophy and Social Criticism. 2001. 27, 2: 1–75. Articles on Jorge Gracia's *Hispanic/Latino Identity*, by Linda Alcoff, Robert Gooding-Williams, Eduardo Mendieta, Gregory Pappas, Richard Berstein, and J. García, with replies by Jorge Gracia.

Rivero, Eliana. 1995. "Cuban American Writing," in *The Oxford Companion to Women's Writing in the United States*, Cathy Davidson and Linda Wagner, eds., 228–30. New York: Oxford University Press.

———. 2005. *Discursos desde la diáspora*. Cádiz: Aduana Vieja.

Sánchez Boudy, José. 1996. *Filosofía del cubano y de lo cubano*. Miami, FL: Ediciones Universal.

Schutte, Ofelia. 1993. *Cultural Identity and Social Liberation in Latin American Thought*. Albany: SUNY Press.

———. 2001. "Latin America and Postmodernity: Ruptures and Continuities in the Concept of 'Our America,'" in *Latin America and Postmodernity: A Contemporary Reader*. Pedro Lange-Churrión and Eduardo Mendieta, eds., 155–76. Amherst, NY: Humanity Books.

———. 2000. "Negotiating Latina Identities," in Jorge J. E. Gracia and Pablo De Greiff, eds., *Hispanics/Latinos in the United States*, 61–75. New York: Routledge.

Smorkaloff, Pamela. 1999. *Cuban Writers On and Off the Island*. New York: Twayne Publishers.

Suárez Virgil, ed. 1996. *Little Havana Blues: A Cuban-American Anthology*. Houston, TX: Arte Público.

Torres, María de los Angeles, ed. 2003. *By Heart/De memoria. Cuban Women's Journeys In and Out of Exile*. Philadelphia, PA: Temple University Press.

Veigas, José, et. al. 2003. *Memoria: Cuban Art of the Twentieth Century*. Los Angeles, CA: California International Arts Foundation.

Viera, Ricardo. 2001. *Latin American Artist Photographers from the Lehigh University Art Galleries Collection*. Bethlehem, PA: Lehigh University Art Galleries/Museum Operation.

Vitier, Medardo. 1948. *La filosofía en Cuba*. Mexico City: Fondo de Cultura Económica.

West, Alan, ed. 2003. *Latino and Latina Writers*, vol. 1, 2. New York: Charles Scribner's Sons.

———. 1997. *Tropics of History: Cuba Imagined*. Westwood, NJ: Greenwood.

———. 1995. "Cuban-American Presence," in *American Journey: The Hispanic American Experience*. CD-ROM. Woodbridge CT: Primary Source Media.

About the Editors

Isabel Alvarez Borland is Professor in the Department of Modern Languages and Director of the Latin American Studies and Latino Concentration at the College of the Holy Cross in Worcester, MA. Alvarez Borland is the author of *Cuban-American Literature of Exile: From Person to Persona* (1998) and of *Discontinuidad y ruptura en Guillermo Cabrera Infante* (1982). Her publications are in twentieth-century Latin American literature, Contemporary Spanish American, Caribbean, Latino and Cuban-American literatures. Her articles have appeared in journals such as *Encuentro, Modern Language Notes, Hispanic Review, Hispania* and *World Literature Today*. She has held Visiting professorships at Middlebury College and Amherst College.

Lynette M. F. Bosch is Professor and Coordinator of Art History at Geneseo State College and has been a Bunting Fellow at the Radcliffe Research Institute, Harvard University. A graduate from Princeton, she is a leading authority on Cuban-American art. Her latest book is *Cuban-American Art in Miami: Exile, Identity and the Neo-Baroque* (2004). In addition she has published *Art, Liturgy and Legend in Renaissance Toledo* (2000), *Ernesto Barreda: Contemporary Chilean Painter* (1996), and many articles in both scholarly journals and widely accessible magazines. She has curated eleven art exhibitions and edited the ensuing catalogues.

Jorge J. E. Gracia holds the Samuel P. Capen Chair in Philosophy at the University at Buffalo, and is State University of New York Distinguished Professor. He has been president of several philosophical societies and has held grants and fellowships from the Canada Council, the National Endowment for the Humanities, and the New York Council for the Humanities. Among his works are: *Surviving Race, Ethnicity, and Nationality* (2005), *Old Wine in New Skins* (2003), *How Can We Know What God Means?* (2001), *Hispanic/Latino Identity* (2000), *Metaphysics and Its Task* (1999), *Texts* (1996), *A Theory of Textuality* (1995), *Philosophy and Its History* (1992), and *Individuality* (1988); also more than 250 articles and two dozen edited books.

Index